Building Democracy?

Building Democracy?

The International Dimension of Democratisation in Eastern Europe

Edited by
Geoffrey Pridham
Eric Herring
George Sanford

In assocation with the
Department of Politics and the Centre for
Mediterranean Studies, University of Bristol

Leicester University Press
LONDON

Leicester University Press
(a division of Pinter Publishers Ltd)
25 Floral Street, Covent Garden, London, WC2E 9DS

First published in Great Britain in 1994

British Library Cataloguing in Publication Data

A CIP catalogue record for this book is available from the British Library

ISBN O 7185 1459 9

Typeset by Florencetype Ltd, Kewstoke, Avon
Printed and bound in Great Britain by
Biddles Ltd of Guildford and King's Lynn

Contents

List of Contributors

Judy Batt is Senior Lecturer in East European Politics at the Centre for Russian and East European Studies, University of Birmingham. During 1992/3, she worked on secondment in the Policy Planning Staff at the Foreign and Commonwealth Office. Her main publications include *Economic Reform and Political Change in Eastern Europe* (Macmillan, 1988) and *East Central Europe from Reform to Transformation* (RIIA/ Pinter, 1990). Her current research interests include the political economy of transition and Central and Eastern Europe, the crises of federal states (Czechoslovakia and Yugoslavia), problems of constitutional reform and nationalism.

Eric Herring is Lecturer in International Politics at the University of Bristol. His publications include *Crisis Behaviour in the Nuclear Age* (forthcoming, Manchester UP 1994) and *A Keyguide to Research in Strategic Studies* (co-author with Ken Booth, forthcoming 1994, Mansell). He is currently writing a book on *The Nuclear Taboo*.

Margot Light is Senior Lecturer in International Relations at the London School of Economics and Political Science. Her publications include *The Soviet Theory of International Relations* (Wheatsheaf, 1988), *International Relations: a handbook of current theory* (edited with A.J.R. Groom, Pinter, 1985). She has recently published an edited volume, *Troubled Friendships: Moscow's Third World ventures* (British Academic Press and RIIA, 1993). Her current research interests include the domestic and foreign policies of post-Communist states.

John Pinder is Visiting Professor at the College of Europe, Bruges, and was formerly Director of the Policy Studies Institute in London. His book publications include *Britain and the Common Market* (Cresset Press, 1961), *The Economics of Europe* (Macmillan, 1971), *Federal Union: the pioneers*, with Richard Mayne (Charles Knight, 1990), *The European Community and Eastern Europe* (Pinter, 1991) and *European Community: the building of a union* (OUP, 1991). In addition to the political economy of the European Community and the Community's relations with Central and Eastern Europe, his main interests include the development of the Community as a federal union. He is Honorary President of the Union of European Federalists.

Geoffrey Pridham is Professor of European Politics and Director of the Centre for Mediterranean Studies at the University of Bristol. He has published books on Germany, Italy, the European Community, Southern Europe and Eastern Europe. They include: *The New Mediterranean Democracies: regime transition in Spain, Greece and Portugal* (editor, Frank Cass, 1984); *Political Parties and Coalitional Behaviour in Italy* (Routledge, 1988); *Securing Democracy: political parties and democratic consolidation in Southern Europe* (editor, Routledge, 1990); and *Encouraging Democracy: the international context of regime transition in Southern Europe* (Leicester University Press, 1991). He is also co-editing with Tatu Vanhanen *Democratisation in Eastern Europe: domestic and international perspectives* (Routledge, 1994) and editing *Transitions to Democracy*, a reader of comparative articles on regime change in Southern Europe, Eastern Europe and Latin America.

N.J. Rengger is Lecturer in Politics at the University of Bristol. His teaching and research is divided between political philosophy and intellectual history and the theoretical, especially ethical, aspects of world politics. He has co-edited *Dilemmas of World Politics* (Oxford, 1992) and *Critical Theory and International Relations* (Harvester, 1994); and has authored *Political Theory, Modernity and Postmodernity* (Basil Blackwell, 1994), as well as a number of articles on ancient and modern political thought.

George Sanford is Senior Lecturer in Politics at Bristol University, where he has since 1966 specialised in European and especially Eastern European and Polish studies. He is author of *Polish Communism in Crisis*, Croom Helm (1983), *Military Rule in Poland*, Croom Helm (1986), *The Solidarity Congress*, Macmillan (1990), *Democratisation in Poland*, Macmillan (1992), the Clio bibliography on *Poland*, Clio Press (1993) and the *Historical Dictionary of Poland*, Scarecrow Press, NJ (in press) as well as numerous articles and chapter contributions. He is currently working on the comparative democratisation and nation-building problems of Poland and Belorussia.

Laurence Whitehead is Official Fellow in Politics at Nuffield College, Oxford. He has been Senior Research Officer at the Latin American Program of the Wilson Center and co-edited with Guillermo O'Donnell and Philippe Schmitter *Transitions from Authoritarian Rule* (Johns Hopkins University Press, 1986). In 1985–6 he was Acting Program Director at the Center for US-Mexico Studies, University of California, San Diego; and since 1989 has been joint editor of *The Journal of Latin American Studies*. During 1990–2 he served as Chairman of the Social Studies Faculty, Oxford University. He is currently directing a research project on the interactions between economic and political liberalisation for the Joint Committee on Latin American Studies of the ACLS/SSRC in New York; and is editing *Studies in Democratisation* (forthcoming, Oxford University Press).

Preface

This book is the outcome of a collective project organised at Bristol by the Department of Politics and the Centre for Mediterranean Studies (CMS). It has involved several members of the Department at Bristol, in collaboration with colleagues and experts from several other institutions in the UK. The project developed in three stages. During the academic year 1991–2, most contributors to this book presented seminar papers (as a form of first draft) in Bristol; and in September 1992 a weekend conference was held there to discuss revised papers. Finally, there followed a further stage during the first half of 1993 when chapter authors completed their final versions based on extensive comments from the three editors.

This has been a collective endeavour on the part of the three editors; and it is difficult to see a substantial difference in the balance of labour. All of us planned this project together, and we were equally involved in the editing of the chapters. Geoffrey Pridham organised the seminar programme, and Eric Herring the conference which followed. George Sanford contributed the Eastern European comparative context to our work and kept an eagle eye on the detail.

There has been a distinct preference throughout the project for work of a comparative nature. We felt that in this way we could best handle the number and variety of simultaneous national transitions; and as this would help us confront analytically a process of democratisation not yet completed. We focus in particular on the region of East-Central Europe, but also discuss the democratisation process in the whole of Eastern Europe. Unfortunately, the chapter we commissioned on the Balkans failed to be delivered, but this region is included in several of the comparative chapters and is treated in some detail in that by Herring.

The project benefited from a research grant from the Nuffield Foundation. This allowed us to meet the conference costs, pay for a couple of field-trips to countries in Central Europe and purchase some research material. We wish to thank the Nuffield Foundation for its support.

We also wish to thank Rozean Marchand for compiling the index.

Geoffrey Pridham
Eric Herring
George Sanford

Bristol
September 1993

Introduction

Geoffrey Pridham, Eric Herring and George Sanford

The international dimension has been central to democratisation in Eastern Europe. It has taken many different forms: unintentional effects (such as market forces) as well as deliberate attempts to exercise influence (such as through trade barriers); non-state actors such as ethnic groups with cross-national allegiances, and entrepreneurs; and not least international organisations as well as national governments. Factors have emanated from beyond as well as within Eastern Europe; there have been unilateral as well as multilateral actions; and accurately gauged as well as misperceived behaviour by external actors has at times influenced the course of events. All these different forms of impact or influence summarised under 'the international dimension' are considered at various points in this book.

Our title deliberately strikes an uncertain note in three senses. First, the extent to which liberal or constitutional democracy is being built successfully to replace Communism in the countries of Eastern Europe is by no means always clear. Various democratic structures and processes have been established; but in some cases they have hardly taken hold effectively, while in others they may be undermined. Second, and related to this, there is no clear agreement on the goal and nature of democratisation and the best way to achieve it. This is distinctly more of a problem than was the case with the earlier transitions to democracy in Southern Europe from the mid-1970s. Furthermore, there is a significant element of those uninterested in or even hostile to democratisation in Eastern Europe. Third, while the removal of the Soviet veto dramatically improved the prospects for democratisation in Eastern Europe, the international dimension has not been unambiguously favourable for democratisation. In particular, the policies of Western countries and international organisations have not always facilitated the building of democracy in that region, and indeed have not always been directed towards that goal. In addition, interstate and non-state relations within Eastern Europe have not always been conducive to democratisation.

Overall, those wishing to build democracy in Eastern Europe are beset with monumental problems and challenges. Some of these problems are quite fundamental and historical in nature. Our study – if one may generalise about the conclusions of eight different authors – tends to portray a sobering picture of the prospects for democratisation where the chances of success seem highly varied cross-nationally. A favourable outcome for the region as a whole similar to that in Southern Europe is by no means a foregone conclusion.

It is necessary at this point to clarify our terms of reference for defining the scope of our book and for placing the current process of systemic change in Eastern Europe in sequential context. 'Democratisation' is seen as the overall process of regime change from beginning to end, including both stages of what are generally called in the comparative literature 'transition' to a liberal or constitutional democracy and its subsequent 'consolidation'. Clearly, this is a process far from completed in Eastern Europe as a whole. Indeed, expert opinion would tend to generalise that the countries of Eastern Europe are still undergoing transition and have not yet embarked seriously on consolidating their new liberal democracies (if that is the accurate term in some cases). It is highly likely their transitions will take rather longer than in Southern Europe.

By 'democratic transition', we mean a process of regime change commencing at the point when the previous authoritarian system begins to be dismantled, abruptly or gradually (in general, this occurred in the year 1989 in the cases of Eastern Europe). The democratic rules of procedure have to be negotiated and accepted; institutions have to be restructured; and political competition has to be channelled along democratic lines. Clearly, the phase of deciding on a new constitutional structure is crucial to transition which concludes once the new democracy begins to function thereafter. The political elites start to work with the new constitution and to adjust accordingly their behaviour to liberal democratic norms. 'Democratic consolidation' is often a lengthier stage but also one with wider and possibly deeper effects. It involves in the first instance the gradual removal of the uncertainties that invariably surround transition and the full institutionalisation of the new system, the internalisation of its rules and procedures and the dissemination of democratic values.

Already, a sizeable literature on the transitions in Eastern Europe has emerged. It has included general works such as from journalist observers of the collapse of the Communist system as well as historical discussions of the countries in question. In other cases it has concentrated on particular themes: the development of new political parties and party systems and patterns of mobilisation in post-Communist politics; the problems of introducing new market economies; and the growth of links with the European Community – to name the most obvious. Given the simultaneous transitions in different countries, there has been a fruitful tendency towards comparative work, although at the same time research on individual countries is growing.

One under-researched area has been a comprehensive analysis of the international dimension of these transitions in Eastern Europe – surprising because of the salience of international factors in this process. The international dimension has been more implicit than explicit in the literature so far published, apart from special work on aspects like the role of the EC. It is our hope with this book to offer the first systematic study of this dimension. In order to do so, we have brought together specialists on democratisation (Pridham and Whitehead), on international relations or European integration (Herring, Light, Pinder and Rengger) and on Eastern Europe and post-communism (Sanford, Light and Batt).

It follows from a previous volume on the same theme in a different region, *Encouraging Democracy: the international context of regime transition in Southern Europe* (Leicester University Press, 1991), edited by Geoffrey Pridham. That was based on a similar project, organised by the Centre for Mediterranean Studies at Bristol University, with the aim of directing attention to the neglected dimension of international factors in the literature on transitions to democracy, with special reference to European countries in the South.

Building Democracy? follows broadly the same analytical approach in focusing on linkages and interactions between domestic politics and external developments in a dynamic period of system change. It is one in which the Bristol Department has specialised through its MSc programme on 'Domestic Politics and International Relations', and reflects the concerns of several colleagues there, whether in comparative politics or international relations. This approach is explained and discussed by Pridham in Chapter 1 which draws comparisons between the transitions to democracy in the countries of Eastern Europe with the earlier experiences of regime change in Southern Europe.

The very salience of international factors in the recent transitions in Eastern Europe provided a further stimulus to this work. As many of the chapters emphasise, the international system as a whole altered dramatically as part of this process of regime change, thus making for a much more uncertain environment than in the Southern European cases. As Geoffrey Pridham shows, there were other signs of a greater prominence of external or transnational influences when comparing with Southern Europe, such as in the discontinuity caused in patterns of national foreign relations and policies in Eastern Europe, the closeness in timing of many more national cases, the emergence of more 'boundary crossing' issues (such as ethnic factors) with repercussions on relations between neighbouring countries and the greater dependence on outside assistance to manage the parallel transformation of economic systems.

The revolutionary changes in Eastern Europe also challenge some previous assumptions in democratisation theory, a theme explored by Laurence Whitehead. Asking whether the cases of Eastern Europe belong to the same classificatory schema as earlier transitions, he discusses the local terminology of democratisation and shows that 'democracy' has had distinctly prescriptive connotations in this region relating to market economy and geopolitical orientation. Taking an historical perspective, Whitehead notes that democratisation theory did not predict what happened in 1989.

Nicholas Rengger looks more fundamentally at the transitions in the

East from the viewpoint of democratic theory. He urges that democratisation be seen as a global question, for only in this way can the legitimacy of new systems be fully acquired. He broaches the problem of the disparate nature of democracy, and in examining these two basic versions comes to the conclusion that 'standard liberal democracy' (as a largely procedural definition) is that espoused by Western governments, while 'expansive democracy' (as having transformative effects) is closer to prevalent attitudes in Eastern Europe. Rengger advocates 'cosmopolitan democracy' as a way of overcoming this dichotomy and facilitating our understanding of change there. In particular ways, international institutions are increasingly taking decisions previously taken by states.

Eric Herring directs our attention to the importance of international security and its multi-faceted and complex relationship with democratisation. He sees the former as comprising different forms – political, environmental, economic, societal and military. This approach makes it possible to differentiate between multiple threats that may arise during democratisation. The dynamics of this relationship can be malign – international security threats undermine democratisation, failed democratisation undermines international security – or they may turn out to be benign. For instance, democratisation itself may soften the edges of different security problems if only because constitutional democracies are better than other systems in understanding the need for compromise and tend to possess more highly developed means for resolving disputes.

John Pinder assesses critically the role of the most important of the international organisations concerned, the European Community. The EC responded quickly to the events of 1989, but it has by and large disappointed the (high) expectations of its contribution to democratisation in the East. The Community has had a 'demonstration effect' of encouraging developments in Eastern Europe, all the more given the eventual prospect of membership. Pinder sees the EC's aims of supporting the move to market economy and pluralist democracy and of promoting international integration as mutually reinforcing, but comes to the firm conclusion that its responses have been inadequate. There is also an urgent task in helping to counter the emergence of intolerant nationalism in the East.

Whitehead likens the change in Eastern Europe to 'decolonisation' by the Soviet Union, whose impact on the countries of Eastern Europe at this time is covered in detail by Margot Light. She argues that Moscow had both a direct and an indirect influence on early democratisation there, the former through *perestroika* and policy change towards Eastern Europe and the latter through the role Moscow played in altering the international system and hence the context of events in Eastern Europe. Once democratisation got under way in Eastern Europe, however, a reverse linkage operated with the Soviet Union becoming strongly affected in turn by those events. Thus, the USSR may have created the necessary conditions for democratisation, but much depends on the countries of Eastern Europe and their international partners for ensuring that what follows is constitutional democracy.

Judy Batt's comparison of Czechoslovakia and Hungary draws out contrasts between the two cases in looking at both the strategies of the two Communist systems before 1989, balancing domestic and Soviet concerns and struggling with the effects of Gorbachev's reform policy, and the impact of international factors in regime collapse and beyond. Nevertheless, similarities have emerged in that Western recognition and the 'return to Europe' form a very important part of the legitimation of the new democracies in those countries (now three with the split between the Czech Republic and Slovakia). At the same time, nationalism has profound implications – positive as well as negative – for the democratisation process.

George Sanford similarly traces the process of democratisation over time and sees a complex and balanced interplay between external and domestic factors in the transition in Poland. In his view, that country was penetrated in two different and conflicting respects: by the Soviet control mechanism as far as the ruling elites were concerned; and, by countervailing Western influences on society through political, economic and cultural pressures since the 1950s. Ultimately, the Communist system could not check the changes favouring the evolution of civil society. Significant transformation had thus occurred before the arrival of Gorbachev, and then the policies he pursued served to isolate the ruling elite there. Furthermore, through promoting international changes (the withdrawal of the Soviet imperial guarantee and improved East/West relations), Gorbachev contributed to the shift of democratisation in Poland from 1989. The prospects for its success are reasonably good according to Sanford, and are enhanced by a favourable security position and international environment unprecedented in modern Polish history. One may be less optimistic about predicting the same for some other countries discussed in this book, especially in the Balkans.

Unlike with the previous project on Southern Europe, we have been concerned with a process of system change that is still under way rather than completed. This entails obvious risks, given the historical importance and magnitude of change in Eastern Europe, the full implications of which are, as yet, still unclear. Conceivably, too, some transitions might not eventually succeed in producing the kind of constitutional democracies familiar in Western Europe. We have sought to limit this problem of assessing present developments not only by comparisons with the earlier transitions to democracy, but also through adopting thematic or contextual directions to our work, including assessments of the role and influence of international organisations. Even the national case-studies which follow are treated in comparative perspective rather than simply as *sui generis*. In combining these different studies, we furthermore look at both 'inner-directed' linkages (the impact of the international system on the domestic system) and 'outer-directed' linkages (vice versa) in order to highlight external/internal interactions within the dynamics of system change.

In sum, *Building Democracy?* more than confirms the initial view behind this collective work that the international dimension is a principal component of the democratisation process in Eastern Europe. It is turning out to be a crucial condition of its success, as is emphasised in different ways in the chapters of this book. The implications and effects of the different problems and challenges for democratisation identified by our study are likely to remain for some time to come and well into the consolidation stage in Eastern Europe.

1

The international dimension of democratisation: theory, practice, and inter-regional comparisons

Geoffrey Pridham

Introduction

Undoubtedly, the different waves of transitions to constitutional democracy – in postwar Western Europe, in Southern Europe in the 1970s, in Latin America in the 1980s and now in Eastern Europe – reveal the influence and importance, if not salience, of international factors in this process, although to varying degrees. It is even arguable that a favourable or supportive geostrategic environment has been an essential, even perhaps crucial, explanation of the occurrence and the success or otherwise of such transitions in a given region. As Schmitter asked in *Transitions from Authoritarian Rule*,

> why have the liberalisations/democratisations of Southern Europe got off to what seems to be a better and more reassuring start [than Latin America]? A partial explanation is that the international context in that part of the world and at this point of time is more supportive of such an outcome . . . (O'Donnell, Schmitter and Whitehead, 1986, Pt. I, pp. 4–5)

However, its importance is more often assumed than proven. The 'international context', really a collective term for different external influences, clearly requires close examination to establish its exact influence on the course of regime change in a particular region.

It is now commonly felt among students of democratic transition that the international dimension has been far more decisive and probably more profound in the regime change in Eastern Europe than in the other regional cases – certainly compared with Southern Europe, and not withstanding the influence or intervention of the regional superpower, the USA, in postwar Western Europe and more recently in Latin America. Thus, a recently published study of democratic consolidation in Latin America and Southern Europe concluded in a postscript on Eastern Europe: 'The international dimension is likely to have a more direct and decisive impact on these transition processes than in most of the countries examined . . . but in no case is the impact of foreign powers on political developments as great as in Eastern Europe'. In the authors' view, while the USSR has withdrawn from Eastern Europe, 'its legacy continues to have a substantial impact on the character of domestic politics' (Higley and Gunther, 1992, pp. 346–7).

Similarly, Kumar has spoken historically of

> the extent to which the 1989 revolutions were an international phenomenon right from the start. In this they continued the general pattern of twentieth-century revolutions, but they appeared to go beyond it in the unusual degree to which they were marked by this feature . . . The causes of the revolutions and the conditions of their success were largely external (changes in Soviet policy); the ideas were mainly derived from external sources (western liberal ideas going back to the Enlightenment and the French Revolution); and the fate of the revolutions in the individual countries is, by general consent, dependent to a large degree on the reactions and intentions of the international community towards the new regimes. (Kumar, 1992, p. 441)

The evidence for this view of the predominance of the international context seems compelling. Not only was the USSR's changed policy line, allowing Eastern European countries to liberalise in their own way, the most decisive single cause of the shift to democratisation in Eastern Europe. But, also, there were many more transitions that commenced in a very short space of time – compared say with Southern Europe – thus enhancing the sense of cross-fertilisation or other transnational influences in the crucial early phase. The very theme of a 'return to Europe', that has surfaced since, highlights both the basic reorientation of these new democracies' external policies as well as the significance of Western organisations and financial institutions in the politics and economics of their regime change. And, then, there are other phenomena of opening up following the abandonment of the Iron Curtain, such as the cultural invasion from the West, the explosion of tourism, the transnational effects of the mass media and the encouragement of the technological revolution in Eastern Europe. Indeed, the events of 1989/90 have sometimes been referred to as the 'media revolution'.

Inter-regional comparisons have the virtue of providing a more definite focus for what is, in the case of Eastern Europe, still an ongoing and incomplete process of change. As argued below and in other chapters of this book, the system change there is still in a state of transition with the prospects for democratic consolidation questionable in some cases (which even raises the question: transition to what?).

Our comparison with the earlier and long since accomplished transitions in Southern Europe generally confirms that international factors were rather less decisive or even prominent there than in Eastern Europe. But we wish to know specifically how and why; and also whether there are any valid inter-regional lessons to draw from the previous experience. Such a comparison is all the more tempting, as political elites in several East European countries have looked to Southern Europe for models to influence their own path of change. This chapter, therefore, sets out some theoretical approaches to our theme, before turning to the Southern European transitions of the 1970s and inter-regional comparisons with Eastern Europe.

The international dimension of democratic transition: concepts and hypotheses

The comparative literature on democratic transitions has tended to conclude that international factors have been essentially secondary in importance, for regime change is primarily a dynamic process which is internally motivated. Thus, the *Transitions from Authoritarian Rule* volume – which examined both Southern Europe and Latin America – marked as 'one of the firmest conclusions' that such transitions and 'immediate prospects for political democracy were largely to be explained in terms of national forces and calculations; external actors tended to play an indirect and usually marginal role, with the obvious exception of those instances in which a foreign occupying power was present' (O'Donnell, Schmitter and Whitehead, 1986, Pt. I, P. 5).

It is, however, the contention here that any bald relegation of external factors to a secondary or subordinate category is too simplistic; and in any case begs a variety of questions about when, how and if. It does not do justice to what Almond has, in a carefully crafted essay, referred to as 'the complex dynamic process' of interaction between international factors and domestic processes (Almond, 1989, p. 257). The *Encouraging Democracy* volume looked comparatively at five transitions in Southern Europe, including postwar Italy and the recent Turkish case, in the spirit of Almond's approach. It concluded that the secondary status of international factors was less clear-cut than originally assumed, for 'as Southern European experience shows, there are different national cases and different kinds of external actors, with different degrees of influence, as well as different time contexts and different phases of transition' (Pridham, 1991, p. 26). Common patterns there indeed are, but the one most evident in Southern Europe – the attraction and influence of the European Community – warns against too sharp a distinction between the external and the domestic, even in the case of countries seeking membership. And, of course, the transitions in Eastern Europe essentially challenge the assumption of external factors as being secondary.

There is little established work as such on the international dimension of regime change. Regime transition theory has, somewhat like comparative politics, focused almost exclusively on domestic political systems. It is, nevertheless, possible here to draw some lessons so far as international factors are concerned. Rustow's 'dynamic model' of transitions to democracy, argues for instance that the 'background condition' which 'must precede all the other phases of democratisation' is national unity and agreed boundaries (Rustow, 1970), which immediately introduces an international aspect – and, one obviously applicable above all to Eastern

Europe. Generally, functionalist theory has given a priority to structural or environmental – notably, economic and social – determinants of political system change. In so far as these may be seen to represent 'confining conditions' (Kirchheimer), it is possible to incorporate for instance the international economy and constraints deriving from it. Similarly, genetic theories focusing on the crucial determinant of political choice during the transition process itself clearly may point, broadly speaking, to external concerns.

At the same time, some early work on the Eastern European transitions has argued that transition theory, related so far to regime change in the West, has limited use for the former as it deals with a capitalist framework (in assuming the existence of an independent civil society) and operates with a too narrow (largely procedural) concept of democracy (Ost, 1990, p. 17). One may hasten to add that democratisation closely tied to economic transformation is a combined process of system change not previously confronted by transition theory. Clearly, theoretical approaches need some rethinking, and indeed may well benefit from the experiences of Eastern Europe. The very assumption of the secondary importance of international factors is a major case in point.

As a whole, the international context may have a general impact through promoting trends of democratisation – in loading the dice in favour of a successful transition to democracy as well as creating pressures during the authoritarian period – or it may contribute to this process at crucial moments of the transition. Thus, one may distinguish between transition 'developments' (as continuous or longer-term, even commencing before transition) and transition 'events' or one-off occurrences, which have an influential or perhaps decisive effect because of their timing or potential for interaction with domestic tendencies in a certain country. They may even be a catalyst in stimulating the final collapse of an authoritarian regime and the consequent shift to democratisation, e.g. the flow of refugees from East Germany in summer 1989; the impact of the dismantling of the Berlin Wall on events in Prague in early November of that year.

Conceivably, too, the international context may sometimes have a negative or deterrent effect on democratisation, or it may hinder or delay the successful course of transition. For instance, 'developments' (such as a persistent deterioration in the international economy) may not be particularly favourable to transition, for they may overload governments when they are primarily concerned with the demanding task of constructing a new democracy. Similarly, some 'events' originating abroad might have a destabilising impact on a fragile system in the making. Instability and the threat of a reversal of reform trends in the Soviet Union in 1991 – the suppression in Lithuania in January, more seriously the attempted coup in Moscow in August – were a source of great concern especially in East-Central Europe.

It is therefore not particularly difficult to recognise the general significance and impact of the international dimension in transitions to democracy. It is 'almost by definition omnipresent since very few polities in the contemporary world are isolated from its effects' (Schmitter, 1991).

However, analysing its real impact or influence on the process of transition is somewhat difficult both theoretically and empirically. This is so because of the intrinsic complexity of the international context (which is clearly an umbrella term for a variety of different external actors, institutions or conditions), but more especially as 'its causal impact is often indirect, working in mysterious and unintended ways through ostensibly national agents' (Schmitter, 1991).

Concerning the first problem of complexity, one simple answer is to *unscramble the international context* by categorising (a) background or situational variables, (b) different external actors and (c) forms of external influence. These may be defined as follows:

a. background of a given country's external policy patterns under authoritarianism (isolation, semi-acceptance or involvement in international organisations); pressures for change in such patterns which in any case will be challenged with the onset of transition; the geostrategic situation, the present state of the international economy and significant international events surrounding the transition process; and, not least, the international system as such and how it is evolving at the time of transition;
b. external actors may be either international organisations (e.g. EC, NATO, IMF, World Bank, CSCE) with possible sub-classifications as to world-wide or regional, traditional or integrative; foreign governments, with the main distinction between superpowers and countries in the same region; and a range or non-governmental actors, both national and transnational, such as parties, interest and pressure groups and social institutions or groups (overall, such relations may be either bi- or multilateral);
c. apart from direct intervention in a country's domestic politics (invasion, occupation), forms of external influence vary in terms of openness and ease with which they may be assessed; they include the political, diplomatic, economic and commercial, moral, cultural and also covert or subversive; and they may be direct or indirect, coercive or persuasive.

It is likely that these inner-directed linkages (i.e. factors originating in the international context and interacting with domestic politics) will vary considerably as to their interest in and activity towards a given country undergoing transition, according to the latter's strategic importance and other conditions listed under (a).

The classification of external actors under (b) also leads us to consider the question of motivation. The superpower which has a special relationship with the region in which countries are undergoing transition is likely to view that change with its strategic or security interests predominantly in mind, the furtherance of democracy being a secondary concern. Liberal democracies in the same region will probably view the same process differently, though not of course to the exclusion of their strategic or particular concerns. Thus, it is conceivable that the furtherance of democracy will be a higher priority for them, albeit one mixed with national interests, probably of an economic kind, and perhaps influenced by traditional bilateral links with a country in transition. For instance, Whitehead distinguished between the USA in postwar Europe and later in Latin America in the former respect; and, in the latter, Western European governments whose attachment to democratic procedures was enhanced by the EC's stipulation that membership was only open to states with pluralist systems (O'Donnell, Schmitter and Whitehead, 1986, Pt. III, pp. 10–11, 18). One may also add that, generally, the USA has paid more attention to formal or procedural requirements and European governments to more substantial requirements for new democracies in other countries.

Furthermore, the time context may well influence the extent to which different external actors seek to influence other countries' regime transitions. The USA was far more intimately involved in the postwar Italian and West German transitions than it was thirty years on when Spain, Greece and Portugal abandoned authoritarian regimes, for meanwhile the international climate had changed – detente had replaced the Cold War – and the EC had emerged as an important regional actor. This last point is even more true when the Eastern European countries embarked on transition, with the EC at the forefront of coordinating Western economic aid to them and generally more visible than the USA as external actor.

The degree of influence by outside actors depends not least on the response or initiative of those countries in transition. It is thus important to focus also on outer-directed linkages, those originally in the domestic system and interacting with external actors. Here, there is much scope for national variation, and on similar grounds it is necessary to *unscramble the domestic context*, as follows:

a. background variables: similar to those under the international environment, they must include standing (treaty and other) commitments of the country in question that remain after the end of authoritarianism (these may in transition be questioned, but that depends on linkage actors, mentioned below); and, generally, the dynamics of the transition process – it may be consensual or gradual, or rapid and involve upheaval – which will condition attitudes towards external actors;
b. the operational environment and domestic linkage actors: specifically, the structure of government and how the changing system/distribution of power relates to external linkages; and the role of different elite groups, both political and non-political (such as economic and military, even ecclesiastical), whose attitudes towards external links must vary according to their particular outlooks and interests and the extent to which they incorporate an 'international dimension' to their transition strategies;
c. the wider domestic environment: this brings into play various societal influences beyond the immediate operational environment, such as the role of public opinion and the media, and the degree of fragmentation or cohesion in the domestic situation, e.g. the existence of cleavages over international issues.

Obviously, there may be different internal reactions within a given country to the international environment during the process of transition. Conceivably, too, the very uncertainties of transition are likely to sensitise domestic actors to external influences, although that may be offset by their absorption in the overwhelming tasks of transition politics. Much depends on factors under (a) concerning the nature of the transition and whether different domestic linkage actors follow lines that are at variance with each other. For instance, an internally contested transition is very likely to force domestic actors to look outwards for support; and it may well tempt external actors to influence directly the internal process of change.

As to the second basic problem identified above – the causal impact or influence of international factors in a transition to democracy – there are greater problems of analysis. It is generally difficult to isolate an effective 'cause' in a process such as regime change, so it is safe to assume there are usually several factors behind this. O'Donnell and Schmitter have commented sceptically on locating international causes in the breakdown of authoritarian regimes, in a way that might appear to question the overwhelming importance of Moscow in bringing about regime collapse in Eastern Europe:

> Ideological constraints at the international level have some effect on actor perceptions of the long-term viability of a given regime, and the negative impact of a downturn in the international economy can accelerate matters. Nevertheless, it seems to us fruitless to search for some international factor or context which can reliably compel authoritarian rulers to experiment with liberalisation, much less which can predictably cause their regimes to collapse. (O'Donnell, Schmitter and Whitehead, 1986, Pt. IV, p. 18).

Implicit here is that international factors are dependent variables, their influence or impact largely conditional on opportunities presented by domestic developments. While perhaps plausible to a conventional student of comparative politics, this assumption has to be challenged as it prejudges situations and does not really allow for cross-national variation. It is necessary therefore to adopt approaches which take us further in specifying how regime change relates to international causes.

One can for instance identify such conditions or patterns as national continuities. For instance, an obvious case in point is those countries which are usually categorised as 'penetrated systems', a term used in the 'linkage politics' school of international studies. According to Rosenau, 'a penetrated system is one in which non-members of a national society participate directly and authoritatively, through actions taken jointly with the society's members, in either the allocation of its values or the mobilisation of support on behalf of its goals', involving a certain 'fusion of national and international systems in certain kinds of issue-areas' (Rosenau, 1966, pp. 65 and 53). This condition is not static, but it can be long term as in states whose penetration, such as by a foreign government or international organisation, was well developed. It is particularly applicable to the Communist regimes in Eastern Europe which were in a special and collective sense 'penetrated systems' subordinate to the USSR.

This is a pattern which cannot readily be dismissed as secondary to a given country's politics. One may also ask whether a condition of 'penetrated-ness' assumes a special form in the event of regime transition. Does such a condition suggest a decisive role for an external actor in bringing this about? Very obviously, we refer again here to the USSR's role in causing the Eastern European transitions. Furthermore, does democratic transition in 'penetrated' countries make new regimes especially vulnerable to outside influences and calculations?

Hypotheses of this kind can provide analytical directions, although they cannot establish exact causality. The term 'penetration', for example, is often employed loosely in the international affairs literature and may mean various conditions ranging from 'influence' through 'interaction' to 'external control'. It may furthermore vary between official or governmental 'penetration' and that which derives more vaguely from transnational influences, such as a 'democracy effect' from neighbouring countries – the German word *Verflechtung* (interweaving) captures this phenomenon. Causality is perhaps more easily established later on through archivally-based historical research. This is likely to flush out details not available to the contemporary investigator, but even here a problem of evaluation still remains. Interviewing key individual actors may of course help, notwithstanding the usual limitations of self-justification or *ex-post facto* rationalisation.

Whatever the individual advantages of these alternative methods, we find most useful the framework of inner and outer-directed linkages outlined above for comparative assessment of international factors in democratic transition. This may be used not merely for identifying the most important actors and their different influences in given cases, but also for examining interactions between the national and international contexts and between elements in both. Thus, we can trace sets of chain reactions, whether originating in the domestic or the external arena, which clearly form part of the dynamics of the transition process.

At the same time, establishing causality requires some sense of sequence. Thus, we may strengthen this comparative approach by focusing on both typologies of transition but also phases of the transition process itself. Baloyra has, for example, schematised patterns of authoritarian breakdown and transition, underlining the importance of timing and locus as to international influences, varying too between different phases of the process. He distinguishes between early-internal, delayed-external, delayed-internal and late-external variations in the sequence of events here (Baloyra, 1987, pp. 297–8). For instance, delayed-external refers to deterioration in the previous regime, with the end-game precipitated by external factors that produce the final breakdown, a situation applicable to several cases of Communist regime collapse in 1989.

The *type of democratic transition* is largely determined by its speed, style and scope which in turn strongly condition the possibilities for impact by international factors. A rapid transition may leave little time for such factors to influence the course of events; while a prolonged and controversial process may well encourage external involvement. At the same time, patterns of pre-transition as well as the conjunction of events behind the shift to democratisation are likely to have a determining effect on the international dimension of transition.

Typologies of democratic transition abound in the comparative literature. Some focus on the mode of initiating transition, such as transaction, abandonment of power or transfer of power; while others focus on the speed of change (evolution, revolution) or the degree of support (consensual or polarised). Transitions may also vary in scope as to whether they are essentially elitist and top-down or participatory and more bottom-up. These are all classifications intended to highlight the *dominant* characteristics of national cases, although in reality the latter may well encompass elements of different styles either in parallel or in succession in the various phases of the process.

External events may be fairly decisive in bringing about the actual shift to democratisation. They may be even viewed as the primary factor at that particular moment, although that is unlikely to be possible without some disintegration of the previous regime's base. The latter may be due essentially to domestic factors, but it is also conceivable that international 'developments' as distinct from 'events' – such as external economic or commercial pressures, or the gradual filtering through of transnational cultural patterns of modernisation – may contribute to this disintegration. It is thus important to include a 'pre-transition' phase for assessing the impact of external factors in the overall process of regime change. At this stage, such change usually takes the form of 'liberalisation', when authoritarian rulers attempt defensively to bolster their regimes through political or socio-economic concessions. How this sensitive phase is handled may help to determine the subsequent course of transition, for invariably such liberalisation is a transitory solution which serves mainly to prolong authoritarian collapse.

Turning to the process of regime change itself, it is possible to identify *different phases of transition*. These may be as follows:

a. inaugural or initial, when the drama of authoritarian collapse is followed by the dismantling of that regime's structure and the first decisions are taken to embark on democratisation – at least, the strategic decision to opt for a liberal democratic type of system should be reasonably clear (this may, for instance, be reflected in the holding of the first free national election);
b. the constituent phase, when the main task is the formulation of a new constitution and other decisions are taken which help to define the particular form of liberal democracy chosen;
c. the completion phase, when the newly defined system begins to operate and basic policy lines are determined – essentially, we are looking here for confirmation of consensus around the constitutional settlement.

The impact or scope for external influences may well vary between such phases. For example, one may hypothesise that these influences could be prominent in phase (a); diminish during (b) when the process has begun to settle down and domestic actors are absorbed in working out the constitutional settlement; then they may reappear in phase (c), when the question of external policy (re)orientation is clarified, if it has not already been a subject of debate.

Of course, in reality such phases may not follow each other neatly; they may overlap or to some extent run in parallel, such as when the fundamental option for a liberal democracy remains contested or when features of the previous regime are not dismantled at the outset. This may well reflect on the form of transition and help to explain its length. One senses this is true of Eastern Europe, where the transitions are generally now in the constituent phase but where, in several cases, the initial phase is not completed and the systemic outcome is not really clear – will constitutional democracy after all be secured; or will there be a reversal to some form of authoritarianism?

International factors and inter-regional comparisons: the transitions in Southern and Eastern Europe

We now turn to the cases of the Southern European transitions, using the above comparative approaches to draw out lessons that may be relevant for the more recent transitions in Eastern Europe (the term 'Eastern Europe' is used for convenience of comparison, although it is now regarded as politically outdated). We start with continuities and sequence before looking closely at the international and domestic contexts.

Typologies of democratic transition

The Southern European cases were sufficiently variable in their speed as well as style, though less their scope, to allow for useful comparisons. As commonly recognised, the two Iberian cases approximated to the revolutionary and evolutionary modes of transition – although the degree to which post-1974 Portugal represented a revolutionary outcome has been disputed among experts of that country's politics. But the transition there was sufficiently volatile and prolonged to occasion external concern particularly in the first years. Spain's experience was a clear-cut case of transition by transaction and it was basically elitist and consensual, leaving little scope for foreign involvement. Greece saw a transfer of power by the military, with a transition that was brief – it was in part a restoration of pre-1967 structures – but one that was not very consensual; and, indeed, party-political polarisation very much included differences over external affairs.

The comparison becomes richer if we include the cases of postwar Italy and Turkey in the 1980s, which also introduce different time contexts from the mid-1970s. Following the defeat of Fascism, Italy experienced an externally monitored installation of democracy, a process marked by a fragile cross-party consensus and later by bitter polarisation. International developments, notably the coming of the Cold War, played a dominant part in that change. Turkey, on the other hand, saw a case of transition initiated by the military as government – as distinct from Greece (initiation by military as institution in overturning a military government). Turkey therefore followed a rather more controlled process, although it was a transition conducted in more tense East/West circumstances than the 1970s.

By and large, these five cases confirm the hypothesis that contested (and probably therefore prolonged) transitions present greater opportunities for external influences than controlled and consensual ones. Similarly, those which witnessed a violent or abrupt end to the previous authoritarian regime (Italy, Portugal, perhaps also Greece) saw a greater presence of such influences than those where transaction between previous regime leaders and new democratic elites resulted in a relatively peaceful process (Spain, Turkey). But, clearly, this kind of comparison has its limitations, for it cannot be divorced from the time context and the particular state of international relations, not to mention geostrategic location.

Eastern Europe also showed intra-regional variation concerning the speed and scope though less in the style of system change. Clearly, if we consider the developments preceding the shift to democratisation from 1989, then the cases of Hungary and Poland represent more gradual processes of change than say East Germany, Czechoslovakia and Romania, where the collapse of Communist rule occurred abruptly. At the same time, Bulgaria in particular and Romania in a more complicated way saw the initiation of change from within the outgoing regime. Some of the transitions were for a time more controlled from above, with some attempts at transaction – such as in Hungary and Poland – but by and large abandonment of power was much more common than in Southern Europe. Again, system change in Eastern Europe was rather more participatory in style with considerable momentum deriving from popular movements.

Despite these differences, it is more difficult to draw conclusions as to the link between type of transition and potential for external influences. The Spanish model of transition, which had initially much appeal for several of these countries, never replicated itself, for as a whole the regime changes in Eastern Europe have shown every sign of being prolonged affairs – more because of the economic crisis and disruption accompanying the political process than because they are internally contested (the latter may be subtly present in cases like Romania where the outcome is far from clear). However, the tragedy of ex-Yugoslavia demonstrates only too well how the chaos of transition can force external concern and involvement. One may simply conclude that the greater degree of international instability surrounding the transitions in Eastern, compared with Southern, Europe itself dictates a more intense relationship between external pressures and domestic change.

Transition events and developments

Southern Europe offers several examples of the impact of international factors in the form of initial transition events. Such events are important both for their timing – they occur at a vulnerable point for the authoritarian regime – and their effect, for they may prove decisive in helping to bring about the shift to democratisation.

In July 1974, the Greek military junta was compelled by their military defeat with the Turkish invasion of Cyprus to hand over government to Karamanlis, who returned from exile. This seems a fairly straightforward instance of an outside event prompting regime change. It was a catalyst for such change, following a process of disintegration of the junta's domestic political base – a problem that had accelerated the previous autumn with the student revolt in Athens. International opinion had to varying degrees been hostile to the military dictatorship, highlighting the regime's lack of legitimacy, although this was apparently not a determinant of its actual collapse (Verney and Couloumbis, 1991). At the same time, while the Cyprus crisis created a crucial opportunity, it was of course no guarantee of a successful democratisation. One can, however, argue that indirectly it had some relevant effects, e.g. in discrediting the military and therefore weakening the authoritarian alternative to the new democracy; also, in sensitising Greek opinion to external affairs during the transition.

In the Portuguese case, we have a classic instance of the corrosive effects of unsuccessful and increasingly unpopular colonial wars on the authoritarian system. There was a direct causal link between these wars in Africa and the military coup of 25 April 1974, through the radicalising influences of their colonial experiences on the middle-ranking officers who led the coup. As such these wars count as a development leading to transition. But if there was any single event, this was the publication of General Spinola's book, *Portugal and the Future*, which was openly critical of government policy in Africa. This encouraged a shift in atmosphere which marked the beginning of the end for the Estado Novo.

These two examples also illustrate the general relationship between 'events' and 'developments'. Transition events may interact decisively with domestic developments so as to instigate the shift to democratisation; but they may also be the culmination of pre-transition developments on the international level. In Spain, it is not possible to identify any particular external event which was decisive in opening the way for democratisation, for obviously it was Franco's death which ultimately made it possible. External developments were present in the international disapproval of his regime and the link between the opening up of the Spanish economy and growing pressures for political change (Story and Pollack, 1991). Their effects may be seen as indirect. In Italy's case, it need hardly be said, a primary international development – national defeat in a world war – brought about the fall of Fascism; while the wartime Resistance proved an important catalyst of early party development in the country's postwar democracy.

This national variation in the incidence of external events or developments is less true of the Eastern European transitions, because they were much closer in time and because they were all influenced strongly by a common development, namely the effects of Gorbachev's reform strategy in the Soviet Union. The reactions of Eastern European leaders to this unsettling change varied somewhat, but the overall effect eventually was to undermine their rule. It particularly posed a challenge to those leaders who maintained some form of Stalinist system, as in East Germany, Romania and Czechoslovakia. In the last case, the unprecedented questioning and self-criticism of Moscow's reform strategy ran directly counter to the severe line of the Husák regime, all the more as the changes were more radical than those voiced during the Prague Spring of two decades before. Gorbachev's refusal to endorse the Warsaw Pact intervention only reinforced this growing sense of alarm (Sword, 1990, p. 63).

In East Germany, Honecker tried to argue defensively that *perestroika* applied only to the particular case of the USSR, but this position was eroded by Gorbachev's growing popularity among the East German public and by first signs of democratisation evident in Poland and Hungary during the course of 1989 (Sword, 1990, p. 77). It is important to emphasise that this common stimulus to change to Eastern Europe formed the background to a special kind of transnational dynamics in regime change in the region. The closeness in time of the different shifts to democratisation enhanced the impact of cross-fertilisation between one case and another, lending considerable plausibility to there being a 'domino theory' at work. A transition in one country was an 'event' in another's own transition. The toppling of the hard-line Communist regimes in East Germany and Bulgaria made the opposition, and the hitherto uncommitted, in Czechoslovakia realise the vulnerability of their own system; and, perhaps more significantly, led to the party leadership there losing confidence (Sword, 1990, p. 65). This phenomenon of 'democracy by contagion' did not really happen in Southern Europe. The Franco regime was clearly unsettled by the Portuguese revolution of April 1974, but the dictatorship continued for another year and a half; and there is no evidence of this revolution seriously affecting the events in Greece a few months later.

Once transition began, various 'boundary crossing' developments ensured that the international dimension of this process in Eastern Europe remained visible. This was particularly true of the problem of ethnic minority issues affecting relations between neighbouring countries. The centre-periphery aspect of building new democracies thus became all the more poignant as it merged with nationalism; and nationalism has been a major source of historical conflict, notably in the Balkans. Needless to say, the explosion of civil war in the former Yugoslavia is the ultimate instance of this kind of problem threatening the prospects of democratic transition. In the Southern European transitions, such 'boundary crossing' issues were confined to the case of the Basque Country which, linked to terrorism, did for a time pose a special threat to the democratic process in Spain as terrorist actions acerbated military discontent.

Phases of transition

One may suppose that the international dimension is likely to fluctuate in salience and intensity between, if not within, the successive phases of transition, according to their different concerns as well as the rhythm of events. The initial phase is likely to engage international attention because of the drama of change and the uncertainties of its meaning for foreign powers; the constituent phase will probably see leaders of a new democracy turn inwards to concentrate on the time-consuming task of constructing its new system; and the completion phase will see them resume a more regular involvement in external affairs by defining or elaborating the country's policy lines and, no doubt, participating actively in international organisations.

This represents an ideal situation, a transition process that is orderly and uncomplicated, somehow disconnected from pressures of unforeseen events. In the constituent phase, for instance, a country's foreign politics cannot of course be held in abeyance; and certain events might force sustained attention to external concerns. We all know that regime transitions are inevitably disorderly if not messy affairs if only through the upheaval they occasion. Spain showed some resemblance to this ideal in that, following international interest in Franco's final crisis and then demise and the early uncertainties until democratic reform was adopted, the new government leaders became immersed in the business of drawing up a constitution, which was an elaborate process as it was based on cross-party negotiations. Once this progressed and the first parliamentary elections took place, the government felt free to make its application for membership of the European Community, Spain's most important external policy decision after Franco.

Portugal was rather different, as the initial phase was much more turbulent and even the other two stages remained somewhat unsettled, as shown by continuing disputes over the constitutional settlement of 1976. This tended to arouse foreign concern, although in the short run that fluctuated. There were times during the domestic upheavals of 1974–6 when international considerations withdrew from centre stage. But the course of events only showed there was quite some variation in the interplay between the domestic and the external. For instance, there were moments during the highly unstable year of 1975 when Western concern over Portuguese affairs was intense, being high on the NATO agenda and the subject of some covert action (Maxwell, 1986, p. 131).

Italy was a classic instance of foreign involvement in the transition process, a pattern especially strong during the long initial phase but also the constituent phase until the USA's internal ally, the Christian Democrats, secured their dominance in the parliamentary election of 1948. But Italy's politics nevertheless remained an object of particular interest abroad because of this special link with Washington and her strategic position in the Mediterranean.

There is therefore some partial truth in the above hypothesis about the salience of the international dimension, but this is much less so with the transitions in Eastern Europe. Certainly, the initial phase occasioned considerable international attention and involvement, if only because these transitions were widely unexpected, and as so many occurred together within a matter of months. It persisted through the first elections held in the spring of 1990 and even beyond. It is possible now to see some lessening of this intense international interest, for the novelty of events has gone, while the countries in question have turned to drawing up constitutions and generally building the new systems.

But it would be rash to assume that, in other ways, international factors have retracted from the scene. This is partly because the main task of the initial phase – reasonable clarity about the systemic outcome of transition – has not yet been achieved in some cases, a consequence being continuing uncertainty about external policy lines. But, also, international sources of conflict have persisted through the subsequent phase. Slovenia may now be settled and has begun to establish westward-looking links with other European states, but Croatia is deeply involved in civil war. Indeed, the whole problem of Yugoslavia makes nonsense of our hypothesis about the different phases of transition; and the tensions it creates clearly affect the transitions in neighbouring Balkan countries. The countries of East-Central Europe are rather more settled into the constituent phase, although by no means free of international repercussions, as illustrated by the division of Czechoslovakia between two new states with rather different policy strategies if not different future systemic outcomes of transition. It remains to be seen what will be the effects of this in terms of their respective international allegiances.

Taken together, these different sequential approaches to democratic transition in the two regions show that, as a main point of difference, international factors have predominated more continuously in Eastern compared with Southern Europe. This is not to say they have not also predominated at times in the latter, but generally the impact of external factors was more uneven, often less direct and possibly less profound in Southern Europe. We now turn to the international and domestic contexts as a more systematic way of comparing the two sets of transitions.

The international context

BACKGROUND OR SITUATIONAL VARIABLES: the geostrategic situation in a given region is rather influential so far as foreign perceptions of a particular transition or set of transitions is concerned. Thus, the Mediterranean had become an area of greater superpower concern by the time of the transitions in the mid-1970s, with the enhanced Soviet naval presence in the East Mediterranean and increased instability in the Middle East. Hence the occurrence of several regime transitions in the Northern Mediterranean was, from the strategic viewpoint, not a welcome development; and it inevitably sharpened the interest of the USA and European governments in the outcome (Chipman, 1988, Introd. and Ch. 1). All the same, the process of detente between East and West nevertheless softened their concern, except at various moments in 1975 during the Portuguese transition.

The time context may indeed sharpen the pressure from geostrategic concerns, as the Italian transition showed. This occurred at a sensitive point given the emergence of the Cold War and the closeness of the Iron Curtain, not to mention uncertainty about the outcome of civil war in Greece. The economic and political instability in Italy, following the end of Fascism, together with the strength of the Communists combined to intensify external, especially American, inclinations to intervene.

The obvious lesson here is that international tension or instability provokes active concern over regime change, which of course only adds to such instability, all the more if an individual country undergoing transition is in a particularly sensitive location, as were Italy and Greece. But the difference in the two time contexts shows that even in the Greek transition from 1974 there was no likelihood of external intervention. It was also a speedy transition with the reassuring figure of Karamanlis at the helm.

As it transpired, there was, despite regime change, considerable continuity of external policy allegiances in Southern Europe. This was least so in postwar Italy, where the country's allegiances still remained to be defined in the transition following Fascism; indeed, they were one of the contentious issues then, given the East/West divide that separated the parties of the Left and Right. But in the four other cases the countries were already part of 'the West', albeit semi-isolated pariahs during their dictatorships. Most strikingly, Portugal was a member of EFTA and NATO before as well as after transition. Spain was under Franco part of the Western alliance by virtue of the bilateral defence agreement with the USA; and Greece had been a member of NATO from 1951. The main difference that transition made was that these countries could now (re-)join the Council of Europe and apply for EC membership, on grounds of being constitutional democracies. The disruption of regime change caused some temporary discontinuity in that anti-American sentiments surfaced, linked with US support for the previous authoritarian systems, leading to Greece's withdrawal from active NATO membership for some years. In Spain, the same problem was reflected in domestic tensions over the decision to join NATO early in 1981, this being settled by the referendum of 1986.

With Eastern Europe, we are talking about an entirely different situation with more momentous implications for the transition process. As a consequence of democratisation and the disbandment of Comecon and the Warsaw Pact, there followed rapidly the end of superpower rivalry and of the politico-military divide in Europe. As Kumar puts it, 'everyone is convinced that, except in the unlikely event of a return to the pre-1989 order in Eastern Europe, the 1989 revolutions have initiated a new phase in international history' (Kumar, 1992, p. 441). While international tension on one plane was abolished, other more localised areas of tension (re-)surfaced in Central Europe and the Balkans. Generally, international instability in Europe mushroomed, not to mention the extra uncertainties deriving from the highly shaky process of reform in Russia and other former republics of the Soviet Union. The international context itself was therefore overturned, with considerable potential for problems in the one context interacting precariously with problems in the other.

By the same measure, external policy discontinuity predominated with a broad need for redefining allegiances both bilaterally and multilaterally.

There was some move towards regional groupings like the Pentagonal (later Hexagonal) association of Central European states, the Black Sea association and some *rapprochement* between the countries of East-Central Europe. But, most importantly, the general tendency among the last was towards prospective membership of the EC, joining the Council of Europe and the Europe (association membership) agreements with Brussels being early instances of this westward redirection of their external allegiances.

EXTERNAL ACTORS: there is much greater similarity between the two regions over external actors, owing to the European Community being the most consistent and influential external actor in both cases. The EC provided moral, economic and political support for the new democracies in the South from the mid-1970s and in the East in the early 1990s, with the USA playing a background role. The main difference between the two examples has been the extent to which the EC itself has developed greater political weight in the intervening period and become an object of enhanced expectations – on the part of the Eastern European states, especially those in Central Europe.

One feature evident in the Southern European transitions is the replacement of bilateral by multilateral special relationships. This had a significance in that bilateral relationships often involve a subordinate client status and can therefore become controversial. They may also, as in Western European experience, be less supportive of democratisation than a multilateral framework like the EC, which specified constitutional democracy as a prerequisite for prospective membership.

Postwar Italy was different from the other Southern European cases, as her ruling elites – the Christian Democrats and their government allies – became political clients of Washington from the time the latter began to provide necessary economic aid. This occurred when the threat from the Left intensified. Through their controlling relationship with the Italian government – supplemented by support for the ruling party organisations and their allied trade unions – the Americans helped to secure Italy's allegiance to the Western alliance and, also, to guarantee the permanent dominance of the centre-Right in Italian politics (Leonardi, 1991). This client relationship was in some respects inhibiting for Italy's democratisation process. Cold War mentalities imprinted themselves on her postwar politics, contributing decisively to the lack of alternation in government which eventually became a principal source of malfunctioning in Italy's system. Indirectly, at least, the American connection was a cause of the prolonged consolidation of democracy there, having been a key determinant of transition in the first place. As Pasquino emphasises, controversy over the transition persisted in Italy and much coloured relations between the various political parties for a long time (Pasquino in O'Donnell, Schmitter and Whitehead, Pt. 1, 1986, pp. 65–6).

The Spanish and especially the Greek transitions were on the contrary marked by a reaction against the bilateral link with the USA due to the latter's support for the two dictatorships. This was significant as it opened the way for the multilateral relationship through EC membership to dominate these new democracies' external policies. It was during the process of Second Enlargement (Greek and Iberian entry) that the Community developed more clearly its principle of democratic conditionality. Its requirements were not merely procedural, such as the holding of free elections and the existence of a constitution, but also included some evidence of the right balance of party strength (pro-democracy parties in the ascendant) and of a reasonably stable government (Pridham, 1991, pp. 234–5). Some EC member states were fairly active through assistance given to particular parties in Iberia in the first years of transition. The lengthy negotiations for entry in effect allowed ample time for testing these requirements. The same is very likely to happen with applicants from Eastern Europe.

The East European transitions have brought the rejection of a bilateral relationship of a very extensive kind. Certainly, the Communist regimes there were in a special and collective sense 'penetrated systems' subordinate to the USSR, to a degree qualitatively different from American penetration of postwar Italy and Greece for example – which was conducted largely via embassies and secret services. As Dawisha notes, 'the CPSU succeeded in establishing a series of binding relationships and mechanisms (the parallel party bureaucracy, the nomenklatura and cells within non-party organisations) for alliance management that was totally without equal in the West' (Dawisha, 1990, p. 98). It was also evident in the way the USSR used security services and the military as major levers of influence throughout Eastern Europe (Dawisha, 1990, pp. 101–2).

With the prospect of eventual EC entry by several Eastern European states, the Community has further refined the principle of democratic conditionality to emphasise democratic values. Thus, negotiations over economic assistance with Bulgaria and Romania were suspended because of human rights abuses. The potential influence of the EC on the recent transitions is enhanced by its prestigious standing in the East, linked to lofty expectations there of a Western style of life. However, the scope for disillusionment is by the same account considerable – there was a foretaste of this in Polish frustrations over the terms of the Europe agreement – and one suspects that generally the EC, with its institutional deficiencies and limited resources, is being asked to assume a burden beyond its capabilities. This is amply demonstrated by the immensely complicated situation in ex-Yugoslavia at a time when the EC has not yet acquired a fully fledged foreign policy role, let alone a defence policy function.

FORMS OF EXTERNAL INFLUENCE: these may be summarised briefly, given this draws on the preceding discussion. The point at issue is that different forms of influence have different effects on the transition process. Conceivably, too, they are not always helpful to democratisation, although as Southern Europe showed this depended on their timing, extent and source.

By and large, the forms of external influence that predominated in the transitions of the 1970s were political and diplomatic, commercial and to a lesser extent economic (in terms of aid), and they were also moral through demonstrations of solidarity. They were generally persuasive rather than coercive, although during 1975 at a sensitive moment in the Portuguese transition contingency plans were formed to counter any worsening of the threat to the option of liberal democracy. While covert activity was not absent from these transitions, it was much more prominent in the Italian case such as in extensive CIA operations in the late 1940s and the 1950s. American economic aid at the crucial moment in the Italian transition, in 1947/8, probably helped to secure the victory for the Right; while, generally, both American and Soviet interference in this period helped to sour relations between the main political forces. It is difficult in the transitions of the 1970s to pinpoint any similar occasion, except possibly threats from Western leaders to Moscow that any interference in Portugal would damage the Helsinki conference (Pridham, 1991, p. 237).

Again, there are similarities with Eastern Europe by virtue of the EC's importance as external actor. The Community's influence is clearly one of persuasion through the link between democratic conditionality and the attractive prospect of membership. The main difference is that economic influence is obviously much more prominent in view of the economic transformation in Eastern Europe and the heavy reliance on Western aid and training and advice. This implies a greater scope for external actors – international financial institutions, the EC and national governments – to influence the outcome of transition there. There are two further points of difference from Southern Europe. The transnational role of the media, in particular television, appears to have been significant in influencing the beginning of transition, especially in the countries of Central Europe, through the broadcasting of transition events elsewhere. This influence may be classified as cultural, and it was less present or more diffuse in Southern Europe as the transitions there were more separated in time. Finally, one cannot ignore pressures for outside military involvement notably in ex-Yugoslavia. The closest it came to this in the South was when the USA formed plans in the later 1940s for military intervention in Italy in the event of a Communist uprising.

The domestic context

BACKGROUND VARIABLES: these refer to past patterns or inheritances from the authoritarian period which have a bearing on domestic responses to international factors during the transition; and, particularly, to how far external policy and allegiances are viewed as a means for democratic support or legitimation.

In Southern Europe, we have already noted the contrast between post-war Italy as a case of external 'penetration' originating in the transition process and Spain and Greece, where transition saw a rejection of client status. Greece had a background of foreign 'penetration' over a long period, American interference in her politics from the civil war being the latest example. Indeed, Greek problems of national identity derived much from this experience going back to the centuries of Turkish occupation. It followed that any attempt to solve this problem – made possible by a return to democracy – is likely to have certain beneficial effects for democratisation (Verney and Couloumbis, 1991).

Regime change usually involves some form of confrontation with national history. This is invariably uncomfortable and perhaps painful, since it requires not merely a rejection of the preceding regime but also a slice of national experience which may have longer roots. It is very likely that international factors are involved here, as such questions like national pride and credibility, the international component of system legitimacy and the need for establishing or reviving national influence in the international community arise. A feature common to the previous authoritarian regimes in Southern Europe was their relative isolation in international or European affairs, and some concern at their exclusion from European organisations. The removal of such regimes thus creates an historical opportunity for redefining a country's role in the world.

In Eastern Europe, there is a similar if not more powerful link between external allegiances and democratisation. The fervent desire for a 'return to Europe, involves a radical redirection of such allegiances and not merely an escape from isolation; and it combines with an opening up of national economies to the world market. There is again an evident link with democratic legitimation. Since the legitimacy of the Communist regimes was closely associated with Moscow, this external relationship inhibited these regimes from acquiring indigenous bases of support (Dawisha, 1990, pp. 131–2). Release from that relationship created space for a new regime to acquire legitimacy more freely.

OPERATIONAL ENVIRONMENT AND DOMESTIC LINKAGE ACTORS: a transition from authoritarian rule to constitutional democracy creates not merely a chance for redefining external policy lines but also a different mechanism for decision-making on external affairs. Notwithstanding the constraints of secrecy in such matters, external relations become more directly or overtly subject to domestic pressures, if only because competing political parties may adopt different or conflicting positions. The basic concern here is how much this affects external policy performance, and hence indirectly the prospects for a new democracy to establish itself.

As Couloumbis has noted in the case of Greece, the state of decision-making over foreign policy changed dramatically after 1974. Whereas before, other actors like the throne, the military (all the more during the junta period) not to mention the USA (as external wire-puller) and the diplomatic service all played some political role here, now it was the cabinet and especially the prime minister who carried responsibility in external affairs (Couloumbis, 1983, pp. 113–14). This clearer concentration of authority made for potentially effective leadership; and during the transition that was evident in Karamanlis's decisive role in pushing through the Greek application to the EC. One can see parallels here with De Gasperi's role in determining postwar Italy's adherence to the Atlantic Alliance and participation in the first European union projects (the dual

Western option), and to some lesser extent in the dominant role of the prime minister in post-Franco Spain.

Admittedly, this also made for some form of monocratic leadership, but it was one subject to various political constraints. With the coming of democracy, external relations became a legitimate area for party debate and media coverage. Spain was the least complicated case, for her embracing of the European option was widely supported at the party-political and public levels. The identification of the EC with democracy was widely recognised and it allowed post-Franco political (also economic) elites a symbolic reference point and also a reason for implementing necessary policies to adjust to future membership. It thus enhanced the chances for effective system performance; and this consensus on Europe furthermore signalled the width of support for the new democracy (Pridham, 1991).

In the other cases in the South, external allegiances were a matter of domestic controversy with some implications for (new) system loyalty. In Italy, the decision on joining NATO in 1949 was a subject of vitriolic debate between left and right, this being associated with not only the Western alliance but also the option for a West European type of parliamentary democracy. In post-1974 Portugal domestic conflict over the type of system became in part externalised, whereby political figures and parties sought external allies through foreign governments or transnational party links, not to mention the solidarity of the EC. The issues of Community and NATO membership became a basic point of difference between the Communists and the other forces (Opello, 1991). And, in Greece, there was for the best part of the decade a polemical divergence over external allegiances between the parties, although this did not have serious repercussions on the transition outcome.

Looking at Eastern Europe, one may apply the same general lessons, although it is perhaps too early to draw conclusions about foreign policy effectiveness and system reinforcement. There is some similarity in that the semi-presidential systems there have allowed scope for political figures like Wałęsa and, earlier, Havel to play an active part in external relations. But there is one major difference from the South in that the extreme overload on these new democracies with the burden of economic transformation (which has an international dimension) is placing and will continue to place a considerable strain on these systems. While there is wide support for the European option, especially in the countries of East-Central Europe, a most serious challenge arises in the form of (ethnic) nationalism. At first sight, the emergence of nationalism in post-Communist Eastern Europe may be a way of redefining state legitimacy; but it also provides, in its more hostile form, a channel for diverting from 'Europe'.

THE WIDER DOMESTIC ENVIRONMENT: this really takes further the point mentioned above about domestic pressures that surface with democratisation, especially in reference to public opinion and the media. The matter of cleavages has already just been covered since political elite differences over external policy issues drew strength from ideological or ethnic differences at the societal level.

In Southern Europe, it is worth noting that recent research on the opinion-policy nexus in the three new Mediterranean democracies of Iberia and Greece has shown that there was a greater consistency between opinion trends and policy on external relations than on domestic issues for the period 1978–86, which overlaps sufficiently with the transition period in these countries (Brooks, 1988, pp. 133–4). This does not have to contradict discussion above about domestic conflict over external allegiances. It may in part be explained by the fact that public knowledge on external matters is usually less than on domestic questions; although, equally, it is quite likely that post-authoritarian societies were relieved if not delighted their countries were once more acceptable to international opinion. This feeling was particularly marked in Greece, where the short-lived Colonels' regime (when European opinion was distinctly adverse) meant people remembered the previous democracy when international responses were different. In general, the media played an important part in the opening up to international influences by dint of their free reporting on foreign events and developments.

In Eastern Europe, it is difficult at this relatively early stage to measure exactly trends of opinion on external issues, except that in broad terms, as just mentioned, there is a strong pro-Europe consensus in several countries, while in others this may be at variance with nationalist feeling. One is tempted here to draw not too fine a distinction between East-Central Europe in the first instance and the countries of the Balkans in the second. What is clear, however, is that the media played a rather visible role in many of the East European transitions from the start. This happened to a degree more dramatic than in Southern Europe, where limited liberalisation under authoritarian rule (e.g. Franco's Press Law 1966) had previously increased the chances for European influences to encourage 'modernising' effects in society; but the media did not play the same direct role in helping to shift the dictatorships.

A few examples illustrate this phenomenon in the transitions of Eastern Europe. Just as censorship in Czechoslovakia found it impossible eventually to stem the flood of new articles appearing in Soviet party journals, expressing the mood of reform in the USSR, so, Honecker censored Gorbachev's statements in the SED organ but could not stop extensive coverage of them in West German radio and television, which was widely followed in East Germany (Sword, 1990, pp. 63, 77). One of the most significant developments in Bulgarian politics in early 1987 was Sofia's agreement with Moscow to boost Soviet television signals so that 90 per cent of Bulgarians were able to view the programmes; and the impact was profound once the public realised what was happening in the USSR (Glenny, 1990, p. 170). Television played a decisive role in the turbulent events in Romania in late 1989 and afterwards. It is widely agreed that Ceauşescu's fate was sealed when he faltered during a speech being televised live from the Central Committee building in Bucharest (Glenny, 1990, p. 116). And, once transition set in train in these countries, then the scope for Western cultural and political influences to cross borders multiplied accordingly.

Thus, looking at the domestic context tends to reinforce the general importance of the societal level in the transitions of Eastern Europe. In Southern Europe, this was not absent but it was a less compelling pressure. And, in Eastern Europe, this had a more profound impact linked as it was to the degree of change being more far-reaching.

Conclusion

The discussion of the two regional waves of transition to constitutional democracy in Southern Europe in the 1970s and in Eastern Europe in the 1990s strongly supports the common view that international factors have had a more persistent and profound effect in the latter case. This is no real surprise since many of these factors have been rather visible in Eastern Europe.

Our main concern in this study has been to identify how, when and why international factors have been important in these two waves of democratic transition. By way of summary, the main differences and similarities between the two regions may be noted as follows:

1. The international system itself altered as a consequence of both Gorbachev's reform strategy and the transitions in Eastern Europe. This set in motion a form of dynamics whereby international and domestic system change interacted and helped to account for the fact the latter was particularly sensitive to the former. In Southern Europe, international factors were at times significant, but they impacted domestically in a less uniform and more national-specific way. They were most evident when transitions were contested internally.
2. Linked to this, there was a much greater break with continuity in external relations when transition occurred in Eastern Europe. The policy redirection that followed required more intensive concern with international affairs during the transition itself than in Southern Europe, where the 'return to Europe' involved a less radical departure.
3. The more extensive wave of transitions in Eastern Europe – there were many more, and they were closer in their timing than those in Southern Europe – reinforced the transnational dynamics of system change in the region. A transition in one country there became an 'event' in another country's own transition.
4. While many of the outside actors were the same in the two sets of transitions – in particular international organisations, above all the EC – there has been a greater dependence on assistance from such outside actors on the part of Eastern Europe, if only because of the demands of economic transformation which have accompanied political regime change.
5. Transition in Eastern Europe has been marked by more regular 'boundary crossing' issues than was the case in the Southern transitions a decade and a half earlier. Problems like the re-emergence of nationalism combined with centre-periphery tensions have meant that internal

cleavages have impacted more frequently on the international context with potentially destabilising effects.

6. There has been a similar shift in both regions from bilateral to multilateral linkages abroad, a general tendency that on past practice has been conducive to democratisation. With the recent transitions, this has happened more in the countries of East-Central Europe than those of the Balkans. This must be one reason among several why the former's chances for successful transition are greater.
7. Most ominously, international military action was not a factor in the Southern European transitions, but it is already a trend in the case of Yugoslavia with a potential threat of this affecting other countries in the region.

A final conclusion from this study is that if anything the international dimension has been somewhat underrated even in the transitions in Eastern Europe, at least after the key factor in the pre-transition phase, the USSR, withdrew from the forefront of events once these transitions started. This only argues for a basic reconsideration of theories of regime transition, which have conventionally assumed that international factors are at best a secondary consideration.

References

Almond, G., 1989, 'Review article: the international-national connection', in *British Journal of Political Science*, April, pp. 237–59.

Baloyra, E. (ed.), 1987, *Comparing New Democracies*, Westview Press, Boulder.

Brooks, J.E., 1988, 'Mediterranean neo-democracies and the opinion-policy nexus', in *West European Politics*, July, pp. 126–40.

Chipman, J., 1988, *NATO's Southern Allies: internal and external challenges*, Routledge, London.

Couloumbis, T., 1983, 'The structures of Greek foreign policy' in R. Clogg (ed.), *Greece in the 1980s*, Macmillan, London.

Dawisha, K., 1990, *Eastern Europe, Gorbachev and Reform*, Cambridge University Press, Cambridge.

Glenny, M., 1990, *The Rebirth of History: Eastern Europe in the age of democracy*, Penguin, London.

Higley, J. and Gunther, R., 1992, *Elites and Democratic Consolidation in Latin America and Southern Europe*, Cambridge University Press, Cambridge.

Kirchheimer, O., 1965, 'Confining conditions and revolutionary breakthroughs' in *American Political Science Review*, December, pp. 64–74.

Kumar, K., 1992, 'The 1989 revolutions and the idea of Europe', *Political Studies*, September, pp. 429–61.

Leonardi, R., 1991, 'The international context of democratic transition in postwar Italy' in G. Pridham, *Encouraging Democracy*, Leicester University Press, Leicester, pp. 62–83.

Maxwell, K., 1986, 'Regime overthrow and the prospects for democratic transition in Portugal' in G. O'Donnell, P. Schmitter and L. Whitehead, (eds), *Transitions from Authoritarian Rule*, Pt. 1, pp. 109–37.

O'Donnell, G., Schmitter, P. and Whitehead, L. (eds), 1986, *Transitions from*

Authoritarian Rule: prospects for democracy, Johns Hopkins University Press, Baltimore.

Opello, W., 1991, 'Portugal: a case study of international determinants of régime transition' in G. Pridham, *Encouraging Democracy*, Leicester University Press, Leicester, pp. 84–102.

Ost. D., 1990, 'Transition theory and Eastern Europe', paper presented to conference on democratisation in Latin America and Eastern Europe, Pultusk, Poland, May, 1990.

Pridham, G. (ed.), 1991, *Encouraging Democracy: the international context of regime transition in Southern Europe*, Leicester University Press, Leicester.

Rosenau, J., 1966, 'Pre-theories and theories of foreign policy' in R.B. Farrell (ed.), *Approaches to Comparative and International Politics*, Northwestern University Press, Evanston.

Rustow, D., 1970, 'Transitions to democracy: toward a dynamic model', *Comparative Politics*, April, pp. 337–63.

Schmitter, P., 1991, 'The international context for contemporary democratisation: constraints and opportunities upon the choice of national institutions and policies', paper, Stanford University, September 1991.

Story, J. and Pollack, B., 1991, 'Spain's transition: domestic and external linkages' in G. Pridham, *Encouraging Democracy*, Leicester University Press, Leicester, pp. 125–58.

Sword, K. (ed.), 1990, *The Times Guide to Eastern Europe*, Times Books, London.

Verney, S. and Couloumbis, T., 1991, 'State-international systems interaction and the Greek transition to democracy in the mid-1970s' in G. Pridham (ed.), *Encouraging Democracy*, Leicester University , Leicester, pp. 103–24.

2

East-Central Europe in comparative perspective

Laurence Whitehead

Introduction

The comparative analysis of democratisation processes was a flourishing branch of political science well before the dismantling of the Berlin Wall, on 10 November 1989. That event, its timing and the transformations through East-Central Europe which it symbolised, were unforeseen not only by virtually all academic observers, but also by world statesmen, foreign ministries and media commentators. Certainly the available stock of 'democratisation theory' was not capable of predicting – or even of strongly suggesting – the course, speed, or sequencing of political developments that converted all the six non-Soviet members of the Warsaw Pact from Communist-ruled regimes into polities operating under more or less competitive electoral systems within about a year. Fortunately such predictive power is not an essential requirement of useful work in comparative politics.

This chapter is based on the assumption that with the benefit of hindsight it can still be helpful to re-examine the political upheavals of 1989 deploying the categories and hypotheses distilled from earlier experiences of democratisation. But equally, these pre-existing analytical tools may have to be revised or refined in the light of East-Central European experiences. This volume focuses attention on one particular aspect of the democratisation literature that may require substantial re-evaluation in view of the collapse of the Soviet bloc, and of post-Cold War developments, not only in Europe but also in various parts of the Third World. Initial approaches to the theory of democratisation derived from a restrictive range of Latin American and Southern European processes which took place within a securely bipolar world, with the result that the 'international dimension' was downplayed and conceived in a restrictive manner. Even with regard to those earlier processes some reconsideration may be called for, given the heightened prominence of international influences apparent in many subsequent cases of regime transition.

However, before the 1989 democratisations can be invoked to justify a possibly wholesale reconstruction of previous analytical work, we need to consider whether these processes do indeed belong in the same classificatory schema as the earlier processes. At the moment of writing it is still too soon to justify the inclusion of the East-Central European cases on the grounds that the eventual systemic outcomes are the same, although that argument is gradually gaining force with the passage of time. Participants in the events of 1989 certainly invoked the same vocabulary – of democratisation, human and civic rights, rule of law and clean and open elections – as their Latin American and Southern European predecessors; and indeed, they drew on powerful and longstanding shared traditions of enlightenment liberalism. To some extent they even made explicit cross-references to non-Communist democratisations. Nevertheless, the regimes they were dismantling (single-party ruled command economies) were very different in structure from the conservative capitalist authoritarian regimes on which most theorising was based. Transition to a market economy was viewed as an integral (possibly even the dominant) component of democratisation. Social structures (universal welfare provision, absence of a strong autonomous civil sphere, or of market-related professional associations) and geopolitical settings were also very different.

The first question to consider, therefore, is whether such key analytical terms as 'democratisation', 'consolidation' and 'transition' carry substantially different connotations when deployed in the East-Central European context. This topic is taken up in the second section of the paper. Then the third section turns to a key feature of the international context that differentiates these from earlier experiences – the persistence for over forty years of a Soviet military veto over full democratisation, and the reasons why that veto was lifted in the late 1980s. The fourth section turns to other distinctive features of the international environment, that can be grouped together under the heading 'the role of the West'. It considers the various influences flowing from 'the West', and their effects in shaping the course and content of local democratising impulses. The fifth section reflects on the interactions that took place once the transitions got under way, and relates this to comparative debates on the prospects for democratic consolidation. The conclusion draws together these arguments about the relative weight of various types of international influence on the East-Central European democratisations, and reflects on the implications for pre-existing analysis.

'Democratisation' in East-Central Europe: the local terminology

In the immediate aftermath of the collapse of the Soviet bloc, it is understandable that East-Central European conceptions of 'democracy' should be viewed essentially as an expression of popular resistance to imposed Communist rule. However such an 'immediatist' perspective is likely to cloud the possibilities of locating the 1989/90 democratisations in a broader comparative framework. Certainly, forty years of living under a Soviet military veto against political reforms that would challenge the legal monopoly on power exercised by ruling Communist parties (together with vetoes against neutralism, privatisation and various freedoms of expression) constituted a profound political learning experience distinctive to this region and common throughout it.[1] By 1989 'democracy' in East-Central Europe was universally equated with the dismantling of an externally imposed system of Communist rule based philosophically on the suppression of private property. Citizenship rights were therefore intimately identified with ownership rights. Indeed, in the prevailing local terminology the re-establishment of a market economy was viewed as a core ingredient of 'democratisation', and was regarded as indissolubly linked with other distinctive aspects of the regime transition, such as the dismantling of Communist structures of political control, the repudiation of Soviet hegemony and the reversal of international alliances. This is a radically different agenda from that associated with the earlier 'democratisations' of conservative authoritarian regimes. Indeed, it is almost exactly the opposite to what 'democratisation' was initially thought to involve in the first of the Southern European transitions (i.e. in Portugal in 1974).

Nevertheless, despite some extremely divergent local connotations of the terminology, some major comparisons between, say, East-Central and Southern Europe remain intact. Such comparisons suggest, for example, that even when such political rigidity is imposed for more than forty years (forty-six in the case of Salazar's Portugal, for example), pre-existing democratic 'memories' and traditions may well persist and retain the power to affect the course and content of an eventual re-democratisation. Moreover, such comparisons also suggest that such a very long period of authoritarian imposition will typically include a variety of different stages, interrupted experiments, lost opportunities and so forth, which are also likely to contribute to the specific form and social meaning of democratisation in each country. Furthermore, of course, the comparative literature reminds us that typically not all the forces which emerge in the course of dislodging an entrenched anti-democratic regime are themselves inherently democratic (there is also scope for considerable diversity of views over the nature of any 'democratising' project); and that not all the power-holders in existing regimes typically remain united in defence of a foundering *status quo*.

It is important to recall that the countries of East-Central Europe had a rich and diverse political history which long antedates the arrival of the Red Army in 1944/5. European liberal values were as well established in eighteenth-century Poland as in many parts of the West; and after 1848 Austrian and German liberalism achieved wide if uneven diffusion in other parts of the region. As liberalism spread eastwards it stirred up subordinated nationalisms, and these two processes did much to undermine the Habsburg and Tsarist empires. However, the international political forces that most powerfully shaped regional democratic potentialities before the imposition of Soviet control were, of course, the two World Wars. Six of the present states came into existence as a result of the Treaty of Versailles, that is under the supervision of the victors of the First World War, and initially all were to some extent influenced by their international sponsors to adopt liberal constitutional forms of government. Such international actors also backed plebiscites to define the new borders and sometimes promoted minority rights through treaty provisions. Czechoslovakia and Estonia both established conventional democratic regimes which lasted for twenty years, until cut down by foreign aggression. Both the initiation and the destruction of these fragile interwar experiments in democratisation were substantially influenced by geopolitical forces beyond their domestic control. This set an enduring pattern, whereby local democratic actors would naturally formulate their strategies having strong regard to their likely international repercussions; and whereby external powers would be watchfully assessed and rated according not only to their stated sympathies, but more importantly according to their real capacities and inclinations to supply help (or to create difficulties) in times of trouble.

In the immediate aftermath of the Second World War there were some indications that post-Versailles regional experiments in democratisation might be given something of a second chance. The Yalta Agreement did, after all, provide for the holding of free elections in all the countries liberated from Nazi occupation, as well as for the negotiating of spheres of influence and the redrawing of national boundaries. Such elections were in fact held, and at least in certain cases (most clearly in Czechoslovakia in May 1946) they were indeed reasonably free. Even where the reality of Soviet control was made more explicit, it would be a mistake to overlook the long-term significance of the three-year period (between early 1945 and the Prague coup in February 1948) during which varying degrees of limited pluralism and non-Stalinist experimentation were tolerated, in deference to Moscow's residual commitments to the wartime alliance. For example, in January 1947 the then Secretary-General of the Polish Communist Party (Władysław Gomułka) could still write that 'we have completely rejected the collectivisation of agriculture . . . our democracy is not similar to Soviet democracy just as our society's structure is not the same as the Soviet structure'.[2] Eight months later the Cominform was launched in Poland with 'the consolidation of democracy' given as one of its stated aims. (It is curious to find such an early use of this term of art, bracketed with 'the eradication of the remnants of fascism', and 'the undermining of imperialism'.)[3]

It was, of course, no kind of pluralist regime that the Cominform was about to 'consolidate'. On the contrary, only five months later the Prague coup led to the fusion of the Socialist and Communist parties, and the adoption of a Soviet-style constitution guaranteeing a political monopoly to the new ruling party. Similar transformations in Poland, Hungary, East Germany and so on ensured that a uniform variant of 'People's Democracy' was rapidly consolidated throughout Soviet-controlled Eastern Europe, an externally underwritten system of centralised political and economic control which survived with only limited variations for the next forty years. Thus, we see that on four successive occasions in the first half of the twentieth century it was major shifts in the *global* balance of power (i.e. processes essentially external to East-Central

Europe) which either initiated (1919, 1945) or terminated (1938, 1948) regional experiments in democratisation.

Following the Prague coup, for about forty years, a Soviet military veto blocked further such experiments and imposed a rather standardised form of Communist political and economic organisation. Although (outside the Baltic republics) the interwar state system was largely resuscitated, and each 'People's Democracy' acquired its own national structure of government enjoying internationally recognised sovereign status, in many respects this was a semi-imperial system of power, with essential decisions requiring if not clearance then at least the tacit approbation of Moscow. (Later in this chapter we will examine the democratisations of 1989 by comparison with earlier experiences of 'decolonisation' leading to democracy.)

Thus, in the first place, without belittling the reforms of this system achieved (in Hungary) or attempted (in Czechoslovakia in 1968, or in Poland and the USSR during the 1980s), it is important from a comparative perspective to remember that the ruling parties retained their legal monopolies on power until 1989 or 1990. Just as the political transition in Spain had to await Franco's death (even though at the social level preparations for such change had long been under way), so the Communist rulers of this region had to acknowledge that their system was not immortal before negotiations over the construction of an alternative regime could get under way. Until such negotiations began there was no way of assessing either the real strength and intentions of the various contenders for power or the substantive bases on which a new regime might be constructed. Thus, in January 1989 the Solidarity movement was legalised in Poland, at about the same time that the Hungarian party decided to abandon its leading role, and accept multi-party elections. Then, in the June 1989 elections Solidarity scored an overwhelming victory (though power-sharing continued to reserve the most strategic ministries for the hands of the Polish Communist Party). In October the Hungarian Party changed its name to the Hungarian Socialist Party and explicitly abandoned its Leninism. Then in November 1989 the Czech and German parties respectively lost their political monopolies through mass protests. Finally, in February 1990 the CPSU abolished clause 6 of the Soviet Constitution, which had for so long formally guaranteed the party's leading role in Soviet society.

If we are to extend the terminology developed in the Latin American and Southern European academic literature on democratisation to these East-Central European processes, we would have to say that there could be no 'transition to democracy' before the ruling party relinquished its legal claim to a monopoly of political representation. From this standpoint, prior to February 1990 *perestroika* and *glasnost* could only be classified as episodes of 'liberalisation', and not of democratisation in the Soviet Union. Similarly, although the Hungarian Communists may have demonstrated an exceptional capacity both for economic reform and for the protection of human rights long before 1989, they too would have to be classified as no more than liberalising authoritarians prior to 11 January 1989.[4] Whether the Polish 'transition' to democracy began just before, or just after, the

Hungarian move is a matter of controversy between democrats in the two countries. It depends whether the bench-mark is the legalisation of Solidarity in January or the 'Round Table' talks in March. In any case, Jaruzelski's reformism did not concede the principle of popular sovereignty before the end of 1988. Similarly, although the 1968 'reform Communism' of Alexander Dubček in Czechoslovakia included the abolition of censorship, and the secret election of party officials, it did not explicitly extend to abandonment of the leading role of the party, and for this reason comparativists should hesitate to apply the term 'democratisation' to it.[5]

At first glance it may seem rather pedantic to worry whether 'liberalisation' turned into a 'transition' to democracy in 1989, or a year or two earlier. It is hardly surprising that in East European parlance processes that an outsider might regard as mere 'liberalisation' were sometimes regarded as the beginnings of democratisation. Well before the explicit surrender of Communist Party monopoly control over the state, such control was *de facto* in retreat. To those accustomed to living under a supposedly 'monolithic' system it was striking to witness the emergence of a significant degree of constitutionalism, a strengthening of the rule of law (except in the most sensitive areas) and increased evidence of 'limited pluralism' at the elite level. Nevertheless, from a broader comparative standpoint these would all be regarded as characteristics of the 'liberalisation' of an authoritarian regime, perhaps foreshadowing an eventual transition to democracy, but still in principle controlled and reversible, and not therefore yet a 'democratisation'.

The issue of precisely when the transition began is quite critical, bearing in mind Judy Batt's observation (elsewhere in this volume), that a distinctive feature of the East-Central European democratisations is that they were accompanied by sweeping transitions in the direction of a market economy, and a wholesale rejection of the Soviet model of the command economy. By contrast, of course, so long as the dominant logic was only that of liberalisation, and not democratisation, the associated goals were to *reform* the command economy and to *re-found* Soviet hegemony rather than to destroy them. In fact at the political level these democratisations were inextricably entwined with movements of national affirmation, and with a comprehensive reorientation of alignments and identities from East to West. In comparison, the authoritarian regimes of Latin America and Southern Europe always regarded themselves as fully identified with 'Western civilisation', even though they may have suffered limited estrangements from some Western governments and institutions because of their human rights violations. The essential point here is that the 'democratisations' under study took place in the context of the longer and larger process of 'decolonisation' which has now shattered the entire Soviet empire. Old political communities reasserted their long suppressed sovereignties, and new national identities were also asserted, in a manner more reminiscent of African and Asian independence struggles than the democratisations of Southern Europe and Latin America. Some fragments of the former empire were well placed to invoke democratic values and aspirations as a guiding principle for national emancipation; other constituent elements of the former empire relied on alternative organising principles. In any case, processes of decolonisation both *precede* and *extend* the democratisation episodes under study in this volume. From a comparative perspective it is important to seek precision over the starting-point of these democratic transitions, not least because they were so pivotal to the broader and more protracted process of dismantling the Soviet empire.

Although the two 'break-points' of 1948 and 1989 both seem unusually clear, abrupt and uniform through the East-Central European region, it by no means follows that Moscow-imposed uniformity blotted out all manifestations of democratic potential across the region and over the entire intervening forty-one years. On the contrary, Soviet policies were of course highly variable in intention and uneven in impact. In part, no doubt, this variability was due to differences in the levels of resistance (and the forms of collaboration) encountered by Moscow in the six distinct and even competitive countries under consideration. As the comparative study of authoritarian regimes has already taught us, too much emphasis on shared patterns of regime control may well conceal more than they reveal about the underlying development of democratic potentialities when considering six distinct nations (or nine including the Baltic states) over a forty-year period. As we have already shown, there *are* some important and distinctive common features shared by these East-Central European Communist regimes. But once these obvious and basic points have been noted, the distinctive (sometimes interacting) political trajectories of these regimes would also require attention in order fully to reconstruct the various 'paths' to democratisation taken in the late 1980s (a task beyond the scope of this chapter).

This variety of interacting trajectories was also, however, in no small measure due to differences of interpretation and even of strategy within top levels of the Soviet leadership. In fact from the death of Stalin onwards the leaders of the CPSU were engaged in a concealed, but more or less continuous, process of debate over how to re-stabilise and legitimise their own political system within the USSR. The questions posed to Moscow by the restless regimes within its security perimeter – how much pluralism could be tolerated, what controls over the intelligentsia and the media were most appropriate, how much historical veracity could be allowed, etc. – all these merely presented in more dramatic form dilemmas that already existed within the USSR as well. CPSU responses to satellite demands for liberalisation were unsteady, in part because leaders in Moscow were divided about how to respond to such demands from within the USSR itself. This interconnectedness between concessions in the semi-colonies, and the pressure for reforms at home, set up an iterative pattern whereby experiments in one country stimulated imitation in others. And when such experiments ran out of control the resulting backlash also spread from country to country. Thus, for example, the frustrated democratic rebellions of 1956 were in part triggered by Moscow's vacillating attempts to de-Stalinise within the USSR; and the backlash against the 'Prague Spring' of 1968 dammed up the impetus for reform not only in Czechoslovakia, but also designedly in the Soviet Union.

Consider the key events of 1956 which gave rise to a reform-minded (or 'liberalised') variant of Communism in Poland and Hungary. Under Malenkov's protection in June 1953, Imre Nagy assumed the Hungarian premiership, curbing the secret police, relaxing policy towards the farmers and promoting a 'consolidation of legality'. His policies of 'liberalisation' stimulated an intense debate among Hungarian intellectuals about how far democracy could progress in a Communist state, and about how far a people's democracy could reach sovereignty within the Soviet bloc. But in the spring of 1955 Khrushchev's stand against Malenkov was followed by the dismissal of Nagy from the Hungarian premiership and an attempt to reassert Communist discipline. Nagy responded by writing a report for the Central Committee, advocating Hungarian independence, neutrality and active coexistence between countries with different systems. In short, a key Hungarian Communist openly advocated policies akin to those of neighbouring Yugoslavia (which had been expelled from the Soviet bloc for its nationalist deviations in 1948). Although Nagy did not at this point advocate an end to the Communist Party's monopoly of power, his arguments went beyond the limits of what was tolerable in Khrushchev's Russia, both on questions of bloc security, and on the issue of political liberalisation.

Although from 1953 to 1955 the strongest impulse for reform took place in Hungary, there was also a parallel process under way in Poland. Following the dismissal of Nagy, leadership of the revisionist movement passed to Gomułka, whose credentials as a reform Communist preceded the split with Yugoslavia. In June 1956 there were workers' riots in Poznań, in response to which in July the Central Committee of the Polish Party invited Gomułka to argue his case. Gomułka subsequently described two main issues under consideration as '(1) the problem of Poland's sovereignty and (2) the problem of democratisation within the framework of the socialist system'.[6] On 19 October 1956, in very tense circumstances, Khrushchev endorsed Gomułka's approach to these questions, and he was restored to the post of Secretary-General of the Polish Party. Soviet troops were then ordered back to their barracks, and the Polish Party proceeded to carry through a wide range of reforms (decollectivisation of agriculture, religious toleration, an enhanced role for parliament and many other measures of *liberalisation*). But the *quid pro quo* for Soviet endorsement of these measures was that the Polish Communist Party should regain its power, and that Polish-Soviet security ties should remain undisturbed. Thus the Polish crisis of October 1956 underscored the connection between continued subordination to a Russian-dominated alliance system and Moscow's veto over democratisation.

The Hungarian uprising of early November 1956 underscored the same connection in a different way. On 20 October 1956 the Hungarian press published the full text of Gomułka's statement accompanying his reappointment to lead the Polish party. This produced a climate of intense mobilisation within Hungary, under which conditions Nagy was appointed Prime Minister. In the following week of intense factional conflict and popular agitation a nation wide demand developed for complete national emancipation. Particularly in the countryside (where no Soviet forces were stationed, and where the local security apparatus had mostly disintegrated) the demand was for general and free elections to be held within two months, with the participation of multiple parties, and the return of Soviet troops, not just to their bases, but to their fatherland. On 30 October Nagy responded by announcing the restoration of a multi-party system and the formation of a four-party coalition government ('like in 1945'). The following day he called for the withdrawal of Soviet troops, and for Hungary's departure from the Warsaw Pact. But rather than acquiesce to the establishment of a neutral, democratic, and no doubt non-Communist Hungary, Moscow used all necessary force to impose a regime (under János Kádár) that would operate within the same constraints as those reluctantly accepted by Gomułka in Poland.

The crushing of the 1956 Hungarian uprising is of course remembered throughout East-Central Europe as a watershed event, demonstrating the limits of Soviet toleration of dissent in the post-Stalinist era. Equally significant, however, was the increased scope for reform allowed within such brutally imposed limits. Khrushchev's memoirs are revealing about the confused attitudes toward political freedom that existed in the higher reaches of the Soviet system after the dismantling of Stalin's apparatus of intimidation. According to Khrushchev, 'the rift which developed (in 1960) between the Soviet Union and Albania stemmed mainly from the Albanians' fear of democratisation'. Following Moscow's break with Albania he claimed to 'stand all the more firmly for those principles of democratic leadership which the Albanians could never accept'. Khrushchev's attempt to explain those principles was a muddle: 'A democratic leader must have a good mind and he must be able to take advice. He must realise that his position of leadership depends upon the people's will to have him as their leader, not on his own will to lead the people . . . In other words he is not above the Party but is the servant of the Party, and he can keep his position only as long as he enjoys the Party's satisfaction and support'.[7]

Later, in 1968 in Czechoslovakia, and then again in 1981 in Poland, the ultimate constraints that had been evident in 1956 were demonstrated yet again, albeit in somewhat different circumstances. In short, between early 1948 and late 1986 the security and integrity of the Soviet bloc system was shown to rest ultimately on Moscow's willingness to use the Red Army (if all other instruments of control failed) *both* to maintain the cohesion of its alliance structure, *and also in an inextricable conjunction* to block dismantlement of the Communist Party's practical monopoly over formal rights of political representation throughout the region. The CPSU invariably barred what we have loosely termed 'decolonisation', and also it limited internal reforms to what we should label 'liberalisation without democratisation', because from Moscow's standpoint these were two aspects of a single integrated process – 'de-Sovietisation', or 'de-Communisation' – rather than two separable issues.

The implied parallel with West European colonialism would naturally have been rejected for one set of reasons; and the liberal theory underlying the language of 'democratisation' would have been rejected for a second set of reasons. Although Soviet political terminology is now mainly of antiquarian interest, it is as well to note that the citizens of the post-Communist regimes of Eastern Europe frequently share an unspoken assumption, inherited from pre-*perestroika* days, that 'democracy' entails a pro-Western geopolitical orientation, and that it necessarily involves a repudiation of state socialism. These are distinctive ideas that were incubated in Eastern Europe by forty years of bitter experience. Prior to 1948, East Europeans were perhaps just as likely as Latin Americans or Southern Europeans to make an analytical distinction between liberal political democracy, on the one hand, and commitment to a market economy system, on the other. They might also (like the Czechoslovak democrat and patriot Eduard Benes in 1947) hold that political democracy could be compatible with a pro-Soviet strategic alignment. It is a historically contingent, rather than logically necessary, feature of the polities of East-Central Europe that, at least for the present generation, 'democratisation' has acquired unusually prescriptive connotations both as to economic system and to international orientation. It is a recurring problem in comparative politics that apparently standard terminology frequently carries strong overtones in one setting that are either absent, or resonate differently, in the next. The analyst must therefore guard against twin dangers of distortion. One source of distortion can arise when local realities are interpreted through an inappropriately rigid and insensitive application of a general terminology; a second equally serious distortion would arise if, for example, the whole spectrum of democratic transitions were to be subsumed under the parochial optic of East European anti-Sovietism. There can be no absolute defence against these twin distortions. The best defence is to be explicit about the contingent and local connotations of more general categories, and to specify the shade of meaning intended at each point.

Why Moscow lifted its veto on democratisation

Using the conventional terminology of the transitions literature, we would have to say that it was not until very late in 1988 that 'liberalisation' (within the framework of a continuance of the Communist system of rule) began to give way to 'democratisation'. However, it would now appear that the most crucial shift in the international context – Moscow's decision to lift its military veto over the unfolding of indigenous political processes – may have occurred and even been announced, as long as two years earlier. Thus, according to Alex Pravda 'it appears that by the autumn of 1986 the Gorbachev leadership had decided to distance itself from the last-resort use of force associated with their predecessors' treatment of East European crises'.[8] In the previous section we saw how, as a result of the Soviet military actions of 1956 and 1968, the issue of democratisation had become deeply entangled with the issue of what may loosely be termed 'decolonisation' within the informal Soviet empire in Eastern Europe. From a comparative perspective, therefore, we need to consider how distinctive this decolonisation-democratisation link may have been.

Elsewhere,[9] I have argued that thirty of the sixty-one independent states that might conventionally be classified as 'democracies' in January 1990 established such regimes in association with processes of decolonisation. In a formal sense the Communist regimes of East-Central Europe were not of course 'colonies', but rather independent sovereign nations recognised as such, for example, through their membership of the United Nations. As we have just seen, however, until November 1986 Moscow kept them under quite a strict system of informal control (stricter, for example, than the restraints on various francophone republics in West Africa, which are also recognised as members of the United Nations, although periodically reliant on French paratroopers, and more constantly reliant on economic supervision from Paris). In particular, Moscow imposed a more constraining limitation on the scope for domestic political expression than is typical of most 'neo-colonial' regimes in the Third World.[10] In that sense, therefore, it may be permissible to analyse the political consequences of the lifting of Moscow's military veto on East-Central Europe's regime transformations by analogy with the more formal decolonisations that sometimes presaged democratisation in other parts of the world.

From a comparative politics perspective it would be misleading to rely on too narrow and formalistic a conception of decolonisation. As John Darwin has pointed out with reference to the British Empire, direct rule was only the most overt manifestation of a much broader structure of imperial controls, which included other kinds of legal concessions, military and demographic provisions, economic advantages and socio-cultural arrangements. Indeed British imperial authorities sometimes sought to avoid the costs of explicit direct rule, believing that the main benefits of colonial domination could better be achieved by other means. Likewise, therefore, the decision to grant formal independence is not necessarily to be equated with 'decolonisation' in a broader sense. Indeed, Darwin's interpretation of the decolonisation of the British Empire bears some striking similarities to the subsequent collapse of the Soviet bloc, in that imperial policy-makers tended to believe they could revitalise their threatened positions of dominance by relinquishing the more objectionable instruments of control. 'For much of the time, we may suspect, those who "made" colonial policy' in London 'were guessing, hoping, gambling – and *mis*calculating',[11] – just like their later counterparts in Moscow.

In reality, of course, the postwar termination of British colonial rule 'did not proceed as a carefully planned rolling programme . . . the actual outcome was largely unexpected and thoroughly unwelcome from a British point of view . . . The rapidity of British withdrawal arose from . . . uncertainties about their ability to check disruptive elements and restore political discipline without losing the co-operation of moderate politicians on whom they depended, were compounded by the fear that confrontation might occur in a number of colonies simultaneously . . .'[12] While this was going on 'British opinion was shaped by a variety of expectations, but one of the most important was the belief constantly reiterated by British leaders, that come what may, Britain would remain a great world power'.[13] In the event, however, 'in South Asia, the Middle East, and then in Africa,

Britain lost her special position with startling speed. It is this, far more than the formal transfer of sovereignty, which indicates the true nature of the changes implicit in the term "decolonisation". In each region, the British found that the effort to move to a less formal kind of superiority proved unworkable in practice.'[14] The parallels with Gorbachev's failed attempt to shift the basis of Moscow's ascendancy within its postwar sphere of influence are notable.

At one level we can view all such 'decolonisations' as conscious strategies for the divestment of a certain type of direct power and responsibility chosen and pursued by imperial decision-makers. This level of analysis requires careful attention, even if the results are unforeseen and the underlying causes are distinct. In the Soviet case this involves analysing the motives and actions of an extremely small group of Moscow power-holders. Between 1985 and 1989 we need to consider above all the political trajectory of Mikhail Gorbachev.

It was by no means a foregone conclusion that he would become Secretary-General of the CPSU, on the death of Chernenko in March 1985 (the Politburo voted 4/4, until Gromyko broke the tie), nor that once in office he would promote such a comprehensive break with the past. What needs to be explained is why, given the enormous concentration of power in the hands of the new Secretary-General, he subsequently came to relinquish ever more of it. In 1989 his power base shifted from the party to a newly empowered Presidency, but the erosion of strength continued until finally, six and a half years later, the entire Soviet structure of command and control had been dismantled, not only in East-Central Europe, but within the USSR as well. With hindsight it can be seen more clearly than at the time that Gorbachev's major decisions concerning his European allies were all largely predetermined by the positions he was developing on East/West disarmament, and in relation to his central concern – the reform and liberalisation of Communist rule in the USSR. Those positions were not uniquely his (their antecedents could be traced back to Khrushchev, and to a lesser extent to Andropov; and for a considerable period they were reinforced by such prominent party figures as Shevardnadze and Yeltsin; together with such influential constituencies as the intelligentsia, parts of the media, and local bureaucracies, e.g. in Leningrad and the Baltic republics), but his authority was essential to sustain and develop them. Given the centralised nature of the Soviet system it was extremely problematic for conservatives (i.e. those who favoured preservation of the apparatus of control) to defy an incumbent Secretary-General who was prepared to use his position to push the cause of reform. Gorbachev may have been misguided, overconfident, inconsistent and opportunistic at various points, but he was never disposed to abandon that cause. Indeed, each time his innovations encountered resistance he identified the opposition as his conservative enemies, and therefore took further liberalising steps in order to reinforce his campaign against them. Given that this was the underlying thrust of his leadership, it was almost certainly never open to him to practise open repression or ally with the forces of conservation in Eastern Europe. To do so would always have been to liquidate his platform for reform within the USSR. It is perhaps unsurprising that democrats in East-Central Europe took quite a long time to recognise this reality, and even longer to feel sufficiently confident of its permanence to act out its implications.[15]

The sequence of events in Moscow was schematically as follows. Even before Chernenko's death, in December 1984, Gorbachev had established a strong following in the Central Committee, with a bold speech advocating '*glasnost*', and even using the term 'democratisation'.[16] On assuming supreme leadership he immediately (April 1985) launched a programme of economic reform (*perestroika*). By June 1986, in the wake of Chernobyl, he was appealing to the intelligentsia and the media for assistance, saying that 'restructuring' was going very badly, and that 'a society cannot exist without *glasnost*' ('openness, publicity, visibility'). One of his advisers, a former speechwriter to Khrushchev, commented that 'the press will be the method of democratic control, not control by administration but control with the help of democratic institutions'.[17] (All this *preceded* the November 1986 meeting at which Pravda believes the CMEA governments may have been told that Moscow was forswearing the last-resort use of force to control them.) By January 1987, recalling how the party apparatus had 'broken Khrushchev's neck', Gorbachev turned explicitly to '*demokratizatziya*',which initially 'applied only to the Communist Party to mobilise the rank and file members to offset the power of the party bureaucracy.'[18] By 1988 the campaign had escalated further. In June of that year Gorbachev proposed a constitutional reform, to create directly elected *Soviets* and a strong elected President, both seen as instruments to advance the cause of reform and overcome conservative resistance. In *perestroika* he asserted that 'everything which is not prohibited by law is allowed' and this was then reinforced by the promotion of *zakonnost* (the law-governed state).[19] In short, by the end of 1988, when the East-Central European transitions began, Gorbachev had taken huge steps towards dismantling the Communist Party's monopoly of power in the USSR.

Prior to 1989 it seems fairly certain that policy-making in Moscow was based on the assumption that a successful programme of economic and political reform could rescue some essentials of the Communist system by liberalising it. ('Everything must change so that everything can stay the same', as Lampedusa's Sicilian aristocrat would say.) This was expected to apply both within the USSR and to those European allied regimes which were agile enough to reform and thereby legitimise themselves. In short, the 'Dubček model' of reform Communism was still thought to be viable, and the real threat to the survival of some variant of liberalised socialism was thought to come from the inflexibility of the conservatives. As we now know, this was all an illusion, a fact that became apparent rather rapidly as the transitions of 1989 gathered momentum. By mid-year the Polish elections had administered a crushing blow to the Polish Workers Party, while the Tiananmen Square massacre had demonstrated that repression could still be effective. On 9 October 1989 the East German government attempted a similar show of force against unarmed demonstrators in Leipzig, only to be told that Russian troops would provide no back-up and that Moscow was opposed to such actions. Once it became clear throughout Eastern Europe that Gorbachev's repudiation of force would remain intact, even *in extremis*, the last external barrier to transition (the fear of a reversal in Moscow) was removed. On 5 December the Warsaw Pact publicly apologised to the Czechoslovak people for the invasion of 1968. With hindsight all this may seem self-evident, but on the information available to them at the time all political actors in the region were bound to fear that the international conjuncture might suddenly turn against democratisation, just as it had done on so many occasions in the past. After all, hindsight also tells us that on 8 December 1991, as a direct consequence of Gorbachev's leadership strategy, the Communist Party of the Soviet Union would itself be dissolved. Given that fact, and the contingent nature of many leadership decisions taken since 1985, it would be ahistorical to regard Moscow's passivity in the face of the 1989 revolutions as natural, let alone inevitable. A Soviet backlash could never be entirely discounted, particularly since Russian troops remained stationed throughout the region, and even though such an extreme change in policy would probably have come too late to salvage anything of the old order, it would most certainly have disrupted all the processes of non-violent regime transition, and might even have thwarted their democratic content. The timing, course, and texture of these democratisations would certainly have been different if Gorbachev had 'reverted to type' at this crucial stage.

This focus on decision-making in Moscow helps to explain the speed, direction, limits and mechanisms of the East-Central European democratisation process. It also invited further comparisons with the British experience of decolonisation which, we have argued, contributed to the establishment of about half the 'democracies' in existence on the day the Berlin Wall came down. In both the British and the Soviet cases, the aim of the for the time being dominant state was not to maximise its immediate power, but to create an international environment that would in the longer run be relatively unthreatening to a former great power in decline. In international politics more broadly conceived, then, there are periods when it may be good policy for a dominant state to be permissive and decentralising in the territories it controls, even though such a situation is hard to express in the terms of strict power politics theory. This is all the more true if we allow domestic opinion within the dominant state to affect its foreign policy. The single-minded pursuit of power politics abroad normally requires fairly unwavering support for a potentially repressive security apparatus based at home. Domestic interests may feel threatened by such an apparatus, in which case the pursuit of apparently inexplicable altruism overseas may reflect a perceived self-interest in detente and the reduction of tension on the internal front. (Compare British support for decolonisation, or French or Portuguese responses to colonial wars. Eduard Shevardnadze's declarations point to a similar pattern in Moscow.)

Neither British nor Soviet decolonising strategies were formulated in an international vacuum. In both cases the dominant authorities had to consider not just the pressures and demands arising within the colonial or dependent territories that they still controlled, but also (and for the purposes of this chapter more crucially) the standpoints and policies of great power rivals and of the 'international community' more generally. In the postwar period British policies were profoundly affected by the requirements of the USA and by the United Nation's commitment to the principles of the self-determination of nations. Similarly, in the 1980s, Moscow's strategy was heavily constrained by the pressure of demands from the 'West' – not just the USA, but also Western Europe and an array of international organisations. To these pressures we shall now turn.

The role of the 'West'

Clearly, in general, the liberal democracies of Western Europe and North America exerted a range of long-term pressures on the Soviet bloc which helped nurture democratic aspirations in East-Central Europe, and which eventually contributed to Gorbachev's decision to risk 'decolonisation'. But any systematic analysis of the role of international factors in stimulating democratisation in this region must carefully specify which pressures were most significant; how, when and where they produced their main effects; and in what historical context they were embedded and constrained. Just as the record of Soviet policy towards the region extends over a long period and contains a variety of distinct phases, with a differential impact on the various countries concerned; so also the policies (in the plural) and influences emanating from the West require disaggregation. Such a deconstruction of the record is required in order to pierce the veil of Western selective recall about the Cold War, as well as to help us situate the East-Central European democratisations in their comparative context, and to clarify the part played by international factors in such processes. Such a re-evaluation is also necessary if we are to understand certain distinguishing features of the regional democratisation experience – the speed of the 'demonstration effects'; the remarkably limited resort to violence; the association between 'democratisation' and 'rejoining the West'.

This chapter is, of course, too brief to accomplish all these tasks. It can only survey some of the major issues and suggest some provisional interpretations. A convenient starting-point is provided by David Deudney and G. John Ikenberry, who have sketched out one influential viewpoint concerning the West's role in spurring changes within the Soviet bloc. They distinguish between the causes of the Soviet crisis, which they describe as primarily domestic, and causes of the Soviet *response* to its crisis (most particularly the foreign affairs response) which they say 'derive from external sources'. 'Many commentators have emphasised the role of Western state policy', they note, 'and particularly American containment policy, in inducing Soviet change'. However, they consider it important to assess the 'full set of environmental factors . . . some of which have been long in the making and some of which are not a reflection of government policy'. They distinguish no fewer than eight dimensions of international influence, ranging through various types of military and economic pressure to the strength of international organisations and a final catch-all 'the character of global society and culture'.[20] After tracing the way all these factors may have affected Moscow's choices of response to the crisis in the Soviet system, they conclude that since the 1950s 'although the West has grown militarily and economically powerful, it has presented the Soviet Union with a more benign and attractive face'.[21] 'The central role of these deeper, long-term forces puts in perspective and shows the limits of the designs and disputes of policy-makers. The real genius of the Western system has been not its coherent and far-sighted policy, but the vitality and attractiveness of its polity.'[22]

This interpretation admittedly offers some rather large hostages to fortune (will the citizens of the new democracies of East-Central Europe continue to admire the vitality of Western polities, no matter how policy-makers behave in the post-Communist era?). And although it seems mainly directed against US conservatives who may feel that the collapse of the Soviet Union vindicates their policies of 'containment', nevertheless it does have the merit of emphasising the multiplicity of channels through which Western influences were exerted, and the cumulative macro-historical impact of these influences. Despite this, it seems to me that certain key decisions by Western policy-makers can be singled out for examination. Had different decisions been taken at critical junctures, I would argue that the pattern, timing and course of democratisation in East-Central Europe might well have been different. In some cases even the outcome itself might have changed.

Most importantly, for example, the artificial postwar division of Germany created the linchpin of Cold War Europe – a German Democratic Republic surrounding a partitioned Berlin. The West never openly accepted this solution (after 1970 *Ostpolitik* involved recognition of postwar frontiers subject to their eventual endorsement by a united Germany), nor did it actively challenge this corner-stone of the Soviet security system, certainly not after the erection of the Berlin Wall, on 13 August 1961. The outcome of this tacit understanding between East and West was that a liberal capitalist democracy came to flourish in West Germany and West Berlin, which never relinquished its claim to the eventual reincorporation of an East German population denied access either to democracy or to capitalism (or indeed to the West in general) by force of Soviet arms. The moment that the people of East Germany realised that Moscow would no longer use military means to block reunification, the linchpin of the entire regional system was removed. The dismantling of the Berlin Wall soon signified not only the reunification of Germany on a liberal capitalist basis, but also the democratisation along similar lines of most if not all of the other countries in the rearguard of the Soviet alliance.

Clearly the basic Western position on German reunification was much more long-term and deeply entrenched than most of the policy debates that consumed the energies of governmental strategists. Moreover, the structural pressures on the Soviet bloc generated by the West's dogged and successful pursuit of 'peaceful coexistence' in Central Europe were much more profound in their effects than most consciously designed strategies of selective reward and punishment. Although such pressures *can* be disaggregated into their military, economic, political and socio-cultural components, it is in practice rather artificial to split up elements that were in reality indissolubly interconnected. However, there is a need to explore how this bundle of pressures changed over time, and how they acted differentially in different parts of the East-Central European region.

Taking a long historical view, it is not so clear that the Western system always displayed great vitality and attractiveness. The Western democracies may have contributed substantially to the creation of a democratic Czechoslovakia in 1919, for example, but they also played a key role in its destruction in 1938. Although they went to war in defence of a much less democratic regime in Poland in 1939, their basic concern was to maintain the balance of power. Hence their intervention only served to maximise the wartime suffering of the Polish people. And even when the war was won neither Polish sovereignty nor Polish democracy were counted as a vital interest of the West.

It is true, and important, that the incorporation of the Baltic democracies with the Soviet Union, (agreed under a secret clause of the Nazi-Soviet Pact), was never fully accepted by the West, but of course for fifty years the issue remained largely dormant in East-West relations. It only returned to haunt officialdom in Moscow when President Gorbachev opened the archives in a misjudged attempt to stabilise the USSR through historical openness. This example confirms the vital importance of retaining a long-term historical perspective when evaluating democratisation processes, since suppressed political memories are frequently so potent. It also illustrates the many complex ways in which the legacy of past actions and inactions (both domestic and international) may hang over and redirect the course of contemporary democratisations. To take one specific example, the consequence of fifty years of Baltic incorporation into the USSR was the 'russification' of these three republics. However, when the international community recognised the restoration of their sovereignty as democratic states in 1991, it made no stipulations as to their treatment of the by this time substantial Russian minority populations within their borders. A consequence of this international inaction was that the Estonian parliament enacted laws restricting citizenship rights to those families already resident in the republic prior to its forced incorporation into the USSR. (This notwithstanding the fact that many Russian nationals had voted for independence in the 1991 referendum.) Thus long historical memories, and the selective application of democratic principles by the West, can markedly alter the character of the democratisation processes under way in parts of East-Central Europe.

One period is of particular interest from our perspective. This is the early to mid-1970s, the era of so-called 'detente', during which a new West German government, led by the former mayor of West Berlin, sought to reassure Moscow and its Warsaw Pact allies that growing Western prosperity and freedom would not be used aggressively to destabilise the postwar *status quo* in the region. Although the broad framework of European detente was inscribed in that phase of international history, a number of specific institutional procedures such as the conference on security and cooperation in Europe (CSCE) were established that were far from inevitable. Particular Western decisions taken at that time contributed significantly to the course and pattern of the democratisations that took place a generation later. Although the Brezhnev leadership group in Moscow remained highly adversarial, Soviet memories of European detente contributed to the Gorbachev team's perceptions of their strategic options (which were of course also shaped by the Reagan administration's more belligerent line in the 1980s). Gorbachev's references to a 'common European house', and his favourable posture towards the CSCE provide tangible evidence of the significance of this contribution.[23]

Detente was formally incorporated into NATO policy on 14 December 1967, with the adoption of the Harmel Report. This reflected a broadened conception of Western security, whereby the military containment of Communism would be supplemented by attempts to stabilise some form of political relationship with it. However, the nature of that political relationship remained controversial within the West, right until the end of the Cold War. Over that twenty-two-year period, perceptions of detente shifted repeatedly on both sides of the East-West dividing line. The West German position underwent a particularly sharp shift when Willy Brandt became Chancellor in 1969 (although the ground was being prepared several years earlier). The earlier position had been that there could be no detente before unification. Now Brandt asserted the reverse proposition. 'The basis of his thinking was that only by accepting postwar reality and giving up unrealistic territorial claims could West Germany exert influence in Eastern Europe . . . *Wandlung durch Annäherung* or "change through rapprochement" was his stated aim'.[24] He thought that by stabilising the *status quo* the West could pave the way for a gradual evolution in the east. Brandt's approach was always controversial in Germany, first resisted by conservatives who said it conferred legitimacy on the fruits of conquest, and subsequently undermined from the left by those who indeed sought only *rapprochement*, reducing the pressure for change.

But at least, according to a careful account by Richard Davy, the original approach was to a considerable degree embodied in the 1975 Helsinki Final Act, which institutionalised the CSCE, and thereby provided a negotiated international framework that helped channel and contain the 'decolonisation' and regime transitions of 1989/91. According to Davy's interpretation, although both Soviet propagandists and some Western hard-liners for different reasons chose to misinterpret the Final Act as an instrument of appeasement, this was far from being the case. 'Instead of endorsing the status quo it was a charter for change. Instead of legitimising the Soviet sphere of influence it legitimised Western intrusion into it. Instead of making frontiers immutable it specifically affirmed the principle of peaceful change. Instead of putting contacts under official control it emphasised the role of individuals. Instead of confining itself to interstate relations it reinforced the principle that peace depends also on how states treat their people.[25] In short, a decade before Gorbachev the West set out in treaty form all the essential principles he would subsequently embrace. On this view it was not just the general 'vitality and attractiveness' of the Western polity, but rather a specific coherent and disputed set of Western requirements, incentives and reassurances embodied in an international treaty that shaped Moscow's foreign policy options in response to the Soviet Union's systemic crisis.

Admittedly the CSCE process only covers a part of the West's role in the democratisation of East-Central Europe. Elsewhere in this volume John Pinder describes the pattern of influences and incentives emanating from the European Community. Both these processes brought maximum pressure to bear on the Soviet bloc system at its weakest point – the German Democratic Republic, (whose five eastern *Länder* were offered immediate and automatic incorporation into the EC via the Treaty of Rome the moment German reunification was agreed).[26] It will never be known whether these positive Western incentives to transform the Soviet system would eventually have achieved their goals in the absence of intensified economic and military competition between West and East in the 1980s. 'Hawks' in the West (now supported by many anti-Communists in the East) argue that it was only by re-escalating the Cold War that the Soviet system could be brought to such a crisis that the Moscow leadership would accept full implementation of CSCE conditions. Arbitration between such rival explanations would require a more precise analysis of the causes of Soviet collapse than can be attempted here. Nevertheless it should be noted that many Western hawks continued until the very end to disbelieve President Gorbachev's protestations of good faith, and to insist that Soviet power could only be destroyed through unrelenting external assault. Some hawks regarded the possibility of a non-violent and negotiated transition as a snare and an illusion, until the very moment when it was upon them.[27]

At any event European detente and the CSCE process produced a range of effects, which varied between countries and social sectors. Not just the possible impact on the Soviet leadership in Moscow requires consideration. The effects were multiple, often indirect and at times quite different from those intended. For example, prior to 1970 the Communist regime in Poland achieved some modicum of patriotic legitimacy because it was seen as defending the nation's post-1945 boundaries against the threat of German revanchism. An unforeseen consequence of Ostpolitik was to deprive the Warsaw authorities of their best claim to the right to rule, thereby contributing to the rise of the broadest and most democratic mass anti-Communist movement known within the region – *Solidarnosc*. Timothy Garton Ash has even argued that without detente there would probably have been no Solidarity. But 'Bonn was not prepared for the Polish revolution any more than Washington was. Solidarity was an embarrassment to the social-liberal government . . . It reacted with palpable confusion, for here (in a process that would have delighted Hegel) a policy had produced its opposite: the policy of reducing tensions . . . had produced tensions.[28]

However, there were also major intended consequences of the policy. Václav Havel's Charter 77, for example, was formed in direct response to the Helsinki Final Act which precipitated Czechoslovakia's signature of the UN Declaration of Human Rights. More generally, as Adam Roberts has argued, 'the existence of international agreements and even of some shared values – exemplified in the 1966 human rights accords, the 1975 Helsinki Final Act, and the 1989 Vienna follow-up document of the CSCE – played a part in facilitating transition, both by stressing the importance of human rights and by helping to establish a framework of general security and confidence that made major change in Eastern Europe and the Soviet Union seem thinkable'.[29] In a similar vein, Richard Davy concludes 'it is incontrovertible that, without the Final Act and the Western interest that it aroused, opposition in Eastern Europe would have been weaker, less coherent, easier to supress and slower to foster the development of civil liberties in Eastern Europe in preparation for the transition to democracy when the opportunity finally came'.[30] Moreover 'by helping to support the development of civil societies in Eastern Europe, detente paved the way for a *smoother* transition to democracy when the old regimes crumbled because it had fostered alternative structures and authorities to take their place'.[31]

After the Wall came down

The immediate post-Communist response throughout the region recalled the democratic honeymoon of 1919, before right-wing dictatorships took over everywhere except in Czechoslovakia ('the only democracy east of the Rhine').[32] This quotation reminds us both that democratisation in the region has historical antecedents stretching back before the first arrival of Soviet imperialism; but also that the consolidation of democratic regimes can be threatened from more than one direction.

As in 1919/20, the years 1990/1 were occupied with the creation of new states and the confirmation of old ones; with the establishment of internationally recognised representative regimes; and with the redefinition of international alignments throughout the region. As in the earlier period these three processes were intimately interconnected. They took place all in a rush, and according to a relatively standardised formula, because although they were obviously initiated and shaped in response to internal political realities, all took place under the vigilance, not to say virtual supervision, of the extra-regional powers. Admittedly the great powers had limited control, and were deeply divided amongst themselves. They sought to sketch out the main elements of an internationally acceptable new order for the region, to substitute for the collapse of German hegemony, in the first instance, and of Russian hegemony, in the second. The main elements of this new order had to be negotiated, and reinforced by international treaty commitments and the appropriate redeployment of economic and military assets, within a fairly short time period, before international attention shifted elsewhere. In each case some international support for representative and constitutional forms of government was expressed, but the depth and seriousness of these commitments could not be gauged in so short a period.

Whether or not international support for the consolidation of fragile democracies will prove more solid and durable in the 1990s than in the 1920s yet remains to be proven. Some moderately encouraging early indications are discussed elsewhere in this volume, although the dismal failure of international policies towards the former Yugoslavia casts a long shadow. As always much will depend upon whether the main international actors can remain united in their support for democratic consolidation in the region, whether their attention becomes distracted by crises elsewhere and whether the objective of democracy promotion remains harmonious with other externally desired objectives (the restoration of capitalism; the control of international crime; the avoidance of warfare; etc.). In the past it has been suggested that the US style of policy-making by crisis management may produce its greatest impact during the brief and turbulent period when a democratic transition is in progress; whereas the more cumbersome and bureaucratic style of the European Community may produce its greatest effects in the long run up to a transition (when it brings cumulative economic and political pressure to bear against the *ancien régime*) and during the subsequent protracted period of democratic consolidation (when it may hold out such incentives as the prospect of full membership of the EC once sufficiently solid reforms have been implanted). While this schema worked reasonably well for Southern Europe or Central America, it requires substantial modification in relation to East-Central Europe. As we have already seen, there is a counterargument concerning the role of military strength and the risks of European detente as instruments for forcing reform out of the Communist apparatus before 1989. At the crucial moment of transition neither Brussels nor Washington played a leading role – Western policy-makers in general were overtaken by events they had not foreseen and could only applaud from the sidelines. Since 1990, despite a torrent of Western rhetoric expressing support for the consolidation of the region's fragile new democracies the actual record has been quite mixed. Both North Americans and West Europeans have shown a tendency to switch attention to their own internal problems, perhaps at the cost of weakening the long-term impact of such support.

From an international relations perspective there is one particularly crucial difference between the earlier democratisations which provided the basis for transitions theory, and those occurring since November 1989. Once the Cold War had ended, the entire international context for democratisation was transformed. Western reactions to earlier democratisations were by contrast shaped and constrained by the overarching context of a bipolar world. Authoritarian regimes had been supported or undermined largely according to calculations concerning their value as allies in the conflict with Moscow. When processes of democratisation received support from the West it was always accompanied by the discouragement of neutralism and efforts to strengthen the electoral appeal of 'centrist' parties against any possible challenge by the far Left. Moscow's approach to democratisation in Latin America and Southern Europe was a predictable mirror image to these concerns of the West. But since the Berlin Wall came down this logic no longer applies. In the euphoria of 1990 there were even Western liberals who argued that in the post-Cold War world the West would become the only important source of external influence, and it no longer has any motive for shoring up authoritarian allies, or for intervening in a discriminatory manner between one set of domestic power contenders and another (provided all observe democratic procedures). On a more sceptical reading, once the challenge of bipolarity is removed the West no longer has a clear *realpolitik* motive for democracy promotion. Liberal idealism is unlikely to have the same staying power. In any case, in the absence of an external threat Western allies are likely to develop a heightened sense of their conflicting interests, and are therefore likely to cultivate rival protégés within each fragile new democracy, and to favour competing client states. Whether or not this proves to be the case, the disappearance of a bipolar order destroys the binary system of classification by which external actors could identify allies and enemies in complex, turbulent and distant political conflicts. So long as the Czechs (or Croats) could be identified as 'liberals' and the Slovaks (or Serbs) as 'Communists', international chancelleries could work out where they stood. Once such spurious systems of classification have been eroded the West is left with a much weakened rationale for sustained involvement in the internal political processes of fragile regimes. The disintegration of the Soviet Union adds to this sense of disorientation, by generating a proliferation of new arenas and untried political actors, often of indecipherable antecedents, few of whom can be regarded as trustworthy democrats, or who can be relied upon to respect the democratic aspirations of their neighbours. Sustained international support for the consolidation of democratic regimes would demand hitherto untapped sources of Western maturity and tenacity in such a context.

Even in the most favourable conditions, such as those prevailing in Southern Europe in the 1970s, something like a decade must pass before a 'transition from authoritarian rule' can progress towards the 'consolidation' of a liberal democracy. East-Central Europe has tried to change itself far more drastically and rapidly than Southern Europe, acting on more fronts simultaneously. The initial conditions ('prerequisites'?) for democratic stability were also much weaker. Consequently it is far too early to pass serious judgement on the prospects for democratic consolidation in the region. A comparative perspective suggests a few provisional considerations, however. If consolidation does occur, it will take time and will develop unevenly. Quite a few regimes could be suspended in an intermediate condition – neither properly consolidated nor clearly headed away from democratic forms. Developments external to the region (e.g. the success or failure of reforms in the former USSR, or shifts in the outlook in Western Europe) will once again exert a strong influence on the political climate in East-Central Europe, and may therefore affect the region's democratic prospects. A final intriguing point concerns the likely character of such consolidated democracies as may emerge. In Southern Europe the initial expectation was that newly empowered popular forces harbouring resentments against earlier authoritarian regimes might press for a more radical and participatory type of democracy than elsewhere. In the event, however, once memories of the transition had faded relatively conventional and unadventurous liberal democracies took the stage. Authoritarian elites were forced to reform themselves, but were in no way disqualified from eventual return to office. Does this mean that in East-Central Europe, once the initial heat of anti-Soviet and pro-market feeling has abated, the democracies that eventually achieve consolidation there will also become reconciled to the preservation of substantial continuity linking them to their Communist past? Will the distinctive overtones of the local terminology concerning democratisation fade, as consolidation progresses?

Conclusion

The recent democratisations in East-Central Europe have introduced some important variations on the themes present in earlier transitions literature; important variations, but not an entirely new tune. Among the most important continuities I would stress the loss of cohesion within the authoritarian coalition prior to the transition; the unforeseen or unintended consequences of its attempts to 'liberalise' the political system without relinquishing ultimate control; the dilemmas this presented to the democratic opposition (how to negotiate a non-violent transition without being co-opted); the rapid turnover of political groupings and projects during the brief quasi-revolutionary phase of full transition; the significance of pacts, constitutional arrangements and other 'bridging institutions' in containing the uncertainties of this phase, and channelling the outcome towards democratic institutionalisation; and the relatively conventional and standardised forms of 'liberal democracy' that emerge rather consistently as the macro-political framework for the post-transitional settlement. The existence of such continuities should be pleasing to those who theorised about democratisation prior to the collapse of the Soviet system. Those who relied on 'totalitarianism' for theoretical guidance, or who regarded Communist political systems as incomparable with pro-Western authoritarian regimes, were by comparison handicapped in their attempts to understand the transformations of 1989 (except in the case of Romania). However, such continuities are imprecise and incomplete. A number of critical features of the East-Central European transition were distinctive to the region, and to the problems of dismantling Communist forms of autocracy.

This chapter, and this volume, have focused on one particular dimension of the democratisation process, and one crucial respect in which East-Central European experiences differed from those of earlier democratisations. The brute fact is that a particularly anti-democratic model of Communism was imposed by Moscow, at Stalin's behest, on all territories occupied by the Red Army, and that post-Stalinist rulers of the USSR nevertheless continued to restrain political liberalisation and to veto democratisation by threat of military force for almost forty years thereafter. This chapter has tried to unravel the major distinguishing features of the 1989 democratisations that flow from this raw geopolitical reality.

There *was* a pre-1945 tradition of attempted democratisation in this region, which provided quite a promising internal basis for *re*-democratisation in at least some of the more influential and prosperous countries of the region following the defeat of Nazism. Not all the local Communist Parties of the region were always pure instruments of Stalinist imperialism. On the contrary, in Poland and Czechoslovakia, at least, more democratic traditions of socialism found brief expression even within the highest party levels. However, wherever such 'soft-line' attitudes materialised they were subjected to the same harsh disciplines that Moscow customarily dispensed to liberal dissidents at home. In consequence, all the Communist Parties of the region without exception were turned into accomplices of foreign imposition, and of the suppression of popular rights and aspirations. This is the fundamental reason why all later attempts to stabilise Communist rule through liberalising it were doomed to failure. In other parts of the world some 'soft-liners' within the authoritarian coalition could manage to survive and even flourish by steering a path to full democratisations. Those who attempted this in East-Central Europe in the late 1980s were swept aside by a tide of popular indignation the moment Moscow withdrew its protection from them. Whether Nagy, Gomułka, or Dubček could have done better in an earlier generation is an experiment the Soviet leadership was not prepared to risk. In consequence, when democracy did finally return to the region it carried very distinctive connotations, not to be confused with the meaning of the term in the abstract, or with the overtones it acquired in other regions. Democracy, private property, anti-Communism and 'embrace of the West' were all rolled into one, and linked to the rebirth of national sovereignties.

This chapter has emphasised two basic factors that probably suffice to explain the durability of the Soviet veto on democratisation, independent of the personal inclinations of individual Russian leaders. One factor is strictly international, or geopolitical; the other is a matter of internal Soviet politics; but the two seem to me so interrelated that it would be artificial to claim that the 'real' explanation was either essentially domestic or primarily international. The first is the strategic imperative of maintaining a divided Germany. This was the core of the postwar settlement in Europe, and the linchpin of Soviet bloc security. It required the imposition of a strict form of Communism on the inhabitants of the Soviet-controlled part of Germany (preferably no doubt with their consent, but finally regardless of their preferences). From time to time experimentation, pluralism and the loosening of Soviet controls in other parts of East-Central Europe might well have been more tolerable to Moscow, but for the repercussions on the GDR. This fundamental geopolitical reality underlay the Soviet veto on all attempts at democratisation in the region.

Equally compelling was the second factor, which must be seen in the context of the first. All Soviet reformers had to consider the implications for their own power base within the USSR of permitting the dismantling of core Communist structures in allied countries. In theory, it might seem as though there could be two alternative routes to reform, regional or system-wide – i.e. liberalism might be allowed in some or all client states, without dictating the content of reform policies within the Soviet Union. In practice, Moscow's scope for permitting deviations within the Warsaw Pact, while blocking them at home, was always highly constrained. If the Hungarians made a success of the price mechanism, that would inevitably (through demonstration effects and the pressures of international rivalry) feed into similar debates throughout the Soviet bloc. If Solidarity's trade unions proved tolerable in Poland, workers elsewhere would certainly wish to emulate the experience. If objective historical enquiry was licensed in any part of the system, it would raise questions that had to be answered throughout the bloc. In short, only a Soviet leader steeled to promote 'openness' at home (and to take the domestic consequences, whatever they might be) would be willing to lift the essential veto on political liberalisation in the neighbouring Communist countries. Prior to 1985 reform-minded Soviet leaders always drew back from the dangers of such far-reaching domestic reform and for that reason they were bound to maintain a wary vigilance over dangerous precedents anywhere in the bloc. The essential link between the two factors just mentioned was provided by the centralising logic of the Soviet command system. Since it was known throughout the system that all essential decisions (military, political, economic, ideological) must be initiated from the top, it followed that whatever the Moscow leadership decided (either by action or inaction) in relation to a particular challenge in a specific policy or geographical arena would be taken to apply more generally. Thus, if Moscow had not crushed the Dubček experiment in 1968, this would have signalled the raising of a veto on reform elsewhere as well (even at home). Likewise, once Gorbachev had decided on extensive liberalisation within the USSR he could never afford to suppress reform elsewhere, without capitulating to the enemies or reform at home. Somewhat similar issues arise with earlier Western experiences of imperial decolonisation.

The 'transitions' literature has sometimes been criticised for focusing too heavily on elite strategies and calculations, the neglect of broader democratic pressures rooted in society at large. This chapter's focus on the Moscow veto might seem an extreme case of such over-emphasis. However, the claim made here is that the maintenance of that veto was a crucial distinguishing feature 'distorting' democratisation patterns and timing in this region. Within the Soviet bloc most pressures from 'below' were heavily suppressed by the Communist system of control (to this extent the 'totalitarian' literature made a valid point, although grossly overstating it). Another distinguishing feature of the regional experience was the role played by 'the West' both in pressing Moscow to liberalise, and in sustaining popular aspirations for democracy in East-Central Europe. This may to some extent be regarded as a partial 'international' substitute for the missing domestic pressures from below – but of course it operated on a different rhythm and according to a distinctive logic, as discussed above.

There is, however, another 'societal' dimension to this process which certainly requires far more attention than it could be given here. The pro-democratic influence of the West came not only through formal treaties and public policies – it was also transmitted through culture, consumption patterns and a proliferation of other demonstration effects.[33] These societal influences are in the long run extremely powerful, but also quite difficult to specify and evaluate.[34] Their impact on different geographical and social sectors within the region was extremely uneven depending on the extent of media control by the regime. (In Romania in 1989, for example, not only were there no private VCR's but every individual typewriter had to be separately registered with the *Securitate*, and photocopying was also rigorously supervised.) In any case it is one thing to show that by example Western social values and practices were in general undermining Communist structures of social control and quite another to link this to specific political consequences. In some cases the greatest practical impact was felt by the ruling elites, whose confidence in their own legitimacy was undermined by demonstrations of the West's superior appeal. Elsewhere the biggest effect may have been to stimulate a wish to travel abroad (particularly in the younger generation) – a wish which once frustrated by bureaucratic edict could be turned into political resistance and the demand for change. It is striking, as Adam Roberts points out, that popular demands for change should have proved so non-violent, as well as so widespread and uncontainable. 'Demonstration effects' across international boundaries were dramatically reinforced by the impact of television news coverage.

In summary then, even though Communism may have traditionally suppressed most forms of 'civil society' in the region, the 'societal' push for democracy became a major independent variable as the transition process got under way. This element in the democratisation process, like the others considered in this chapter, surely contained a major international component. But whether one stresses pressures from below, or the importance of elite strategies, in any case the domestic and international components were so intermingled that it would be arbitrary and artificial to disentangle them, let alone to present the former as dominant over the latter.

Notes

1. The 'region' in question therefore extends from the former German Democratic Republic to the Baltic states, and from Poland to Bulgaria. It excludes the former Yugoslavia and Albania, which were not under Soviet control.
2. Quoted by Ghita Ionescu, 1965, *The Break-Up of the Soviet Empire in Eastern Europe*, Penguin, Harmondsworth, p. 27, which also contains a discussion (pp. 25–6) of the ambiguities of the term 'people's democracy', which still retained some pluralist connotations until late 1947.
3. The speaker was Andrei Zhdonov, as quoted in Alan Bullock, 1991, *Hitler and Stalin: parallel lives*, Harper-Collins, London, p. 1023. By this point, of course, the anti-Fascist alliance was breaking up, and Zhdanov's speech is primarily remembered for enunciating the doctrine of the 'two camps'.
4. According to Adam Roberts 'in acceptance of multiparty democracy (though not in the holding of actual elections) Hungary was significantly ahead of

Poland'. Adam Roberts, 1991, *Civil Resistance in the East European and Soviet Revolutions*, The Albert Einstein Institution, Monograph No. 4, p. 174.

5. Alex Pravda is generally cautious and precise in his use of such terminology, but to my mind he goes too far when describing Dubček's influence on Gorbachev's entourage, saying 'many of the ideas underlying the Czechoslovak reform programme coincided with and perhaps catalysed the thinking and aspirations of the Gorbachev generation to a *communist-party led democratisation* of the Soviet command system' (my emphasis). Alex Pravda (ed.) 1992, *The End of the Outer Empire*, Sage, for the Royal Institute of International Affairs, London, p. 3. It might be safer to substitute the term 'liberalisation' here.
6. G. Ionescu, 1965, *The Break-Up of the Soviet Empire in Eastern Europe*, Penguin, Harmondsworth, p. 64.
7. *Khrushchev Remembers*, Sphere Books, London, 1971, p. 438. This may seem hard to take from the man responsible for the execution of Nagy, but it is of great importance that Khrushchev could be removed by a collective decision and without bloodshed. So were all subsequent Communist rulers of Eastern Europe, other than the Albanian and Romanian dictators. So was Gorbachev.
8. Alex Pravda, 1992, *The End of Outer Empire*, Sage, p. 70. Indeed he thinks it 'likely' that CMEA leaders were informed of this decision when they met in Moscow on 10–11 November 1986 (pp. 17–18).
9. L. Whitehead, 'International aspects of democratisation: three perspectives' in J. Richardson and S.W.R. Samarasinghe (eds), *Democratisation in South Asia* (forthcoming).
10. Interesting attempts to compare the US sphere of influence in the Caribbean with the Soviet sphere in East-Central Europe include Jan F. Triska (ed.), 1986, *Dominant Powers and Subordinate States*, Duke University Press, Durham, 1986 and Paul Keal, 1983, *Unspoken Rules and Superpower Dominance*, Macmillan, London.
11. John Darwin, 1988, *Britain and Decolonisation: the retreat from empire in the post-war world*, Macmillan, London, p. 20. He adds that Harold Macmillan's retrospective claim that African independence was the longstanding object of British policy, and the triumphant culmination of Britain's mission to endow less fortunate peoples with her democratic heritage, was 'a picturesque invention worthy of Disraeli'.
12. Darwin, 1988, *Britain and Decolonisation*, p. 334.
13. Darwin, 1988, *Britain and Decolonisation*, p. 331. However Darwin does not attempt to answer Max Beloff's highly pertinent question, 'Why were British governmental institutions and even the party system so little affected by the retreat from Empire when the collapse of almost all other imperial systems has entailed the most profound repercussions upon the domestic polity?': Beloff, 1969, *Imperial Sunset, Vol. I*, Alfred A. Knopf, New York, p. 7.
14. Darwin, 1988, *Britain and Decolonisation*, p. 335. Britain's Caribbean possessions were something of an exception, and that is where many of the more successful recent decolonisation-cum-democratisations took root (with US support).
15. Paradoxically, the first Moscow-watcher to grasp the full significance of what was happening, and to act consequentially in order to protect his position, was almost certainly Fidel Castro, who launched an implicitly anti-Moscow campaign of 'rectification' in 1986.
16. Robert V. Daniels, 1983, *The End of the Communist Revolution*, Routledge, London, p. 12.

17. Daniels, 1993, *The End of the Communist Revolution*, Routledge, London, pp. 15–16.
18. Daniels, 1993, *The End of the Communist Revolution*, p. 19.
19. Daniels, 1993, *The End of the Communist Revolution*, p. 24.
20. David Deudney and G. John Ikenberry, 1991–2 'The international sources of Soviet change', *International Security*, Winter, Vol. 16, No. 3, p. 77.
21. Deudney and Ikenberry, 1991–2, 'The international sources of Soviet change', p. 117.
22. Duedney and Ikenberry, 1991–2, 'The international sources of Soviet change', p. 118. In essence, then, it would seem that the West could do no wrong.
23. 'One symptom of the change was the revival of the CSCE, which entered a wholly new phase of its existence at the Vienna follow-up meeting of 1986–9. The Soviet Union now wanted to be accepted as a member of the world community, and especially of Europe, so it had to be seen to accept European values. The CSCE was its ticket to admission'. Richard Davy (ed.), 1992, *European Detente: a reappraisal*, RIIA, Sage, pp. 25–6.
24. Davy (ed.), 1992, *European Detente*, pp. 10–11.
25. Davy (ed.), 1992, *European Detente*, p. 19.
26. See Laurence Whitehead, 1993, 'Requisites for admission' in Peter H. Smith (ed.) *The Challenge of Integration: Europe and the Americas*, Transaction Publishers, New Brunswick.
27. Those wedded to the theory of a 'totalitarian' Soviet bloc had to conclude that it was only through outright defeat in war or a violent and catastrophic internal revolution that the system could change. By contrast, as early as 1980, Richard Davy was pointing out the heavy drain on Soviet military, economic and political strength arising from the East European dependencies. 'We should not write off the possibility that the Soviet Union will gradually become more flexible, perhaps under a new leadership. It has good economic reasons for encouraging East European trade with the West, and it is learning to live with greater unorthodoxy even, for the moment, in Poland. Peaceful evolution is still possible', he wrote in *The Times* (London), 18 December 1980.
28. Timothy Garton Ash, 1991, *The Polish Revolution: Solidarity*, Granta Books, London, p. 336. Not that *Solidarnosc* should be viewed as relentlessly destabilising – on the contrary, prior to the declaration of martial law there were some serious efforts at 'pact-making'.
29. Adam Roberts, 1991, *Civil Resistance in the East European and Soviet Revolutions*, The Albert Einstein Institution, Monograph No. 4, p. 32.
30. Davy (ed.), 1992, *European Detente: a reappraisal*, RIIA, Sage, p. 251.
31. Davy (ed.), 1992, *European Detente*, p. 263 (my emphasis).
32. Daniels, 1993, *The End of the Communist Revolution*, Routledge, London, p. 132.
33. There were en estimated 700,000 VCRs in Poland in 1987, 300,000 in Hungary and 150,000 in Czechoslovakia. Miklos Sukos, 'From propoganda to "*Öffentlichkeit*" in Eastern Europe: four models of the public sphere under State Socialism', p. 25, Paper presented to the conference 'Contemporary Societies in Comparative Perspective: Eastern Europe and Latin America in the Twentieth Century', Polish Academy of Sciences, Pultusk, Poland, 29 May – 1 June 1990.
34. Adam Roberts goes so far as to argue that 'television played a key role in the events of 1989–91. It made East Germany aware of the flight to the West, Czechs and Slovaks aware of what was happening in all the neighbouring countries and in their midst, and Romanians aware that Ceauşescu was vulnerable: indeed, much of the Romanian revolution was conducted from the television studio in Bucharest.' Adam Roberts, 1991, *Civil Resistance in the East European and Soviet Revolutions*, p. 33.

3

Towards a culture of democracy? democratic theory and democratisation in Eastern and Central Europe

N.J. Rengger[1]

The rise of democracy in the modern world is surely one of the greatest questions for students of political science. In the last two hundred years an idea that had disappeared from the accepted lexicon of political language by the time of the Roman principiate has become the closest thing to a universal ideology that the modern world possesses. As John Dunn has said in a recent book, part of its charm is that democracy is a deceptively simple idea, though in the forms in which it is practically relevant to us it is anything but simple; its power in the modern world lies in the ordinariness of modern democratic institutions and in their peculiar aptness to the world in which we live, especially, Dunn thinks, the economic aspects of that world (Dunn, 1992, pp. vi–vii).

Such a view poses more questions than it answers. Despite this, however, democracy has become more and more unchallenged, at least in symbolic terms. The latest recruits to the cause of democracy are those countries and peoples in Eastern and Central Europe who have emerged from externally imposed Communist regimes since 1989 and have since attempted to 'democratise' their governments and societies. In this endeavour they are being aided by those states who, in their own terms, sought to defend democracy during the so-called Cold War, the western liberal democracies.[2] The West, we are told, is engaged in 'building democracy' and 'encouraging a culture of democracy' by virtue of extending credit, allowing at least associate membership of the relevant international clubs (the IMF, IBRD, etc.), developing a 'culture of democracy' through the training of Eastern and Central European politicians (and, perhaps, citizens) including seminars on how to run democratic parliaments, encouraging the establishment of a free press, freedom of worship and assembly and so on, and providing an environment conducive to, and supportive of, 'democratisation' (Pinder, this volume).

In this chapter, I want to suggest that in order best to understand what is at stake in questions about democratisation, we need simultaneously to raise our eyes from what appears the immediate and pressing agenda and also to lower our expectations as to what we expect from democratisation *per se*. In brief, I shall argue that 'democratisation' (for all of us, not just for any one state or region) must be seen as a global question under modern conditions, however much it is also a question about particular states or issues. I shall also argue that, as a consequence, an equally important concern must be the presence and strength of constitutionalism and civil society as much as of democracy as such. However, I shall also seek to suggest (though it cannot be part of my main argument in this chapter) that both democracy and constitutionalism must be seen in the context of a more general rearticulation of political understanding.

Before I can turn to any of these questions, however, I want to say something about the disparate nature of democracy itself. For in order to discuss democratisation sensibly we must first try to acquire a clear understanding of the available senses of democracy as they currently stand.

Democratic theory agonistes

Given everything that has occurred in world politics since 1989 it is hardly surprising that democratic theory has become something of a growth industry. Of course, it has always been an important concern of twentieth-century political science (Michels, 1915; Dahl, 1956; Lipset, 1960; Sartori, 1962; Huntington, 1991) but its contemporary significance has elevated it still further in importance and popularity. While there are many different varieties of democratic theory (Held, 1987; Graham, 1986) it is commonly held that this variety can be divided into two broad groups. Mark Warren, in a recent paper, puts it as follows: 'One group seeks to balance democratic participation against other desirable rights of political order . . . by limiting the spheres of society that are organised democratically. The other group . . . sees such limits to democracy as an important cause for many of the ills of contemporary liberal democracies' (Warren, 1992, p. 8).

Both groups of theories premise their accounts on particular understandings of the self and its relation to politics. The first group work with theories about the self that see it as being in fundamental ways pre-political and emphasise, therefore, democracy as a procedure to cope with the inevitable clashing of such pre-political interests. Warren calls these accounts 'standard liberal democracy' (SLD). The second group argue for an 'expansive democracy' (ED) in which 'increased democracy transforms individualistic and conflicting interests into common and non-conflicting ones . . . transformations reduce conflict [and] allow reduced use of power as a medium of political interaction . . . [and] . . . democracy is necessary to the values of self-development, autonomy and self-governance' (Warren, 1992; p. 8). These three theses taken together illustrate what is distinctive about the second group of accounts which Warren calls the 'self-transformation thesis' (STT).

This dichotomy is similar to those proposed by many other contemporary theorists (Plamenatz, 1973; Weale, 1989; Held, 1992; Habermas, 1993), though all would recognise the great variety that exists within groups as well as between them. Benjamin Barber, for example, suggests that while you should distinguish between direct and representative democracy (corresponding very roughly to ED and SLD respectively),[3] it is also important to distinguish between types of democracy within these two groupings. For Barber, representative democracy is divided into authoritative, juridical and pluralist modes, direct democracy into unitary and strong modes (Barber, 1984, p. 141, Fig. 1). Each of these different modes has slightly different referents, dominant values, institutional bias, citizen and government postures and groundings. None the less, Barber is clear that each *is*, so to speak a family grouping.

Despite this variety, however, it is clearly the case that it is Standard Liberal Democracy, in various guises and to varying degrees, that dominates discussion of democracy today, particularly in the West. In part this is because it is this form which has taken root in those countries which are the main advocates and inheritors of the liberal tradition more generally, that is to say, Western Europe, the United States and countries such as Australia, Canada and New Zealand. As many, probably most democratic theorists would argue, democracy needs liberal values.[4] The questions revolve around whether liberalism on its own is enough or whether more radical views are also necessary.

A second reason for the dominance of SLD is well put by Samuel Huntington in a recent study of what he calls the 'third wave' of democratisation (understood as transitions to democracy from 1974 to 1990 and beyond). Huntington unambiguously adopts an SLD definition and trenchantly gives his reasons.

'Serious problems of ambiguity and imprecision arise,' he says, 'when democracy is defined in terms of either source of authority or purposes and a procedural definition is used in this study . . . (Since) the central procedure of democracy is the selection of leaders through competitive elections by the people they govern . . . (and) following in the Schumpeterian tradition, this study defines a twentieth-century political system as democratic to the extent that its most powerful collective decision-makers are selected through fair, honest and periodic elections in which candidates freely compete for votes and in which virtually all the adult population is eligible to vote' (Huntington, 1991; pp. 6–7). Building on earlier work of Dahl, Huntington goes on to argue that this understanding of democracy involves two key dimensions, to wit contestation and participation, and further implies 'the existence of those civil and political freedoms to speak, publish, assemble and organise that are necessary to political debate and the conduct of electoral campaigns' (Huntington, 1991, p. 7).

Huntington's version is only one possible way of reading SLD of course, (it would be, for example, a 'pluralist' model as Barber sketches it) and a slightly different one is visible for example, in John Dunn when he refers to the 'representative democracy of the modern constitutional state, which has enjoyed such a sudden and striking recent triumph' (Dunn, 1992, p. vi), a clear reference to the events of 1989. Dunn's view here seems to be rather closer to Barber's juridical view, as would the views of much mainstream American political theory, especially that deriving from the work of liberal political philosophers such as John Rawls, Bruce Ackerman and Ronald Dworkin.[5] The main point, though, is that all extant liberal democracies are largely, as Barber admits, more or less happy compromises between all three forms of representative democracy.

Notwithstanding this, however, most contemporary forms of SLD are versions of what is usually called 'elite democracy'. This view is clearly Huntington's cited above, for example, though he is clearly echoing one of the earliest, and perhaps the most influential, articulation of such a view, to wit Schumpeter's famous argument that democracy is merely a method, a particular institutional arrangement for arriving at political decisions 'in which individuals acquire power to decide by means of competitive struggle for the people's vote' (Schumpeter, 1943, p. 269). In formal democratic theory in political science, this version remains perhaps the most influential form of SLD and it is perhaps for this reason that many criticisms of SLD are often more properly seen as criticisms of the elite model. I shall return to the significance of this a little later on.

Expansive Democracy, too, has different groupings within it. Many versions of ED are rightly seen as close to traditional republican accounts of politics drawn from a variety of sources running from the Renaissance civic humanists, Montesquieu, the Scottish Enlightenment or, more radically, Rousseau. One very recent version of republican theory has suggested that Machiavelli is the most appropriate source for such accounts (Bok, Skinner and Viroli, 1992), a point touched on, in different ways, by earlier accounts of the republican tradition (Pocock, 1975). Other versions of ED draw on much more recent trends or developments. While not denying its links with older forms, for example, Barber claims that his 'strong democracy' is 'a distinctively modern form of participatory democracy . . . not intrinsically inimical to neither the size or the technology of modern society and is therefore wedded neither to antiquarian republicanism nor to face to face parochialism' (Barber, 1984, p. 117).

However, and despite Barber's caveat, increasingly much modern political theory that wishes to depart from SLD assumptions has taken a 'republican' form to a greater or lesser extent (Bellamy, 1992; Mouffe, 1992; Pettit, 1989).[6] While there are many differences between individual republican theories and while in many respects the republican tradition is also a liberal one, the ways in which republican theories differ from traditional (nineteenth-century) liberalism are also those ways in which ED most differs from SLD.[7] Two points deserve particular mention in the current context. The first is that republicans (and strong democrats) tend to emphasise the transformative and identity-creating aspects of participation. (Barber, 1984; Pettit, 1989; Skinner, 1992); the second is that, for republicans (and strong democrats) the public sphere and its institutions has what Pettit calls a 'formative' role whereas for SLD, the more usual assumption is that the public institutions take a largely neutral role.[8] I shall return to this point a little later on.

The continuing debate between the different sets of democratic approaches has led to some who seek a way to synthesise the insights of SLD and ED, as well as some who reject the language in which they couch their democratic theory altogether. Representative of the latter approach are writers such as William Connolly, Rob Walker, Michael Shapiro, James Der Derian, Richard Flathman and Bonnie Honig who have begun to develop readings of contemporary political theory in a poststructural vein that emphasise the radically contingent and necessarily ongoing aspects of politics that, in their view, much traditional theory (including democratic theory) tries to ignore, marginalise or displace, while articulating a strong democratic (and in Flathman's case, at least, liberal) ethos.[9] These writers all suggest in various ways that, to use Honig's words, 'politics never gets things right, over, and done with. (This) conclusion is not nihilistic but radically democratic. To accept and embrace the perpetuity of contest is to reject the dream of displacement, the fantasy that the right laws or constitution might some day free us from the responsibility for (and, indeed, the burden of) politics' (Honig, 1993, pp. 210–11). This view is one to which I shall have to return later on in this chapter; for now let me just note that it sidelines the traditional SLD/ED debate by treating varieties as variations on a theme of 'displacement', though clearly it has more in common with some ED conceptions than with any version of SLD.

Perhaps most important among those who seek to synthesise SLD and ED approaches are those who take as their starting point the work of Jurgen Habermas.[10] In a thoughtful recent paper Habermas has argued that both traditional forms of democratic theory (he calls them liberal and republican) are problematic. 'The republican trust in the force of political discourses', he suggests, 'stands in contrast to the liberal scepticism about reason. Such discourses are meant to allow one to discuss value orientations and interpretations of needs and wants and then to change these in an insightful way' (Habermas, 1993, p. 5). However, contemporary republicans, Habermas suggests, tend to give this public communication a 'communitarian reading' and therein lies the problem. For 'Political questions may not be reduced to the type of ethical questions, where we, as members of community, ask ourselves who we are and who we would like to be' (Habermas, 1993, p. 6). Habermas suggests that, *pace* republicans and communitarians, and important as these ethical questions unquestionably are, they must, under modern conditions, be subordinate to moral questions understood in the Kantian sense of being basically questions of justice; 'the question having *priority* in legislative politics concerns how a matter can be regulated in the equal interest of all. The making of norms is primarily a justice issue and is gauged by principles that state what is equally good for all. And unlike ethical questions, questions of justice are not related from the outset to a specific collective and its form of life' (Habermas, 1993, pp. 7–8).

The implication of this is that those who emphasise the procedural aspects of democracy are more likely to be able to accommodate this insight. Such, indeed, is Habermas' view. However, he is careful to stress that this does not commit him to an SLD view (or as he terms it, simply a 'liberal' view), for here too, there are problems. Specifically, for

Habermas, liberal arguments are indeed vulnerable to the kind of criticisms levelled at them by republicans in that they over-emphasise the interest/appetitive aspects of democratic practice and see democracy as simply 'the task of programming the government in the interest of society, where the government is represented as an apparatus of public administration, (and) society as a market structured network of interactions among private persons' (Habermas, 1993, p. 1).

Habermas' own solution to these problems is to suggest an integration of aspects of the two views along the lines he has already sketched out in his work on communicative rationality and discourse ethics (see Habermas, 1983 and 1984; Baynes, 1992). That is to say, what he calls his 'proceduralist, deliberative model of democracy' 'invests the democratic process with normative connotations stronger than those found in the liberal (SLD) model but weaker than those found in the republican model' (Habermas, 1993, p. 13). I shall not attempt to outline the general theory of democracy that this view leads to. Rather, I want to offer one particular reading of this project and indicate its significance for our current concern.

This reading highlights the twin elements of constructivism and constitutionalism in Habermas' project. The project is constructivist in the sense suggested by Onora O'Neill of a theory that occupies the space between realist and relativist accounts of ethics (O'Neill, 1989, p. 206). It also at least purports to be a *Kantian* constructivism. It is constitutionalist in that Habermas' proceduralism suggests that as a basic minimum, at least initially, a just state must subscribe to the rule of law free from despotic or arbitrary government, which, as many have pointed out, is as good a definition as any of constitutional government (McIlwain, 1947; Linklater, 1993).

Without necessarily subscribing to what he thinks follows from them, these two aspects of the Habermasian project point in the direction in which we need to travel in order to develop a satisfactory account of democratisation in contemporary world politics. However, there are problems with all of the forms of democratic theory just mentioned.[11] In all cases, there is insufficient attention paid to the question of the category and classification of the political units within which 'democracy' must now take place. In general terms the unit is usually perceived to be some version of the state. On the republican view, for example, we would have a tight, focused, participatory state (though it might also be a federal or even confederal one as Rousseau's arguments about the government of Poland suggest) (see Hoffmann and Fiedler, 1992). On the liberal/SLD views we would have a loose, rule-governed, neutral one (whether this is understood in authoritarian, juridical or pluralist ways).

However, the European state in which both these views originated was itself something which grew, evolved and changed over time (Oakeshott, 1975; Skinner, 1978) and the idea and practice of the state seems to be continuing to evolve in the face of profound socio-economic changes at all levels (Robertson, 1992). It is doing so, moreover, in ways that now make it very difficult to see how 'democracy' can be sustained if we do not go beyond the boundaries of particular states, certainly if anything like expansive democracy or the Habermasian agenda is to be met.

Thus, one can agree with Habermas that traditional dichotomies between SLD and ED models need to be overcome but I would also suggest that democratic theory in general must take a turn away from its exclusive focus on the state. Significantly, this focus is even present where, as in the case of Barber, a theorist stresses regional and local concerns. Of course, it should be emphasised here that the main issue, as we shall see, is not simply moving beyond the territory of particular states; it is the need for issues (and not just territories) to be democratised, if democracy is to work. Thus freeing democratic theory from its overconcentration on the state does not mean that the state level is to be ignored. On the contrary, it is to claim that only by taking into account the significance of democratising *issues* can the possibility and applicability of democratising *states* be properly assessed. What we need, as Michael Walzer has recently emphasised, is a political theory above and below the level of the state (Walzer, 1992).

The complexities and confusions of democratic theory on these issues, however, need to be contextualised for the full difficulties to become apparent. So, let me now turn to the region with which we are primarily concerned here, Eastern and Central Europe.

Democratisation in Eastern (and Western?) Europe

Even a cursory reading of much of the available literature from Central Europe[12] indicates fairly clearly that, while Western governments – and many in Eastern and Central Europe too – have adopted a relatively straightforward SLD case, there are a significant minority of Eastern and Central European thinkers and movements who are in many ways much closer to ED accounts. As James Turner Johnson has pointed out, there are four themes in contemporary Central European 'democratic theory' that form a kind of 'nested set'. Firstly, there is the idea of civil society, deployed in an analogous way to Locke, though with significant and important differences; secondly, the theme of the relationship of the member of civil society to participatory membership in a state; thirdly the question of pluralism (again significantly different from more familiar Western accounts); and finally the concept of rights in the context of pluralism (Johnson, 1992).[13]

The way that these themes are deployed indicates that many of the most influential Central European ideas about democracy are closer to varieties of ED than to SLD. To suggest exactly how this is the case, let me just briefly spell out the implications of some of these ideas. Perhaps the most important, as we shall see, is the idea of civil society. Writers like Michnik and Havel modify the standard Lockean notion of civil society in that they argue that rather than government being created out of civil society, civil society is created in opposition to government and therefore depends, in a way that Locke's does not, upon mutually reinforcing patterns of responsibility and interconnectedness. As Johnson and Scruton both, in their different ways, point out (Johnson, 1992, pp. 45–6; Scruton, 1988a, pp. 456–7), this implies that for the creation of democratic societies there must first be a democratic culture and that this culture consists precisely in the existence and independence and of free associational groupings. It is, therefore, a phenomenon that arises from the community as a whole rather than being imposed by, or directed from, a particular elite.

Given that the conception of democracy espoused by SLD sees democracy as 'primarily a means for aggregating pre-political interests (which) should be limited in scope just because it is instrumental to pre-political interests and not a good in itself' (Warren, 1992, p. 8). The views of those Eastern and Central European writers just cited seem clearly to be much closer to versions of ED. The emphasis placed on notions of association and free groupings is also reminiscent of early guild socialists like Figgis and Cole, for example, and of their modern heirs like Paul Hirst (see Hirst, 1992).

This analysis is borne out by perhaps the most thorough investigation of Eastern and Central European thinking on civil society, Jean Cohen and Andrew Arato's *Civil Society and Political Theory* (Cohen and Arato, 1992, pp. 31, 36, 58–82, 487–91). They comment that in its earliest (and largely Polish) form the idea was always 'the protection and/or self organisation of social life in the face of the totalitarian or authoritarian state' (Cohen and Arato, 1992, p. 31). However, there were also considerable problems with this version, the most fatal of which was the lack of clarity concerning the type of civil society to be constructed (or reconstructed). This ambiguity in part accounts for the very divided character of Eastern and Central European thinking on democracy and civil society for it allowed some versions very strongly reminiscent of SLD models to develop as well.

This leads on to a second area in which these conceptions of democracy are analogous to ED. This can be found in the fact that they amount to a modified communitarian view of democracy.[14] As Johnson puts it, for these writers, 'democratic identity flows from the experience of membership in a plurality of community relationships and the growth of a democratic society depends on the protection of such plurality' (Johnson, 1992, p. 49). This is effectively a re-articulation of Warren's first argument for the STT. It also makes clear why many 'communitarian' writers have found so much common ground with Eastern European theories of democracy (see Walzer, 1992). In the West, writers often termed 'communitarians' (Michael Sandel, perhaps, or Charles Taylor) will make criticisms of liberalism that amount to attacks on notions such as the idea of procedural democracy, for failing to see the centrality of their project of the embedding of cultural pluralism in communities (see Sandel, 1982; Taylor, 1990).[15]

One plausible reason for the differences between West and East lies in the differential characteristics of state/society relations in Western Europe on the one hand and in Eastern and Central Europe on the other. There are two aspects of this. Historically, those parts of Central and Eastern

Europe that were part of (for example) federal or quasi-federal structures (Austria-Hungary, for example, and Germany both before and after 1870) had a history of powerful local and associational groupings, that is a natural bedfellow for ED accounts, once you allow any form of democracy at all (Stone, 1983; Taylor, 1948).

Secondly, the experience of state/society relations *after* the Second World War might, paradoxically, have reinforced such tendencies. Especially significant in the latter case is the imposition of forms of government from above (locally unpopular Communist regimes) and, indeed, from outside (such regimes imposed and sustained by a Soviet Union clearly viewed by a majority as simply Imperial Russia in new clothes). The consequence seems to have been that home-grown and solidarist notions of self-rule and the centrality of groupings other than the state came very much to the fore,[16] and the obvious result has been notions of democracy that emphasise its transformative potential (especially immediately after 1989) and that are, as a result, closer to ED than SLD.[17]

There is, however, a separate question here. It is clear that behind the proliferation of aid programmes and structural reform programmes in both West and East lies a general set of assumptions drawn from SLD. Individuals are seen as 'rational maximisers of preferences', thus political institutions should be designed to separate political judgements from those of individuals; political interests are inherently conflicting because they are oriented towards scarce resources, so politics is an allocative activity taking place under scarcity. Thus, economically, the West is concerned to support market-driven reforms, and so it makes the aid necessary conditional on the establishment of democracy understood as a framework of institutions designed to maximise the opportunities for the market. A similar phenomenon is observable in relations between the West, and the international organisations that it largely controls such as the World Bank and the IMF, and developing countries more generally (Hewitt, forthcoming).

The issue here, however, is whether such 'reforms' are appropriate or suited to the needs of the countries wherein they are being applied. There is much evidence from many parts of the world that this is simply not the case; that, in fact, such 'reforms' as the installation (from above) of 'multi-party democracy' actually exacerbates or even creates ethnic, religious or tribal differences which create unrest, leads to further problems with foreign investment, further strictures from international organisations and so the cycle begins anew. Much of the time such unrest is fanned by political elites themselves for electoral or narrowly partisan purposes or is present at a visceral level in communities anyway; but this does not negate the main point which is to suggest that such 'reforms' are not always in the best interests of the countries that are adopting them.[18]

We should also note that the structure of the world economy acts as a constraint on the assumptions of SLD. This can be viewed in a number of ways (see Gill, 1989; Mazrui, 1990; Keohane, 1990). However, given the West's preponderant power in the international system and in the major organisations that are active within it, and given the general predominance of SLD views amongst the political elite, the agenda of 'democratisation' in

Eastern and Central Europe, at least in so far as it is dependent upon Western economic aid and access to Western-dominated economic institutions, will be dominated by Standard Liberal Democracy models. Even assuming complete integrity in Western policy on this issue (and there is some evidence that many Western and Western-inclined states seem uncomfortably reluctant to take the medicine that the West is prescribing for Eastern and Central Europe, either economically, or constitutionally),[19] the question still remains, will this form of democratisation produce what is expected of it, that is to say, rising living standards and greater freedom for the East and greater stability and security for the West?

Global politics, democracy and constitutionalism

In order to look at this question, I now want to return to the question raised at the end of the first section of this chapter. Most especially, I want to examine the argument that democracy should now be seen in a global context.

The political theorist who has most persuasively articulated the view that democratisation is now a global phenomenon and advocates, as a result, what he calls 'cosmopolitan democracy' is David Held.[20] Held's argument is premised on the assumption that what he calls the 'Westphalian model' of the international system, i.e., an international order focusing on independent sovereign entities and an international law that reflects this, has now been at least partially replaced by the 'UN Charter model'. This view holds that international law is not simply about interstate relations and that states are not the sole bearers of international rights and obligations. States are still sovereign but are linked together in a myriad of relations. (Held, 1992, pp. 27–8)

At the heart of this shift, Held thinks,

> lies a conflict between claims made on behalf of individual states and those made on behalf of an alternative organising principle of world affairs: ultimately a democratic community of states, with equal voting rights in the general assembly of nation states, openly and collectively regulating international life while constrained to observe the UN charter and a battery of human rights conventions. (Held, 1992, p. 29)[21]

The point for Held, however, is that both models are at variance with the transformations being wrought in the international system in the wake of a globalisation which is placing both models of international governance under strain. Held believes that the best way of altering contemporary world politics (both ethically and practically) is to move towards a transformation to a system of cosmopolitan democracy. Such a democratic politics has three distinct requirements, he thinks;

> (firstly) that the territorial boundaries of systems of accountability be recast so that those issues which escape the control of a nation state . . . can be brought under better democratic control; secondly, that the role and place of regional and global regulatory and functional agencies be rethought so that they might

> provide a more coherent and useful focal point of public affairs (and) . . . thirdly, that the articulation of political institutions with the key groups, agencies, associations and organisations of international civil society be reconsidered to allow the latter to become part of a democratic process. (Held, 1992, p. 33)

In order for this to take place Held, like Habermas (whose writings are an acknowledged influence on him),[22] thinks that we need to recognise that democratic politics needs both standard liberal and expansive democracy conceptions. Democracy must become transnational and this will require an expanding framework of institutions and agencies that will rely on the transformative power much stressed by ED theorists, but it will also clearly require many of the liberal assumptions on which SLD depends, as well as many of the practices and assumptions that SLD champions procedurally and of which there is a good deal of practical experience (elections, parties, free press etc.)[23] It will require, in other words, a global civil society and public sphere.

Of course, there is no guarantee that the processes of globalisation will encourage such developments. It is quite possible that the vested interests that would be harmed by such a movement as well as the logics and trajectory of world politics more generally, will be successful in stopping or corrupting such cosmopolitan democracy as does emerge. That is something to which I shall have to return in my concluding remarks. However, we should not let it prevent us from examining the requirements of such a view in general terms.

Let us, then, assess the implications of this cosmopolitan democracy. If the most appropriate focus for 'democracy' in the contemporary world is the cosmopolis, the world as a whole, not simply the nation state, then it is surely at the 'global' level that justification must be found for political systems *tout court*, both in terms of the interests they serve and the values they hold to (they will, of course, also have other, local or regional justifications and explanations; economic, social, traditional). Such a 'global' justification does not require the emergence of some 'global morality' (the rubbishing of which is a common way of dismissing such views) but rather the acceptance that decisions, actions and events cannot be evaluated outside a global context.[24] Thus, political communities cannot, on this argument, simply assert (for example) that their 'internal affairs' are not the business of anybody else. They might be able to show that, under certain circumstances this is, indeed, the case. But *making* such a case at all requires them to address the world community; to give reasons to the said community, not simply to assert an allegedly obvious or legal fact.

Such a view is, of course, out of step with contemporary public international law as well as with the rhetoric (and practice) of most states. However, there are reasons for looking behind both the structure of contemporary international law and the rhetorical practices and tropes of states (Carty, 1986; Walker, 1992); as Robert Jackson has convincingly argued (Jackson, 1990) the vast majority of states today in any case acquire their 'legitimacy' through the working of the international legal order. They are 'juridical states' in that their capacity for statehood is largely, and in some cases entirely, generated by the 'fact' of recognition from the international community as a whole. Dorothy Jones has added weight to this thesis by pointing out (Jones, 1989) that during the nineteenth and twentieth centuries the international community has hammered out a set of principles that govern its activities and through which it gives and withholds legitimacy. We might equate this with what Held regards as the 'partial' amalgam of the Westphalian and UN Charter models that he thinks now constitutes world politics.

If this is so, we should recognise that today (whatever might have been the case in the past) legitimacy can only be acquired globally and that, as a consequence, we must discuss questions of legitimacy in a global context. This means that those institutional forms that we hold to convey legitimacy – democracy, for example, – must also be global in reference, if not always in reach. The implications of such a view can only be briefly mentioned here. In order for it to be at all convincing, we must either develop, as I hinted above, an account of practical reasons immune from charges of relativism or scepticism or accept the logic of those like Connolly and Walker who suggest it is in part the attempt to achieve such an Archimedean point that is the problem. The work of those like Habermas, Apel and others in discourse ethics, of Onora O'Neill and Thomas Hill in Kantian ethics and Charles Beitz and Andrew Linklater in international political theory are all, in this respect, designed to attempt to provide a ground (or rather different grounds) for practical reason that is non-relative but also not dependent on any of the grander metaphysical accounts of truth or meaning; they are, in other words, constructivist projects as I defined the term above.

This implies that questions of justice and democratisation cannot solely be concerned with the *state*. As the growth of the literature on regimes, multilateralism and interdependence suggests (Krasner, 1982; Keohane and Nye, 1987; Ruggie, 1992), international institutions are increasingly taking decisions that, in previous centuries would have been taken by 'legitimate states' (or not taken at all, because impossible or impractical) and yet, in most cases, such institutions are almost entirely undemocratised. In order to legitimise them, and the decisions they take, it is the international community as a whole, the world order, if I can use a grand phrase, that we must 'democratise' and make accountable. In order to do this, however, the first step must be to support and ensure the minimum basis of any such attempt, which is not liberalism, but constitutionalism. Thus, in order to democratise adequately world politics we must first constitutionalise it and in order to do this we must understand the relations between civil society and constitutionalism.

Democratisation and constitutionalism in Eastern and Central Europe

We appear to have moved a long way from the problems of building democracy in Eastern and Central Europe. However, in the last two sections of this chapter, I shall try to show how this discussion provides a way both to understand the transformations in Eastern and Central Europe and to help us structure our responses to them, both individual and institutional.

To begin with, on the argument offered above, it is unlikely that the characteristics of civil society in Eastern and Central Europe will respond well to the sort of 'marketisation' of society being advocated in the West, at least at the pace currently being suggested. One would have thought that we had far too many examples already in twentieth-century history of the failed attempt to create democracy by simply adding institutional experience from other political cultures and circumstances and allowing it to stew until, surprise, the dish boils over.[25] This is not a criticism simply aimed at Western policy. It is also true of the governments of the new democracies themselves. In the first place, the policies which many of these governments are following consist in variously serious attempts at 'market reform' coupled, in most cases, with strong statist, even nationalist, tendencies.[26] It is hardly surprising in this context that strong nationalisms have emerged once more; indeed, the wonder is that, so far, they have not been stronger.[27]

This brings us to the first paradox of contemporary democratisation in Eastern and Central Europe. The logic of cosmopolitan democracy outlined above suggests that, while state institutions will be crucially important, those concerned with democratisation must pay much more attention than has been common to regional and local concerns and to the democratisation of transnational issues, especially the economy (Dahl, 1985 and 1989). Yet in the Eastern and Central European cases it is the 'state building' aspects that tend to be emphasised and this will provide only the illusion of democratic control in many cases. The result is likely to be the perception that 'democracy' does not work, in that decisions are still made in ways that people will find difficult to follow or whose logics they will deny and this will lead to decreasing support for the 'democratic' institutions on which they had pinned so much hope.

This raises the general question of the relationship between nationalism, political identity and democracy. Historically, nationalism has often gone hand in hand with liberalism and with demands for self-rule. In this sense, there is no necessary antagonism between nationalism and democracy. In the contemporary situation, however, it is surely the case that the nationalisms we are witnessing in Eastern and Central Europe, composite phenomena though they may be, are quite likely to work against the establishment of both the local, regional and transnational elements of democracy that the cosmopolitan account requires. Writers such as Charles Taylor have recently emphasised the centrality of the notion of recognition to contemporary politics and the central place within that notion that ideas of national autonomy and cultural identity can play (Guttmann and Taylor, 1992). He is undoubtedly correct in delineating this phenomenon as one of the most significant political beliefs of the modern age and rightly sees it as going hand in hand with many of the assumptions that are also requisite for democracy. However, if the cosmopolitan model of democracy is even partially correct, we have to be careful about how we understand such identity claims and we should try to re-articulate how we might interpret such beliefs for a rapidly changing world (as, in many ways, Taylor does; for a contrasting attempt to think this through, see Rengger, 1993).

The most obvious general assumption that such a re-articulation would seem to qualify is that most sacrosanct of modern shibboleths, the 'right of national self-determination'. Cosmopolitan democracy seems to me to rightly assume that *people* (as individuals) have such a right, but peoples (that is nations) only do secondarily and derivatively. This position need not be simplistically individualist, in that its emphasis can be as much on the rights of groups and communities as well as individuals, although of course such rights need filling out in particular ways (for two contrasting discussions of this see Waldron, 1993, pp. 1–34 and Rengger, 1993). It simply refuses to give *priority* to the notion of a discrete 'people' understood as a linguistic or cultural group defined as a nation, in terms of the demarcation of political legitimacy. Within the network of agencies and institutions that make up world politics, the rights of particular communities must be enshrined (and there might be legitimate disagreements about the best way to do this), but it need not be done in the way that the traditional assumption of self-determination requires (i.e. full 'state' sovereignty). Such an argument will require a much more thorough investigation of the cultural and societal elements of contemporary world politics than we currently have and considerable attention will also need to be paid to the question of the securing of rights for individuals and groups within multi-ethnic associations (for discussions see Kymlicka, 1989; Taylor, 1992; Rengger, 1993).

The implication of all of the above is that the problems of contemporary policy in Eastern and Central Europe is that in trying to 'encourage' or 'build' democracy (anyway understood largely in SLD terms), a very real risk is being run that respect for constitutionalism will be destroyed. On the argument presented here, it is the task of building, sustaining and supporting constitutionalism which is the essential precondition of any successful democratisation.

A second problem that grows out of this is that the democratisation process in Eastern and Central Europe has been only fitfully related to the expanding network of international agencies and institutions either regionally or globally. These too require embedding in a 'constitutional' framework – and a civil society – and yet the task of doing this has barely even begun. Even within the European Community, where it might be supposed that such discussions were frequent, there is very little real constitutional discussion that is not 'problem solving' legal argumentation or political quick-fixes[28] and similar problems are visible in other European organisations such as the Conference on Security and Cooperation in Europe (CSCE) (Birnbaum, 1991, p. 85; Baylis, 1992). Indeed, the response of the European organisations like the EC, as well as international organisations like the UN, to both the collapse and the horrifically violent dissolution of Yugoslavia gives due warning of the dangers of what (aside from the depressing lack of political will), an inability to constitutionalise the principal international institutions may well presage.

Thirdly, while we can accept (as I remarked above) that the structural aspects of the international system, most especially the international economy, are among the most resistant to change that would lead to increasing democratisation, it is precisely here that change is most necessary. By this I do not mean the 'conversion to capitalism' of Eastern and Central European state economies, though clearly some change here is necessary. Rather I mean, for example, the ability of large corporations and of the financial markets generally, to influence and even to set the political agenda (a point rightly emphasised by Held and which is discussed from a slightly different point of view by Dahl, 1985 and 1989) as well as the structural imbalances in the international economy as a whole that work as an inhibiting factor on democratisation and responsiveness. The point here is to agree with those who see these as impediments to democratisation, (and what I think are still more central) but to disagree with those who argue that they are inevitable and immovable. It is unlikely that they can be easily changed but it is not impossible (for suggestions as to how see Held, 1992; Dahl, 1989).

There are, of course, many other problems. As I said earlier, there are many problems with democracy that are not specific to Eastern and Central Europe but that are the common lot of those who support, however, critically, the achievements that 'democratisation', at least when understood as going hand in hand with constitutionalism, can bring. The implication of this, however, is that we should see the debates and choices in Eastern and Central Europe in an even more obviously 'global' way; 'they' are, after all, engaged in the same project as 'us', (though rooted in their own contexts and circumstances); as Benjamin Franklin once said, in a rather different context, 'if we do not hang together we shall all, most assuredly, hang separately'.

Constitutionalism, global civil society and the persistence of the state

I now want to turn to what might be attempted as more positive steps towards the building of constitutionalism and democracy in Eastern and Central Europe before making some final concluding remarks. I want to divide what I have to say here into two categories. The first might be called pragmatic, in that there is the potential for doing them with very little structural change. The second have do with what I shall term 'constitutional' change, and are the most wide ranging, the least likely and the most problematic.

Let me take the pragmatic category first. Here, I assume that all would agree that democratisation requires a degree of stability (in the sense of a relative absence of social unrest and upheaval whether economic, political, cultural or ideological) and at least a minimum degree of goodwill from the populations at large. To that extent, current opinion poll evidence, such as it is, is worrying in that it indicates that there has been a marked decline in support for 'democracy' since 1990 and the beginnings of the reform process. Part of this is unquestionably due to economic hardship created by the 'marketisation' of Eastern and Central European economies (see Przeworski, 1991)[29] To an extent such hardship is an inevitable concomitant of emerging from years of Communist rule and its associated economic strait-jackets. However, it does not seem very likely that, left unchecked, such hardship will create a groundswell of support for the system that permitted it to happen. Thus the first step of any serious 'marketisation' of Eastern and Central Europe must be for the groups with the most to lose (after the Eastern and Central Europeans themselves, of course) to do as much as they can to stabilise the situation. This will involve a twofold programme: first, substantial aid to ease the path of marketisation (i.e. NOT conditional on particular structural political reforms as at present (see, for example, Pinder, this volume), but rather simply to help create basic welfare provisions for those hardest hit by the marketisation of the economy). We might also bear in mind that there is considerable evidence from the West, too, that citizens are unhappy about what they see as unfettered market policies creating unacceptable social costs.

It is clear also that the tasks of supporting the Eastern and Central European economies, reviving the currently stagnant Western European economies and attempting to ensure at least minimum ecological standards are unlikely all to be done without the necessity for some lowering of expectations both as regards economic growth and increased prosperity in the currently richer (Western and Northern) parts of Europe and as regards the time-scale of reform in the Eastern parts. Such lowering of expectations is unlikely to happen without a deliberate attempt to make people aware of the reasons for it. Politicians (amongst others) here must lead, not simply follow.

The second pragmatic strategy should focus on the strengthening of support for the embedding of civil societies in Eastern and Central Europe that would make any return to authoritarian rule (of whatever political flavour) increasingly difficult; in other words the embedding of constitutionalism. This would not necessarily include 'multi-party systems' and all the usual apparatus of the liberal democratic state (though it might include that, where possible) but it certainly would require support for plural centres of influence and power (trade unions, churches, universities, the media) and opposition to arbitrary or despotic rule. There is the minor point that in at least some Western countries such agencies have been under attack to varying degrees by their own governments and so it is, to put it mildly, difficult to see that they will support such agencies abroad if they dislike them at home. None the less, such a policy seems to me to be the minimum that is both practical and necessary given current conditions. This support will have to be financial but, at least as important, it must also be political and cultural. Some work of this kind is already happening (Pinder, this volume). Such a policy would benefit both Western and Eastern groups and associations involved and it should by no means be seen simply as the 'West' teaching or training the 'East'.

The point about this, therefore, is that the embedding of 'civil society' cannot be an activity restricted to a particular country or region. Given the arguments discussed earlier, it has to be a much more general activity and indeed, as Cohen and Arato argue, it will have to be part of a much more general process of political rearticulation. Their view is that their conception of civic society can help resolve what they see as the three most fundamental political arguments of the past twenty or so years, that between elite and participatory democracy, that between 'rights oriented liberalism and democratically oriented communitarianism' and that between welfarism and neo-conservative anti-statism. In terms of the current discussion it is clear that their argument would lend support to the argument that in attempting to apply 'market focused' solutions and SLD political institutions Western governments are failing to see the significance of the emergence of new forms of civil society. However, their argument also suggests that such versions of civil society require both fairly elaborate philosophical defence and considerable changes in the way in which contemporary world politics operates. They require, in other words the embedding of a global civil society. I shall return to this point a little later on.

A third pragmatic point, of course, is to stress the international sources of domestic tension and take steps to resolve them. It is a by now familiar point that a relatively secure and stable international environment will aid security and stability internally (Waever *et al.*, 1993; Skocpol, 1978; Herring, this volume). There are a number of areas where this needs to be remembered. Trade, and economic relations generally, is again one central area but also, of course, military security relations in Europe. It is for this reason, amongst others, that the failure of the EC in former Yugoslavia is so debilitating. As is already obvious in Albania, Macedonia, Greece, Bulgaria, Hungary, Romania, Austria and Germany, the instability and violence in the Balkans have set in train much instability outside their 'region', narrowly defined. Thus, great care must be taken to ensure that the mistakes that have characterised Western responses to these events (in both ethical and strictly practical spheres) do not occur again.[30] As in the past, the main responsibility for this must, at least in the short run, lie with the major European powers, to wit, Germany, France, the UK and Italy. It would be best if they could agree to increase their commitment to a common EC foreign and security policy with binding majority voting, but in the absence of that they should operate in the form of quasi-European concert of powers (Kupchan and Kupchan, 1991).

Of course, these pragmatic points are inevitably relatively short term and a consideration of the longer term inevitably leads on to my second category. I shall term these steps 'constitutional', in the larger sense that I have followed in the rest of the paper, i.e., conducive to constitutionalism in world politics as a whole.

To begin with, we should take two things as givens. First, as Charles Taylor suggests, people will continue to want 'recognition', i.e., the greatest degree of self-rulership consistent with their economic well-being (efficiency, practicability etc.), cultural (including ethnic and religious) loyalties and historical experience. This implies that some form of the state is likely to continue to be the most important single unit in world politics for the foreseeable future. Secondly, and contrarily, the structures of contemporary world politics, especially the world economy, and of European politics in particular, mean that such units will have to be supplemented in a number of ways, in order for such communities to retain the independence and self-rule that is their *raison d'être*.

What, then, can we do? We seem to have three possibilities. First, we can remain more or less as we are, or engage in largely incremental, piecemeal damage control, passed off as reform. This seems to me to be the preferred option (or at least the option that is being taken) by most European states at present, both Western and Eastern. Consider, for example, the haphazard way that the Treaty of Rome is 'reformed' (as in the Maastricht process). A similar strategy seems to be behind the calls for the EC to be 'widened' rather than 'deepened', on the grounds that the larger the number of members the less likely it is that any really radical change will be tried or, if it is tried, will be successful.

Secondly, we might attempt a 'deepening' of the existing European Community (with perhaps two or three new members)[31] fully federating the institutions and beefing up the powers of the Commission and the Parliament and perhaps weakening the powers of the Council of Ministers. This seems to be the idea that animates many Eurofederalists, and is influential (unsurprisingly) in the European Commission. This option would be worse than the previous one. As far as democratisation in Eastern and Central Europe is concerned it would effectively leave the new democracies to wither on the vine, while the richer Western half of Europe attempted to bind itself closer together with the likely result that the Eastern European states would not gain significantly in democracy, freedom or stability and the Western Europeans would be continually responding to crises and security problems in the East. There is also no guarantee it would strengthen the Community and there is a good deal of circumstantial evidence that the peoples of Europe, already deeply disillusioned about the EC, would rebel against such a further stage of integration (Gallup, 1993). There is also little in these ideas that speaks to the sort of constitutionalism that I have suggested is important here.

The third option is the most radical. That option is to assume that the experiment in institution building that we call the EC has gone as far as it practicably can go by incremental, *ad hoc* decision-making. Either we must declare the experiment over or we must take it into its next stage. By this I mean that we must reconsider what sort of organisation we require if we are to fulfil the aims that we all have in terms of democratisation, economic prosperity, sustainable development and so on. In the past, such a grand reconsideration of Europe and its structure has only self-consciously taken place after a major war (as, for example, at Westphalia, Utrecht, Vienna and Versailles), and has usually been restricted to the question of political borders and regimes. However, not only have we just finished a major (if Cold) war, but we can surely learn from experience that there might be occasions when there would be a need for a such a reconsideration even in the absence of a major war.

This undertaking would unquestionably be immensely ambitious. Given modern conditions and the range of issues to be discussed such a conference would have to combine elements of a peace conference, with a rolling economic summit and a constitutional convention. It would also, clearly, have to take place over several years, with the evolving incremental structure still in place while it ran. Moreover, such an endeavour would have to be wider than the EC as currently structured. Criteria for participation should be those states which could materially affect the security, prosperity and way of life of the states of Europe. Thus, the 'new democracies' in Eastern and Central Europe and (at least) the Western states of the former Soviet Union, as well as states such as Turkey, would have to be included.[32] Only through such an endeavour are we likely to evolve political structures that can meet the inevitable changes that will affect politics as we move into the twenty-first century in ways that give us the best chance of good (that is constitutional) government and democracy (however conceived). This convention would have to address itself to many aspects of contemporary life and politics: citizenship; the public/private distinction; welfare provision; migration and asylum; governmental structure; the appropriate forms of democracy for local, regional, national and transnational dealings (some might be direct, some indirect, some a combination of the two) and the appropriate ways that these new forms of political institutions might fit into the existing world political system as well as the local and national political systems.

It will be said that such a view is ridiculously Utopian, that I am ignoring the vested interests that exist in defence of the *status quo* and the huge collective action problems that exist even in contemporary states and that would be even greater in the sort of situation I envisage. It will be argued also that the account I have given is heavily underspecified; that I have not said enough about the character of the political units that might emerge from any such convention, or how such an enormously different set of political structures would work. Huntington's claim about the 'fuzziness' of non-procedural understandings of democracy, many might think, will be amply justified.

It is certainly true that the view I have just sketched is highly speculative. However, I suggested at the outset that if my task was to discuss 'democratisation' in Eastern and Central Europe (or, indeed, anywhere else) then we would have to both raise our eyes and lower our expectations. The meaning of this phrase is now, I hope, clearer. Democratisation, under contemporary conditions, is a vast, complex and multi-faceted task which cannot be restricted to a particular state, or to a particular view of democracy. It must involve a much more wide-ranging rethinking of our categories of politics, the units that we assume politics to consist of and the values which we hold to be relevant to politics. 'Minimal' definitions of democracy, however convenient, however 'rigorous' they may appear to be, and however preferable to non-democratic alternatives, are actually normative choices working in defence of the *status quo*. Such a choice may – and often will – be better than what has been the case before but in the longer term it cannot avoid dealing with a much broader set of issues.

Conclusions

There remains the task of assessing these various arguments. The last point is, deliberately, both controversial and in practical terms, at least at the moment, extremely unlikely. The first question, therefore, is to ask just how desirable it actually is and how much we will lose if something like it is not attempted. It is at this point that the question that has hovered in the background of much of this debate comes centre stage. The central task here must be to articulate a sense of how 'democracy' in any sense can be grounded, or at any rate legitimated and how such a grounding relates to the emerging forms of (global) civil society and to the (legal and institutional) constitutionalism that, together, are the only proper guarantors of any kind of political freedom. Thus, the central task of legitimating democracy becomes one of articulating a sense of politics that ties political things and ethical things together – in other words a theory of practical reason.

It is worth bearing in mind here the argument of those like Connolly and Honig that I mentioned earlier. Their point, it will be recalled, is that there is no point trying to 'displace' politics or assume that any constitutional 'settlement' or 'procedure' (however formally democratic) will take from our shoulders the burden of action and of choice. I agree. However, seeing the problem of democracy in contemporary politics as I have, does not suggest that any such settlement or prodecure could possibly do that. Of course, politics is an ongoing, never completed process even more so assuming the difficulties of constitution building and democratisation in the countries of Eastern and Central Europe, but it must be a process that takes place within certain parameters if people are to have any hope of understanding it, learning from it, and building communities through it.

Those parameters are what civil society and constitutionalism create, whether we see them in terms of a Habermasian communicative rationality, a Kantian derived practical reason or other equally interesting forms of legitimation. Civil society creates the arena and the actors, constitutionalism the formal parameters (which are always open to change and evolution, of course) within which are communities (not necessarily states in the traditional sense) which exist and have their being. They also provide the seed bed of democratisation for without them there is no soil in which a democracy, saving only perhaps the crudest elite form, can take root.

It is unquestionably true that taking our quest for democratisation this far carries with it very considerable risks of overextension or impracticability and we should, of course, weigh up whether under current circumstances we should take such risks. However, given the increasing and ever more complex aspects of globalisation, the overlapping and interdependent patterns of exchange, influence and control some such considerations are the only way in which responsibility, accountability and genuine constitutional oversight are likely to be possible at all. Without them, there would surely grow an increasing (and justified) sense that accountability and responsibility was slipping out of the control of those very systems (liberal democratic ones) that had made such virtues the centre of their construction and appeal.

That would perhaps be the most dangerous development of all, for it would presage the collapse of widespread support for constitutional and democratic government in its very heartland. If we are to ensure that such a disaster will not befall us, we must be as inventive, articulate and skilful in pinpointing the difficulties and dangers of democracy (as well as its advantages) as were the people to whom we owe the concept in the first place. Let us not forget Plato's warning (for so I believe it to be) that those who value constitutional government should examine the bad as well as the good in all systems of rule and should be aware of how easily democracy can become tyranny.[33] If we are to avoid that fate then the creation, defence and maintenance of constitutionalism in the sense given here in Eastern and Central Europe will be the surest policy to start building a 'culture of democracy' in Europe but it can only be the beginning of such a project.

Notes

1. I am very grateful to a number of friends and colleagues for their comments on this chapter. The other contributors to this book made acute and perceptive (if painful!) comments at the conference in September 1992 at which all the chapters were discussed. The editors all made additional comments on a revised version. On a number of the issues with which the article is concerned I have benefited from disucssions with Chris Bertram, Terrell Carver, Bill Connolly, Keith Graham, Bonnie Honig, Andrew Linklater, Judith Squires, Rob Walker and, especially, John Charvet and Onora O'Neill. As usual, I am responsible for what use I have made of the benefits that they have so liberally bestowed upon me.
2. Which is usually said to include Japan. There are many interesting things to be said about the inclusion of Japan in the 'West', especially given the West's history of anti-Japanese actions (the refusal to include a racial equality clause at Versailles, for example) and Japan's own unique brand of 'democractic' politics to give just two examples. However, for the purposes of this chapter I shall say nothing more about this.
3. It is worth pointing out here, however, that it might be possible to envisage a direct democracy that was not expansive. A state, for example, like that beloved of science fiction writers which uses the forms of democracy to entrench its power, by means of electronic referenda and the like (always constructed in very specific ways and with very close control over the available information), might formally fulfil the description of direct democracy. Although such a state is not what Barber has in mind, it is worth making the point that such distinctions need to be held to their spirit rather than their letter. As I discuss later, the crucial missing ingredient there, would be deliberation.
4. Understood essentially as being such things as toleration, free expression, some form of accountable representative government, the rule of law and so on. This does, of course, beg the question of how one should best understand liberalism. For discussions of this see Bellamy, 1992; Waldron, 1993; and Rengger, 1993.
5. See Rawls, 1971 and 1993; Ackerman, 1980; Dworkin, 1986.

6. The current debate in contemporary political theory of the Anglo-American type is said to be between liberalism and communitarianism. However, the so-called 'communitarians' are, in fact hardly a unified group. They are usually said to include Alisdair MacIntryre, Charles Taylor, Michael Sandel and Michael Walzer, amongst others. Of these four, MacIntyre adopts a straight-forward anti-modernism, overtly Thomistic in its most recent variant that is decisively outside both liberal and republican traditions. Sandel and Walzer, meanwhile, adopt variants of an indentifiably republican position. Taylor, in many respects, is the most complicated and interesting of all, having elements of nineteenth-century liberalism, republican liberalism as well as elements that are neither, drawn rather from his commitment to Hegel. As far as democracy is concerned, anyway, the central division is between 'standard' liberal and republican liberal accounts. I have discussed this phenomenon in more detail in Rengger, 1994. For other good discussions see Mulhall and Swift, 1992; and Kymlicka, 1989.
7. I have explored the differences in varieties of liberalism in Rengger, 1994.
8. For discussions of liberal neutrality see Dworkin, 1986, pp. 191–204; Ackerman, 1980, pp. 10ff. For Barber's version of the formative role of the public sphere see Barber, 1984, Chs 6 and 9.
9. See, for example, Connolly, 1987, 1992; Walker, 1992; Der Derian, 1992; Flatman, 1992; Honig, 1993.
10. I am thinking here of those who work in discourse ethics and critical theory. See, for example Benhabib, 1992; McCarthy, 1990; Cohen and Arato, 1992; Dallmayr, 1991; Baynes, 1992; and, for a focus on international relations, Linklater, 1990 and 1993. For Habermas himself, see especially Habermas, 1983 and 1992.
11. I should emphasise that writers such as Connolly and Walker do stress the deeply problematic nature of the state and sovereignty so my strictures do not really apply to them. However, they face other difficulties to which I shall return.
12. I cannot forbear to add that 'Central Europe' in this sense is the Europe of the Višegrad memorandum and of Milan Kundera's MittelEuropa, i.e. it is the Europe of Poland, Czechoslovakia and Hungary, not of 'Eastern Europe' (i.e. Romania, Bulgaria and the Balkans). The distinction is, of course, an uncommon one for Westerners to make. It is a common one for Central Europeans to make, as was pointed out to me in no uncertain terms by representatives of all three states at a conference at Strasbourg in October 1991.
13. For samples of eastern and central European writing on democracy, see Michnik, 1985; Keane, 1985; Havel, 1992; Zizek, 1992; Squires, 1991; Scruton, 1988a and 1988b; Rau, 1991.
14. Here it is fair to argue that the so-called communitarians, especially Walzer and Sandel, do emphasise 'the community' in specific ways that relate very clearly to those widely used by Central European writers.
15. To some extent this judgement makes clear why writers like Roger Scruton are attracted to and supportive of many Eastern and Central European ideas. While Scruton is clearly not a 'communitarian' in the same way as, for example, Charles Taylor, the link is partly to be found in the centrality of the role of the notion of community in each writer, in its turn strongly influenced by their shared admiration for Hegel. At the risk of trivialising a serious and instructive difference, their relationship might be seen as that of 'right' Hegelian and 'left' Hegelian respectively. Scruton's 'conservatism', which emphasises traditional concerns (social order, the centrality of the family as the

building block of civil society, the importance of an organic conception of community), has always been of a very different kind from that of the 'New Right' in the UK and the USA which has a very clear SLD message, although there was clearly a tactical alliance in the early 1980s (Scruton, 1988a and 1988b; see also Scruton, 1988c. For a balanced view of the New Right phenomenon as a whole, see King, 1987). Not the least of the lessons that might be taken away from this is the narrowness of the usual definition of 'communitarian': while 'communitarian' is a fair enough term to use in certain contexts, it is rapidly emptied of all meaning if it is seen as an 'ism'.

16. General evidence for this can be found, for example, in Johnson, 1992 and Tilly, 1990; also see Schopflin, 1993.
17. I am, of course, aware that there are a great variety of other political persuasions, including some extremely atavistic nationalisms, active in Europe as well. Without denying the risk that this poses, I would point to the arguments of thinkers such as Hannah Arendt, who argued persuasively that it is in the revolutionary moment, if properly understood, that democracy has its real chances to affect genuine transformative change. See Arendt, 1965 and, for an interesting and stimulating fugue on Arendt's main melody, Honig, 1993, Ch. 4.
18. For evidence of this see, for example, McHenry and Bird, 1977; Sen, 1981; Leftwich, 1983; Druze and Sen, 1991.
19. See, for example, *The Economist*, 'People who live in glass houses . . .', 20 July 1991, p. 46.
20. Held, 1992; see also the discussion in Rengger and Hoffman, forthcoming, 1994, and the special issue of *Alternatives*, Summer 1991.
21. A similar sort of argument is made in Rosenau, 1990.
22. Held, 1977, is an introduction to critical theory and Held, 1987, amplifies some of these themes. See also the references to Habermas in Held, 1992.
23. A number of other writers, from a wide variety of perspectives, have recently emphasised similar or related arguments. See, for example, Giddens, 1990; Booth, 1991; Linklater, 1989 and 1993; Walker, 1992; Connolly, 1991.
24. Though to be fully comprehensible it clearly will require some method for judging 'globally' which will, in effect, mean some form of practical reasoning immune to scepticism and relativism. I cannot discuss this further here, however,
25. Weimar and any number of post-colonial societies provide examples of this phenomenon.
26. Good general discussions of nationalism that trace a variety of different approaches to, and versions of, the phenomemon are Gellner, 1993; Smith, 1971; Seton-Watson, 1977; Anderson, 1983; and Mayall, 1990. A short but elegant essay that makes a point similar to mine is MacCormick, 1979.
27. I exclude from this, of course, former Yugoslavia and parts of the former Soviet Union, where the policy has not even included economic reform.
28. I am aware that such a view is controversial. Evidence for it can be found in Moravscik, 1991 (though I do not suggest that he would agree with my interpretation).
29. The exception is Albania where expectations started from a very low base. I owe this point to Eric Herring.
30. The mistakes are open to debate. I would suggest that they basically fell under two headings: (1) sins of omission (e.g. failing to intervene credibly enough early enough; i.e. on the secession of Slovenia); and (2) sins of commission (e.g. the practice of the so-called 'mediation' effort, which simply caved in to

the realities of largely Serbian military strength).

31. Say Austria, Norway and Sweden, the most likely new members initially.
32. To those who ask why such a conference should not be a global one, I reply that in the context of a regional network, such as Europe, where there is a tradition of cooperation and a commitment to some degree of integration, to say nothing of historical, cultural and at least some degree of evaluative consensus and a (relatively) shared political culture in many cases, there is at least some chance of a relative degree of success. In a less favourable context there is virtually none. Moreover, such a conference would clearly be highly experimental and only in such a situation could it even be contemplated.
33. See Plato, *Republic*, Bk. VIII, 562 a–b.

References

Ackerman, Bruce, 1980, *Social Justice and the Liberal State*, Yale University Press, New Haven.

Anderson, Benedict, 1983, *Imagined Communities*, Verso, London.

Arendt, Hannah, 1965, *On Revolution*, Penguin, London.

Barber, Benjamin, 1984, *Strong Democracy: participatory politics for a new age*, University of California Press, Los Angeles.

Baylis, John, 1992, 'European security after the Cold War' in John Baylis and N.J. Rengger (eds), *Dilemmas of World Politics*, The Clarendon Press, Oxford.

Baynes, Kenneth, 1992, *The Normative Grounds of Social Criticism: Kant, Rawls, Habermas*, State University of New York Press, New York.

Bellamy, Richard, 1992, *Liberalism and Modern Society*, Polity Press, Cambridge.

Benhabib, Seyla, 1992, *Situating the Self*, Polity Press, Cambridge.

Birnbaum, Karl, 1991, 'Civil society and government policy in a new Europe', *The World Today*, May.

Bok, Gisela, Skinner, Quentin and Viroli, Maurizio (eds), 1990, *Machiavelli and Republicanism*, Cambridge University Press, Cambridge.

Booth, Ken, 1991, 'Security in anarchy. Utopian realism in theory and practice', *International Affairs*, Vol. 67, No. 2.

Carty, Anthony, 1986, *The Decay of International Law*, Manchester University Press, Manchester.

Cohen, Jean and Arato, Andrew, 1992, *Civil Society and Political Theory*, MIT Press, Cambridge.

Connolly, William, 1987, *Political Theory and Modernity*, Basil Blackwell, Oxford.

Connolly, William, 1991, *Identity/Difference: democratic negotiations of political paradox*, Cornell University Press, Ithaca.

Dahl, Robert, 1956, *A Preface to Democratic Theory*, University of Chicago Press, Chicago.

Dahl, Robert, 1985, *A Preface to Economic Democracy*, Polity Press, Cambridge.

Dahl, Robert, 1989, *Democracy and its Critics*, Yale University Press, New Haven.

Dallmayr, Fred, 1991, *Between Frankfurt and Freiberg*, Polity Press, Cambridge.

Der Derian, James, 1992, *Anti-Diplomacy: speed, spies, terror and war*, Basil Blackwell, Oxford.

Druze, Jean and Sen, Amartya, 1991, *Hunger and Public Action*, The Clarendon Press, Oxford.

Dunn, John, (ed.) 1992, *Democracy: the unfinished journey*, The Clarendon Press, Oxford.

Dworkin, Ronald, 1986, *Law's Empire*, Fontana, London.

Flatman, Richard, 1992, *Willfull Liberalism*, Cornell University Press, Ithaca.

Gellner, Ernest, 1983, *Nations and Nationalism*, Cambridge University Press, Cambridge.

Giddens, Anthony, 1990, *The Consequences of Modernity*, Polity Press, Cambridge.

Gill, Stephen, 1989, *American Hegemony and the Tri-lateral Commission*, Cambridge University Press, Cambridge.

Graham, Keith, 1986, *The Battle for Democracy*, Harvester, Brighton.

Guttmann, Amy and Taylor, Charles (eds), 1992, *Multiculturalism and the Politics of Recognition*, Princeton University Press, Princeton.

Habermas, Jurgen, 1983, *Moralbewusstein und kommunikatives Handelns*, Suhrkamp Verlag, Frankfurt.

Habermas, Jurgen, 1984, *Theory of Communicative Action*, Vol 1. MIT Press, Boston.

Habermas, Jurgen, 1992, *Factizitäte und Geltung*, Verlag, Frankfurt.

Habermas, Jurgen, 1993, 'Three normative models of democracy', Paper presented to the annual *Conference for the Study of Political Thought*, Yale University, April.

Havel, Václav, 1992, *Summer Meditations*, (trans. Paul Wilson), Faber, London.

Held, David, 1987, *Models for Democracy*, Polity Press, Cambridge.

Held, David (ed.), 1992, *Prospects for Democracy*, Polity Press, Cambridge.

Herring, Eric, 1994 forthcoming, 'International security and democratisation in Eastern Europe' in G. Pridham', E. Herring and G. Sanford (eds), *Building Democracy*, Leicester University Press, Leicester.

Hewitt, Vernon, 1994 forthcoming, *North/South Relations after the Cold War*, Manchester University Press, Manchester.

Hirst, Paul, 1992, 'Assocational Democracy' in D. Held (ed.), *Prospects for Democracy*, Polity Press, Cambridge.

Hoffmann, Stanley and Fiedler, David, 1992, *Rousseau on International Relations*, The Clarendon Press, Oxford.

Honig, Bonnie, 1993, *Political Theory and the Displacement of Politics*, Cornell University Press, Ithaca.

Huntington, Samuel P., 1991, *The Third Wave: democratisation in the late twentieth century*, University of Oklahoma Press, London.

Jackson, Robert, 1990, *Quasi States: sovereignty, international relations and the Third World*, Cambridge University Press, Cambridge.

Johnson, James Turner, 1992, 'Some thoughts on democracy and its cultural context', *Ethics and International Affairs*, Vol. 6, pp. 41–55.

Jones, Dorothy V. 1989, *Code of Peace: ethics and security in the world of the warlord states*, University of Chicago Press, Chicago.

Keane, John, 1985, *The Power of the Powerless: citizens against the state in Central Eastern Europe*, Hutchinson, London.

Keohane, Robert O., 1990, *International Institutions and State Power*, Westview, Boulder.

Keohane, Robert O., and Nye, Joseph S., 1987, *Power and Interdependence: world politics in transition*, 2nd edn., Little-Brown, Boston

King, Desmond S., 1987, *The New Right: politics, markets and citizenship*, Macmillan, London.

Krasner, Stephen (ed.), 1982, *International Regimes*, Cornell University Press, Ithaca.

Kupchan, Charles and Kupchan, Clifford, 1991, 'Concerts, collective security and the future of Europe', *International Security*, Vol. 16, No. 1.

Kymlicka, William, 1989, *Liberalism, community and culture*, The Clarendon Press, Oxford.

Leftwich, Adrian, 1983, *Redefining Politics*, Methuen, London.

Linklater, Andrew, 1989, *Beyond Realism and Marxism: critical theory and international relations*, Macmillan, London.

Linklater, Andrew, 1990, *Men and Citizens in the theory of International Relations*, 2nd edn., Macmillan, London.

Linklater, Andrew, 1993, 'Liberal democracy, constitutionalism and the New World Order' in Richard Feaver and James L. Richardson (eds), *The Post Cold War Order*, Allen and Unwin, Canberra.

Lipset, Seymour Martin, 1960, *Political Man*, Doubleday, New York.

MacCormick, Neil, 1979, 'Nation and nationalism' in Colin Maclean, (ed.) *The Crown and the Thistle*, Scottish Academic Press, Edinburgh.

Mayall, James 1990, *Nationalism and International Society*, Cambridge University Press, Cambridge.

Mazrui, Ali, 1990, *Cultural Forces and World Politics*, Heineman.

McCarthy, Thomas, 1990, *Ideals and Illusions: on reconstruction and deconstruction in contemporary critical theory*, MIT Press, Cambridge.

McCilwain, C.H., 1947, *Constitutionalism, Ancient and Modern*, Cornell University Press, Ithaca.

McHenry, D.K. and Bird, K., 1977, 'Food bungle in Bangladesh', *Foreign Policy*, Vol. 27.

Michels, Robert, 1915, *Political Parties: a sociological study of the oligarchical tendencies of modern democracies*, The Free Press, Glencoe, 1966.

Michnik, Adam, 1985, *Letters from Prison and Other Esssays*, University of California Press, Berkeley.

Moravscik, Andrew, 1991, 'Negotiating the Single European Act: national interests and conventional statecraft in the European Community', *International Organisation*, Vol. 45, No. 1.

Mouffe, Chantal (ed.), 1992, *Dimensions of Radical Democracy*, Verso, London.

Mullhall, Stephen and Swift, Adam, 1992, *Liberals and Communitarians*, Basil Blackwell, Oxford.

O'Neill, Onora, 1989, *Construction of Reason*, Cambridge University Press, Cambridge.

Oakeshott, Michael, 1975, *On Human Conduct*, The Clarendon Press, Oxford.

Pettit, Philip, 1989, 'The freedom of a city: a Republican ideal' in Hamlin, Alan and Pettit, Philip (eds), *The Good Polity: Normative Analysis of the State*, Basil Blackwell, Oxford.

Pinder, John, 1994 forthcoming, 'The European Community and democracy in Central and Eastern Europe' in G. Pridham, E. Herring and G. Sanford (eds), *Building Democracy*, Leicester University Press, Leicester.

Plamenatz, John, 1973, *Democracy and Illusion: an examination of certain aspects of modern democratic theory*, Longman, London.

Pocock, J.G.A., 1975, *the Machiavellian Moment: Florentine political thought and the Atlantic Republican tradition*, Princeton University Press, Princeton.

Przeworski, Adam, 1991, *Democracy and the Market Political and Economic Reforms in Eastern Europe and Latin America*, Cambridge University Press, Cambridge.

Rau, Zbigniew, 1991, 'The state of enslavement: the East European subsitute for the state of nature', *Political Studies*, Vol. xxxix, No. 2.

Rawls, John, 1971, *A Theory of Justice*, Harvard University Press, Cambridge.

Rengger, N.J., 1993, 'Liberal identities, democratic differences', paper to

European Identities conference, Faaborg, Denmark, June.
Rengger, N.J. 1994, 'Constitutionalism, indices of democratisation and world politics' in Beeham (ed.).
Rengger, N.J. and Hoffman, Mark (eds), 1994, *Critical Theory and International Relations*, Harvester, Hemel Hempstead.
Robertson, Roland, 1992, *Globalisation*, Sage, London.
Rosenau, James, 1990, *Turbulence in World Politics: a theory of change and continuity*, Harvester, Hemel Hempstead.
Ruggie, John Gerard (ed.), 1992, *Multi-Lateralism*, Westview, Boulder.
Sandel, Michael, 1982, *Liberalism and the Limits of Justice*, Cambridge University Press, Cambridge.
Sartori, Giovanni, 1962, *Democratic Theory*, New York.
Schopflin, George, 1993, *Politics in Eastern Europe*, Polity Press, Cambridge.
Schumpeter, Joseph, 1943, Capitalism, Socialism and Democracy, Unwin, London.
Scruton, Roger, 1988a. 'The New Right in Central Europe Part 1', *Political Studies*, Vol. xxxvi, No. 4.
Scruton, Roger, 1988b. 'The New Right in Central Europe Part 2' *Political Studies*, Vol. xxxvi, No. 4.
Scruton, Roger, 1988c, *The Meaning of Conservatism*, 2nd end., Penguin Books, London.
Sen, Amartya, 1981, *Poverty and Famines*, The Clarendon Press, Oxford.
Seton-Watson, Hugh, 1977, *Nations and States*, Methuen, London.
Skinner, Quentin, 1992, 'On justice, the common good and liberty' in C. Mouffe (ed.), *Dimensions of Radical Democracy*, Verso, London.
Skocpol, Theda, 1978, *States and Social Revolutions*, Cambridge University Press, Cambridge.
Smith, Anthony D., 1971, *Theories of Nationalism*, Duckworth, London.
Squires, Judith (ed.), 1991, *New Formations*, special issue 'On Democracy'.
Stone, Norman, 1983, *Europe Transformed 1878–1919*, Fontana, London.
Taylor, A.J.P., 1948, *The Hapsburg Monarchy 1815–1918*, Oxford University Press, London.
Taylor, Charles, 1990, *Sources of the Self*, Harvard University Press, Cambridge.
Tilly, Charles, 1990, *Coercion, Capital and European States*, Basil Blackwell, Oxford.
Waldron, Jeremy, 1993, *Liberal Rights*, Cambridge University Press, Cambridge.
Walker, R.B.J., 1992, *Inside/Outside: international relations as political theory*, Cambridge University Press, Cambridge.
Walzer, Michael, 1992, 'The civil society argument', in C. Mouffe (ed.) *Dimensions of Radical Democracy*, Verso, London.
Warren, Mark, 1992, 'Democratic theory and self-transformation', *The American Political Science Review*, Vol. 86, No. 1.
Weale, Albert, 1989, 'The limits of democracy', in Hamlin and Pettit, (eds), *The Good Polity: Nomative Analysis of the State*, Basil Blackwell, Oxford.
Zizek, Slovaj, 1992, 'Eastern Europe's republics of Gilead' in C. Mouffe (ed.), *Dimensions of Radical Democracy*, Verso, London.

4

International security and democratisation in Eastern Europe

Eric Herring

The question of the relationship between international security and democratisation in Eastern Europe is a pressing one.[1] Two implicit concerns and links are that the presence or perception of international security threats undermines democratisation, and that the failure of democratisation undermines international security.[2] While both hypotheses have some validity, they understate the complexity of the concepts of security and democratisation and the relationship between them. In some circumstances, as will be shown below, threats can boost democratisation and democratisation can exacerbate threats.

A number of claims are made in this chapter. First, the positive correlation between international security and democratisation exists to the extent that democratisation embodies liberal values. Second, a broad concept of security which looks at its political, economic, environmental and societal as well as military dimensions is vital because they all interact with each other and because non-military threats are in some cases equally as dangerous as military ones for democratisation in Eastern Europe. Third, various related concepts developed in security analysis – such as the idea of the security dilemma – are of value in understanding threats to democratisation in Eastern Europe, especially when their definitions are broadened so that they are not solely military and state-centric. Fourth, the emphasis on the international dimension of security is appropriate because the fate of individual attempts at democratisation in the states of Eastern Europe is strongly influenced by, and strongly influences, events, attitudes, values and policies elsewhere. In particular, it will be shown that the policies of the West and organisations such as the European Community (EC), the North Atlantic Treaty Organisation (NATO), the International Monetary Fund (IMF) and the United Nations (UN) have sometimes helped but have sometimes been very damaging for security and the prospects for democratisation in Eastern Europe. Furthermore, it will be argued that the flaws of the policies of the West are not only a product of limited resources and inadequate understanding undermining good intentions, but also flow from the ways in which the West's commitment to the building of democracy is tempered by the protection and pursuit of personal and national power, wealth and prestige.

Democratisation and liberal values

Democratisation refers to the process of becoming democratic, and, at its most crude, democracy is simply popular or majority rule. Democracy requires procedures such as elections or referenda to ascertain the will of the majority. In some cases the criteria for deciding the majority can be disputed. The Albanian majority in the Serbian province of Kosovo argues that the Serbian suspension of Kosovo's autonomy is undemocratic, while the Serbs argue Kosovo is part of Serbia and that the Albanian Kosovars are only a minority in Serbia as a whole. When perceptions of the basis of the majority clash, liberal values are threatened. In the West, the kind of democracy people have in mind is liberal democracy, with its connotations of individualism, compromise, tolerance, respect for the rights of minorities and free, regular elections.

Democratisation and the spread of liberal values are often treated in popular discourse as necessarily closely related. However, the experience of the former Yugoslavia, where illiberal political parties have had much electoral support, underlines the fact that democratic procedures do not guarantee liberal outcomes. That said, the increasing degree of repression under Serbian President Slobodan Milošević as the costs of war in Bosnia-Hercegovina and Croatia mount suggests that once an illiberal political party finds itself in electoral difficulties, it can seek to undermine the democratic procedures which put it in power in the first place. Hence there is a degree of symbiosis between liberal values and the sustainability of democratic procedures although there is not a necessary connection between them at all times. The democratisation in Albania and the former Yugoslavia has been the least liberal in Eastern Europe as it has become a tool of extremely intolerant nationalists. Liberal democracy has been built up to a much greater extent in East-Central Europe (Poland, the Czech Republic, Slovakia and Hungary) but is of variable and debatable stability. Somewhere in between the two lies the democratisation which has taken place in Romania and Bulgaria.

A broad concept of security

Political, economic, environmental, societal and military security

Security refers to perceived and actual freedom from threat. In recent years there has been much advocacy of the need for a broad concept of security: in particular, Barry Buzan (1991) has argued systematically for consideration of political, economic, environmental and societal as well as military security. This is valuable in that it takes into account the multiplicity of threats in existence and does not elevate military security to such a level that the political, economic, environmental and societal costs of attaining it are neglected. While it is perfectly possible to think about economic and other issues without doing so in relation to the concept of security, the value of the concept is that it allows the analyst to concentrate on the most threatening problems in each area.

The impact of the economic, environmental, societal and military dimensions of international security upon the political security of democracy in Eastern Europe is the main concern of this chapter, where political security is defined as 'the organisational stability of states, systems of government and the ideologies that give them legitimacy' (Buzan, 1991, p. 19). In the case of Czechoslovakia, there was a clash between the organisational stability of the state (due to the decision of Slovakia's leaders to press for the dissolution of the federal union in July 1992) and the legitimating ideology (liberal democracy) because Czechoslovakia could not have remained a single state without the suppression of the Slovaks. This tension was resolved in favour of liberal democracy and the dissolution of the federation on 31 December 1992 because the Czechs felt no strong desire to keep Czechoslovakia together. In contrast, in the Yugoslav case, the federal armed forces attempted to hold the state together by force: limited democratic procedures were in operation, but liberal values had little hold.

Individual, group, state and international security

Two conceptual questions remain. First, is there a distinctly international level of security? Second, what are the other levels? The answers offered here are that, in theoretical terms, there is such a level and that there are also individual, group and state levels of security, but that the domestic and the international are becoming much less insulated from each other and much more similar as interdependence increases. At their most simple, international factors are simply any factors which originate outside the borders of a particular state, such as the role of the IMF in influencing Polish economic policy. The international security environment is having many important effects on attempts to build democracy in Eastern Europe: as will be discussed at length, international economic insecurity is a severe threat to democratisation in East-Central Europe. while international insecurity in both military and societal terms has already seriously undermined democratisation in the Balkans. Furthermore, the internal policies of states, for example towards ethnic minorities, also tend to have international repercussions, intended or unintended. What results is an interaction and even blurring of the domestic and the international.

The concept of international security has been examined thus far only from a state-centric level of analysis: the sub-state and systemic levels of analysis also need to be considered because they also have important effects on the process of democratisation. The security of the state is often a precondition for the security of its citizens: the state can protect its inhabitants from external and internal threats posed by states and non-state actors. When the security of an individual is threatened, it is often because that person is a member of a particular group such as an ethnic minority. Cases of this kind of insecurity are now common in Eastern Europe. Indeed, individuals and groups can be threatened because of the inaction of the state. In Poland, the concept of citizens' security – protection of citizens from anarchy caused by the actions of organisations such as the Self Defence trade union and party – has been used in the debate on the revision of the laws regarding the roles of the State Protection Office (UOP), police and Ministry of Internal Affairs to bolster arguments in favour of increased state powers (BBC, *Summary of World Broadcasts – SWB* – EE/1462 B/9–10, 18 August 1992). In this type of formulation, the protection of the state and the citizen are seen as synonymous or at least as complementary: democratisation increases the probability that this will be the case by giving the people within the state – especially the more powerful or better organised – some control over it. However, in the advanced capitalist liberal democracies, the elites try to retain their power and maintain order through the exercise of ideological, economic and, if necessary, military power (Herman and Chomsky, 1988; Parenti, 1988; Chomsky, 1988, 1992, 1993). Hence the contradiction between state and individual security continues to exist even in those states.

Domestic and international politics: a difference of degree

The view that what happens within states is radically different from what happens between states is based on the idea that, unlike domestic politics, international politics takes place in the context of anarchy. However, Helen Milner (1991) argues persuasively that the concept of anarchy is used too vaguely in international relations theory and that the dichotomy between domestic and international politics is overstated. Anarchy in the sense of disorder, chaos and the perpetual threat of violence is not the norm in relations between states and is sometimes the case within states (Milner, 1991, pp. 69–71). Hedley Bull perceived the existence of international order, which he saw as a pattern of behaviour which sustains the main norms of the system. According to Bull, those norms involved a reasonable degree of commitment to minimal use of force, the avoidance of breaches of agreements and support for some stability of possession of territory and other assets (Bull, 1977; Buzan, 1991, pp. 166–74; Rengger, 1992a,b). In Buzan's terms, an 'immature anarchy' is an international system in which the norms of international order are weak or non-existent (1991, p. 175). The frequent breaches of cease-fire agreements by all sides in what was Yugoslavia are an indication of immature anarchy in the region. In contrast, in a 'mature anarchy', states abide by the main norms of the international order to an extent that it is worth referring to the existence of an international society.[3]

In international relations theory, anarchy is usually defined not in terms of chaos but in terms of the absence of overall government or authority (Waltz, 1979; Buzan, 1991, pp. 146–53; Buzan, Little and Jones, 1993). As Milner argues, this begs the question of what we mean by government or authority. The executives, legislatures and judiciaries of international organisations such as the UN or EC are not as well developed as most national ones, but they do exist. Government in the Weberian sense of the possession of a monopoly of legitimate force is problematic on two counts (Milner, 1991, pp. 71–2). First, within states, governments never have a complete monopoly of the use of force and often do not have anything like it. Second, the legitimacy of the use of force by governments domestically (such as by Croatia against its Serbian minority or by Iraq against the Kurds) or internationally (such as by Serbia against Croatia) can be challenged by the international community. Similarly, while states assert their sovereignty, those same states often appeal to the authority of international law and the UN Charter.

There seems to be a strong correlation between liberal democracy and mature anarchy. The relationships between the states of Western Europe are conducted on this basis, and the states of East-Central Europe are well on their way to mature anarchy, although the possibility of regression cannot be ruled out. Bulgaria, Romania and the ex-Soviet states are further down the scale, and the former Yugoslavian states are closest to the bottom. While the international system is essentially a mature anarchy amongst the dominant states, regional security tends to be much more variable. International politics in Europe as a whole is significantly less chaotic, more ordered, more law-governed and more liberal than politics in the former Yugoslavia.

The point of the foregoing is that the difference between domestic and international politics is more one of degree than of kind. To this can be added Milner's other main point, namely, that interdependence – the way in which the ability of an actor to achieve its objectives is strongly influenced by the ways in which others will behave – is as important a structural feature of the international system as anarchy. The implications of interdependence are that perceptions, communication, anticipation and information are vitally important to the exercise of power (Milner, 1991, pp. 81–5). This perspective sits well with the focus of this volume: democratisation in Eastern Europe has been strongly influenced by international factors within and beyond Europe, and the fate of East European democratisation has been having a substantial impact on international problems and opportunities.

The spectrum of security

Security relations can be seen as lying along a spectrum. At one end there is a 'security community' – a group in which none of the actors perceive any of the others as a threat: the relationships are dominated by what Buzan terms 'amity' (Deutsch *et al.*, 1957; Buzan, 1991). NATO has been a military security community for most of its members for most of the time. The obvious exceptions are the relationship between Turkey and Greece over territory, and occasionally between the United States and Western Europe over Western European fears of being dragged into wars by the

United States. At the other end of the spectrum is a 'conflict formation' in which relationships are dominated by enmity which is limited only by short-term calculations of self-interest (*cf.* Buzan, 1991). This has been most obviously true of relations between Croatia, Bosnia and Serbia since the breakup of Yugoslavia. In the middle of the spectrum is the idea of a 'security regime', that is, a set of principles, rules and norms which permit restraint on security matters in the expectation of reciprocity amongst actors whose relations are a mixture of amity and enmity (*cf.* Jervis, 1983; Buzan, 1991). The preconditions for the formation of a security regime are that the actors must want it; that they perceive a mutual desire to have it; that none of them believe that they would be better off by measures that threaten others; and that the unilateral pursuit of security is perceived as costly (Jervis, 1983, pp. 176–8). Attempts to increase security can provoke countermeasures which to a significant degree nullify the value of the initial actions – this is the 'security dilemma'.[4] The dilemma is that both inaction and action result in insecurity. A security dilemma may exist but may not be perceived: or one may be perceived where it does not exist. Security measures may make others feel insecure either because the measures are clearly offensive in some way, or because others cannot tell whether they are offensive or defensive and assume the worst (Jervis, 1978). As will be made clear below, the interaction of democratisation and the security dilemma plays a central role in explaining where relations between political actors lie on the spectrum of security.

Economic security and democratisation

Problems of economic security – that is, 'access to the resources, finance and markets necessary to sustain acceptable levels of welfare and state [or non-state] power' (Buzan, 1991, p. 19) – are the primary threat to democratisation in Eastern Europe, with the exception of former Yugoslavia, where issues of societal and military security have dominated. The international dimension is vital to the transformation from socialism to capitalism in Eastern Europe. Organisations such as the IMF and the EC are setting the terms for Western assistance for that shift, and the East European states have their sights fixed firmly on membership of the EC. Some protectionism and subsidisation of inefficient industries are policies which provide a degree of economic security. However, economic security also requires the efficiency gains from a substantial degree of competition, and competition involves winners and losers. Hence the paradox that economic security requires a degree of economic insecurity (Buzan, 1991, Ch. 6). This means that full economic security communities are unattainable, even when economic cooperation is extensive.

Cooperation in hard times

The countries of East-Central Europe have managed to avoid entrapment in an economic security dilemma by deciding to cooperate with each other in order to demonstrate their worthiness as candidates for membership of the European Community. The nature of their cooperation seems to amount to an economic security regime. Although the balance between short-term and long-term self-interest underlying their cooperation is debatable, there is no doubt that they want to cooperate and have little confidence that they would be better off trying to make unilateral deals with the EC or by increasing protectionist measures against their neighbours.

Economic insecurity and popular discontent

In spite of their cooperation, the new democracies face desperate economic problems, and the potential for the breakdown of their economic security regime is significant as the incentives to gamble on unilateral measures increase.[5] They are caught between a rock and a hard place: their economic systems must be transformed to free them from their Communist legacy, but the process of transformation may be more than their fragile political systems can take. Popular discontent with this situation is mounting to the benefit of forces linked to the former regimes and to a lesser (but more dangerous) extent the extreme xenophobic right-wing. In Poland in September 1993, the former Communists – renamed the Democratic Left – took one-third of the seats in a general election and, as the biggest single party, formed a coalition government, while the ex-Communists in Hungary under former Prime Minister Miklos Nemeth and the far right are gaining in popularity. In Bulgaria, the ex-Communists secured minority party support to bring down the coalition government of Prime Minister Filip Dimitrov in October 1992 due to popular opposition to the government's austerity programme which has subsequently been watered down. A similar process has been under way in Albania, and in Romania the former Ceauşescu ally, President Ion Iliescu, won comfortably a second election in September 1992 (*Guardian*, 19 November 1992). In Lithuania, the Democratic Labour Party (DLP) swept Vytautas Landsbergis' nationalist party Sajudis from power in the election of November 1992, as industrial output fell by 48 per cent in 1992 and lack of money to buy gas meant the absence of hot water in most Lithuanian cities for weeks. The DLP leader, Algirdas Brazauskas, another former Communist but one with a solid nationalist record in resisting Soviet pressure in 1990, argued that cooperation with the IMF was necessary, 'but under conditions which soften the blow on people' (*Guardian*, 17 November 1992).

Votes for former Communists primarily reflect a desire for less painful economic policies rather than a rejection of democracy or a return to Communism. However, for democratisation (in a liberal form) to survive marketisation, the state and the international community still have a large role to play in providing a safety net for ordinary people (Nelson, 1993; Pereira, Maravall and Przeworski, 1993; Snyder, 1993). As Jonathan Luxmoore and Jolanta Babiuch put it: 'Having been told repeatedly that democracy and the free market are linked, many seem to have ended up convinced of the natural corollary – that if the market offers them few advantages, the democratic system itself is at fault . . . So far, most east Europeans have had little to associate democracy with except growing poverty and insecurity, matched by a rapid decline in all forms of authority and an erosion of confidence in the future' (*Guardian*, 2 November 1992). Socialism provided important basic necessities and full employment. Now people in Eastern Europe have no confidence in their access to those conditions, and many people throughout the region have seen their living standards crash.

Western policies, economic security and democratisation

Although the West is trying to provide a degree of economic security to make the process of transformation easier (*The Economist*, 1 May 1993), the state of the economies in Eastern Europe and the rise of protectionist nationalist and right wing anti-democratic forces suggest that not enough is being done. Economic conditions are particularly desperate in Romania. In addition to an energy shortage, drought combined with lack of investment in the water and sewage systems has raised the possibility of water rationing in the major cities. However, the government is under pressure from the IMF to cut spending – hardly a recipe for flourishing liberal democracy (*Guardian* 1 March 1993). Hungarian Foreign Minister Geza Jeszensky argued that if the Soviet Union had not collapsed, Hungary would have received much more economic aid (*SWB*, EE/1666 A1/2, 19 April 1993). Hence Western military insecurity would have increased Hungarian economic security.

The real problem is less a lack of aid and more the EC's barriers to free trade. Former Polish Prime Minister Hanna Suchocka made it clear that the countries of Eastern Europe needed to be given much freer access to EC agricultural markets. In an attempt to appeal to EC self-interest, she argued that Poland was not a high-risk country and that 'It is dangerous naivety to expect that western Europe can isolate itself with a cordon sanitaire from the problems which came into existence after the fall of communism' (*Guardian*, 4 March 1993). The EC prefers aid to free trade as it believes that free trade would hurt EC economies (*The Economist*, 1 May 1993).

Destabilisation and demilitarisation

Economic insecurity has been further exacerbated – and thus further strain put on the process of democratisation – by the fact that most of Eastern Europe is demilitarising as well as marketising. Demilitarisation has improved confidence in the sphere of military security but not in the sphere of economic security. When he first came to power in Czechoslovakia, President Václav Havel suspended all of his country's arms sales in a gesture of idealism, but felt forced to recommence them on economic grounds. The Slovak government is finding it difficult to convert its arms industries into civil industries. In 1992, 140,000 people worked in the Czechoslovak arms industry (two-thirds of them in Slovakia), and the Slovak government spent only 5 per cent of the funds set aside for the purpose (*SWB*, EE/1464 B/7, 20 August 1992). East-Central European demilitarisation is doing less than in Russia to undermine the process of democratisation (due to the economic insecurity of demobilised personnel), as the East-Central European armed forces have nearly all been garrisoned on home territory. The German government is paying the full cost of the former Red Army's withdrawal from former East Germany and has arranged a transit agreement with Czechoslovakia (*SWB*, EE/1460 B/4, 15 August 1992). The world has certainly changed when all it takes to get the Russians out of East-Central Europe is the rail fare.

Environmental security and democratisation

Environmental security 'concerns the maintenance of the local and the planetary biosphere as the essential support system on which all other enterprises depend' (Buzan, 1991, pp. 19–20). Global environmental problems for which there is incontrovertible evidence (such as depletion of the ozone layer) or for which the evidence is disputed and inconclusive (such as global warming) are minor when compared with the much more pressing and obvious environmental problems in Eastern Europe. The worst pollution in Eastern Europe is in the triangle of former East Germany, Poland and former Czechoslovakia, but with Romania close behind.[6] The least damaged country is Albania, where the environment has been preserved as an unintentional effect of the xenophobia and anti-consumerism of former dictator Enver Hoxha (Glenny, 1993, pp. 158–9).

Democratisation and increased environmental security

Democratisation has been beneficial for one aspect of Hungarian environmental security. In August 1992, Hungary withdrew from the joint Czechoslovak-Hungarian hydroelectric project on the Danube (*SWB*, EE/1464 B/3, 20 August 1992). Hungary cancelled its dam at Nagymaros for environmental reasons while Czechoslovakia (and then Slovakia) pressed on with the Gabcikovo dam (Rich, 1991). Slovaks deny that the dam will create environmental problems and see the technical achievement of building the dam as a source of national pride (*Guardian*, 3 November 1992). The Hungarian and Slovak governments agreed on 7 April 1993 to have the legal aspects of their dispute arbitrated by the International Court of Justice in The Hague (*SWB*, EE/1661 A2/6–7, 13 April 1993), but this will not resolve the economic and political aspects of the dispute. Slovak democratisation did not result in the same degree of increased mobilisation of concern for the environment because this international dispute was manipulated by the country's ambitious nationalist politicians.

Environmental insecurity and increased democratisation

Environmental insecurity boosts democratisation when it motivates previously politically apathetic and repressed individuals and groups to organise and involve themselves in the political process. In some cases this is 'NIMBY' (Not In My Back Yard) activism. NIMBYs do not care about pollution: they just want it to happen elsewhere. However, some of the activism is a product of thinking which reflects the Green slogan 'Think globally, act locally'. In Bulgaria, the perspectives have been local and national. The opposition to the Bulgarian Communist Party (BCP) crystallised around environmental issues in the late 1980s in organisations such as the Rusé Defence Committee (RDC) which challenged the poisoning of the atmosphere of the city of Rusé by a metallurgical plant. The most important national ecological association in Bulgaria was an offshoot of the RDC, Ecoglasnost, which operated on the principle that 'there can be no ecological security unless there is proper public discussion of, and full democratic control over, all policies affecting the environment' (Crampton, 1990, p. 25; Glenny, 1993, p. 171). In a process similar to what happened to Green parties in Western Europe in the 1980s, Ecoglasnost was eclipsed by mainstream political parties which added green elements to their agendas (Glenny, 1993, p. 94). The potential electoral costs of the most palpable and obvious pollution such as unbreathable air and undrinkable water have created incentives for the Polish government to tackle the environmental problems of Upper Silesia caused by mines, steelworks and related industries (*SWB*, EE/1660 B/8, 12 April 1993).

Marketisation, democratisation and environmental security

The primary international influence on environmental security in Eastern Europe is marketisation. On the one hand, increasing economic insecurity caused by the failure of a large proportion of Eastern Europe's industry to survive under market conditions is improving environmental security. East European production has tended to be extremely wasteful in terms of energy and raw materials. The discipline of the market will require that such waste be eliminated and the environment will benefit as a result. Furthermore, in order to achieve EC membership in the future, Eastern Europe will have to evolve towards EC environmental standards. On the other hand, some Western European companies are taking advantage of the lack of regulation to dump large amounts of toxic waste in Eastern Europe with total disregard for damage to the environment (*Guardian*, 4 June 1993). In addition, very little is being done to make safe nuclear reactors which were built shoddily and with totally inadequate safety procedures. There are 58 such reactors in Eastern Europe and the former Soviet Union which could be made much safer and some of them replaced with gas-fired power stations for around $10 billion (*The Economist*, 15 August 1992, pp. 14, 60; 24 July 1993, pp. 21–6). Little aid has been forthcoming for this due to a combination of governmental complacency, lack of concern about the future and a short-sighted unwilllingness to foot the bill.

Matters are made worse by the fact that most (but not all) East Europeans are too preoccupied with shoring up their own short-term living standards to exercise much democratic power to protect the environment. The dilemma between economic and environmental security is common to all societies which have not developed environmentally sustainable economic systems: the dilemma is simply more stark in the wake of a Communist economic system in which disregard for the effects of unfettered industrialisation on human life and the environment was extreme. Higher living standards will bring little relief if rising expectations fuelled by marketisation increase consumerist pressures from electorates. Overall, democratisation makes it more likely that obvious environmental emergencies will be dealt with but reinforces the more insidious long-term effects of marketisation.

Societal security and democratisation

Societal security refers to 'the sustainability, within acceptable conditions for evolution, of traditional patterns of language, culture and religious and national identity and custom' (Buzan, 1991, p. 19). The most prominent conflicts over societal security which have arisen in the wake of democratisation in Eastern Europe have been ethnic ones.[7]

Ethnicity and the societal security dilemma

The view that the existence of inter-ethnic tensions in Eastern Europe can be explained as the inevitable result of ancient hatreds which could be mobilised through the newly available democratic procedures is inadequate. The situation is too complex to bear out fully that conclusion. As a number of writers have pointed out, it cannot be explained why the degree of ethnic tension has varied so much across Eastern Europe (de Nevers, 1993; Posen, 1993; Snyder, 1993). The explanation offered here is that the key factor has been the degree of intensity within states and across borders of the societal security dilemma – the efforts of some ethnic groups to protect their identity have threatened the identity of other ethnic groups and provoked aggressive countermeasures. The societal security dilemma has been exacerbated by international factors, especially the policies of some states to protect their minorities abroad and to a lesser extent by the policies of other states. Before an explanation of the differing intensity of the dilemma and conclusions on whether its effects could have been mitigated are offered, the main cases – Slovenia, Croatia, Bosnia-Hercegovina (commonly referred to simply as Bosnia), Kosovo, Macedonia, Slovakia, Transylvania and Vojvodina – will be examined in turn.

SLOVENIA, CROATIA AND BOSNIA. Slovenia declared its independence in June 1991 following on from its referendum in December 1990 with only a brief, half-hearted attempt by the federal Yugoslav army to suppress it. While Slovenia had only a tiny Serb minority and was territorially insulated by Croatia from the Serb-dominated rump of Yugoslavia (Serbia, Montenegro and, until its declaration of independence in April 1993, Macedonia), Croatia and Bosnia were not so lucky. Croatia and Bosnia seceded primarily because they did not believe that they could achieve societal security as long as they were part of Yugoslavia. Those fears were fuelled by memories of a millennium of struggles between Serbs, Muslims and Croats, by Serbian expressions of ambitions for a greater Serbia, by the way the federal Yugoslav army and its weapons were increasingly coming under Serb control and by the fact that both had large Serbian minorities.

The way in which Croatia and Bosnia went about achieving their independence exacerbated the feelings of insecurity of Serbs within their territory. Non-Croats formed (before the 1991 war) 21 per cent of the Croatian population, most of whom were Serbs (Thompson, 1992, p. 252). In April 1990, the Croatian Democratic Union (HDZ) won the election under Franjo Tudjman on a nationalist platform which even included talk of absorbing western Hercegovina or even all of Bosnia-Hercegovina into a greater Croatia. The government adopted symbols which evoked memories of Croatian concentration camps for Serbs while Croatia was allied with the Nazis in the Second World War and ignored the rights of Croatian Serbs in the new constitution (Zametica, 1992, pp. 16–17). Not surprisingly, the Croatian Serbs took up arms in August 1990 and declared a still unrecognised republic in the Croatian region of Krajina. Serbia soon intervened with force on their behalf.

Events in Bosnia followed the same pattern as those in Croatia. The Bosnian Muslims and Croats were provocative in March 1992 in abandoning the equal nations concept for the new state in favour of the concept of majority and minority nationalities. One month earlier, the Bosnian referendum, in which the Muslims (44 per cent of the population) and Croats (17 per cent) voted 99.7 per cent for secession, was boycotted by most of the Serbs (33 per cent) who had not been reassured that they would not be persecuted. Once the civil war began in Bosnia in June 1991, Serbia backed the Bosnian Serb minority. Since then, 'ethnic cleansing' – that is, the terrorising, expulsion and often large-scale slaughter of other ethnic groups to bring about numerical domination in an area by one's own ethnic group – has been carried out mainly by the (Bosnian and Serbian) Serbs, to a lesser extent by the Bosnian Croats and least of all by the Bosnian Muslims. The Bosnian Croats were initially allied with the Bosnian state against the Serbs, but in October 1992 many of them turned on the Bosnian state in order to take advantage of their military superiority.

The war in Bosnia is widely but wrongly portrayed as a war between Croats, Serbs and Muslims. In fact, it is a war between advocates of a Greater Croatia, advocates of a Greater Serbia and advocates of a multiethnic Bosnian state. Although the army of the Bosnian state (drawn from local militias to replace and fight the Yugoslav federal army) is mostly Muslim, it was and continues to be multi-ethnic. Similarly, although the Bosnian National Assembly has been dominated by ethnically-based political parties since the November 1990 elections (Zametica, 1992, p. 37), the central government is multi-ethnic, as are the local town councils. There are many ethnically mixed marriages in Bosnia, and many Bosnians saw and continue to see themselves primarily as Bosnians rather than as members of separate ethnic groups.

MACEDONIA. Macedonia was admitted to the UN as a sovereign state in April 1993 under the temporary compromise name of the Former Yugoslav Republic of Macedonia. The new state simply wants to call itself Macedonia, but a northern region of Greece is also called Macedonia, and Greece fears a possible territorial claim. Historic Macedonia is divided between three states: Vardar Macedonia (39 per cent of the territory of historic Macedonia) which corresponds to present-day independent Macedonia: Aegean Macedonia (51 per cent) in northern Greece; and Pirin Macedonia (10 per cent) in south-western Bulgaria (Zametica, 1992, p. 34). Although Greece has great military superiority, Macedonians are making provocative statements. For example, in a typical statement the Deputy Speaker of the Macedonian Assembly, Tito Petkovski, asserted that Greece 'has no legitimate rights over' Aegean Macedonia (*SWB*, EE/1659 C1/12–13, 9 April 1993). For its part, Bulgaria sees the Macedonians as Bulgarians: hence it has recognised the Macedonian state but not the Macedonian nation. Twenty one per cent of the two million population are Albanian Muslims and 8 per cent are Serbs. The Albanian minority has called for recognition as a 'state-building nation' and not simply, as the Macedonian authorities classify them, a minority (*SWB*, EE/1659 C1/12–13 9 April 1993; *Guardian*, 17 November 1992). Like the Serbs in Bosnia, the Albanians boycotted the Macedonian referendum on independence. The Macedonian authorities are determined not to make any concessions as they see this as the first step towards the unification of western Macedonia with Kosovo and Albania. They point out that the 150,000 ethnic Macedonians in Albania have few political and cultural rights while the ethnic Albanians in Macedonia have many, and that the Albanians do not accept the right of those ethnic Macedonians to the status of nation (*Guardian*, 19 November 1992).

KOSOVO. The Macedonia dispute is linked to the one over Kosovo because Yugoslavia is concerned that Macedonian Albanians may go to fight in Kosovo if violence breaks out there, while Macedonia fears invasion by Yugoslavia as well as by Greece (*The Economist*, 1 August 1992, pp. 31–2; 29 August 1992, p. 13). Kosovo used to be an autonomous province of Yugoslavia, but was absorbed forcibly into Serbia in 1990. The population is 90 per cent Albanian Muslim, but the Serbs see it as the historic birthplace of their nation, are steadily settling more and more Serbs there and have no intention of letting go of the territory. Kosovo's Albanians want an independent state in which, they claim, Serbs would have equal rights. Repression and discrimination are fuelling a greater Albanian separatism which may eventually provoke brutal Serb violence.[8] Although Albania might be drawn into a conflict over Kosovo, it would be no match for Serbia militarily.

SLOVAKIA, TRANSYLVANIA AND VOJVODINA. Frequent references have been made by Hungarian leaders to Hungarian minorities in Vojvodina, the Transylvanian region of Romania (which is dominated by over two million ethnic Hungarians) and Slovakia. Those references are made in the hope of protecting Hungarian minorities and trying to bolster electoral positions within Hungary, but they could produce an anti-Hungarian backlash. Slovak Prime Minister Vladimir Měciar has argued that, if the Hungarian government objects to infringements of the rights of Hungarians abroad, it should identify those infringements and should go through the Council of Europe rather than claiming a unilateral right of investigation (*SWB*, EE/1443 B/6, 27 July 1992; *SWB*, EE/1428 A2/2, 9 July 1992). In August 1992 in the days before the convening of both the World Congress of Hungarians and World Conference on Transylvania in Budapest, the Romanian Foreign Minister Adrian Nastase warned the Hungarian Foreign Minister Geza Jeszensky that Hungary should not try to stir up nationalism amongst ethnic Hungarians in Transylvania and urged that the two countries conclude a bilateral treaty which would incorporate a clause in which both sides would renounce any territorial claims upon each other (*SWB*, EE/1463 i, B11–13, 19 August 1992).

Romanian efforts to counter allegations of discrimination have not been successful. It set up a Council of Ethnic Minorities composed of 14 state representatives and 36 representatives of Romania's 17 ethnic groups (*SWB*, EE/1665 B/6, 17 April 1993). However, it did not appoint Hungarians as the prefects of the two Romanian counties with the highest proportion of Hungarians (Harghita and Covasna), and this has caused friction. Jeszensky and Hungarian Bishop Laszlo Tokes reacted by referring to Romanian ethnic cleansing of the Hungarian minority. Romanian authorities countered by arguing that the prefects were born in the two counties and speak Hungarian well, and one of the prefects said that the demand that only a Hungarian ethnic be appointed to the post showed a tendency to carry out ethnic cleansing.[9]

Mutual suspicions are also rife in the autonomous Yugoslav republic of Vojvodina: the Vojvodina Serbs accuse the Hungarian minority of wanting their territory to become part of Hungary, while the Hungarian Secretary of State for Refugees and Migration, Istvan Morvay, has accused the authorities of deliberately settling large numbers of Serbs from Croatia and Bosnia in the area. He is concerned that those Serbs could try to drive out the Hungarian minority of 100,000 people (*SWB*, EE/1662 C1/10, 14 April 1993; Zametica, 1992, pp. 28–30). The Vojvodina Hungarians have stated a desire for autonomy and have denied that the border issue is settled. Hungarian authorities claim that over 50,000 Hungarians and 35,000 Croats have left Vojvodina since 1991 due to Serb oppression (*SWB*, EE/1653 C1/12, 2 April 1993).

Illiberal democracy and the societal security dilemma

In trying to ensure their own societal security – their ability to preserve and promote their own ways of life – why have so many ethnic groups acted so provocatively in threatening the societal security of others? Some can indulge themselves because of their military superiority. However, provocative behaviour has been common even amongst the militarily vulnerable. The backlash has been disastrous for the Bosnian state and costly for the separatist Bosnian Croats (although their tactical alliance with the Serbs is allowing them to carve up Bosnia). The potential backlash against the Albanian Kosovars by the Serbs, against Albanian Macedonians by the Macedonian majority, and against Macedonia by Serbia and Greece is also horrendous. The basic reason is that in most of the former Yugoslavia (with the exception of the Bosnian state discussed below), the models of national self-determination have been highly intolerant ones: Macedonian domination of Macedonia, Croat domination of Croatia, Serb domination of Kosovo and so on. Most were never interested in liberal democracy but only in democracy as a majoritarian device to be manipulated. Once committed to this ideological position, they were trapped in the societal security dilemma. From that point on, most Croats, Serbs and others have employed many devices to bolster their resolve. They have convinced themselves that they have no other choice, that it is better to have war now rather than later, that (in some cases) they can find external allies and arms, that the fulfilment of their ideological dreams and historic missions is worth the risk and that their opponents are evil subhumans with whom coexistence is intolerable and unworkable.

Would it have helped the Bosnian Croats and Muslims if they had not acted so provocatively? Was there a way to avoid entrapment in the societal security dilemma? Possibly, but probably not. The transition to independence could undoubtedly have been handled a great deal more sensitively by the Bosnian Muslims and Croats. However, it is likely that Serbia and many Bosnian Serbs would have acted no differently even if they had received assurances of their rights. This is mainly because, especially with the example of Croatia in mind, there were many Serb expressions of the view that the only acceptable place for Serbs is within a Serbian state. On this basis, Bosnian Serb security could only be achieved at the expense of the security of non-Serb Bosnians.

The impact of the main international actor in the region – the EC – on the societal security dilemma has not been very positive overall. After the Bosnian independence referendum in February 1992, the Bosnian Serbs, under great EC pressure, agreed reluctantly that Bosnia did not have to break up if it were governed internally according to ethnic territories (Zametica, 1992, p. 39). However, the EC did not put equal pressure on the Bosnian Muslims and Croats to guarantee the rights of Bosnian Serbs. The replacement of the Bosnian Serbs' equal nation status with minority status – even though all three ethnic groups were meant to have a political veto – guaranteed outright rebellion. The EC recognised Croatia and Slovenia in December 1991, followed by the United States in April 1992.

The United States and the EC simultaneously recognised Bosnia in April 1992. The failure of the international community to make international recognition conditional on guarantees of the rights of minorities encouraged the illusion that compromise was not necessary or achievable. Even-handed external pressure may or may not have worked: it should at least have been tried.

Some general conclusions on the dynamics of the societal security dilemma can be drawn from the foregoing (*cf.* de Nevers, 1993; Posen, 1993, pp. 29–31). First and foremost, if the form of nationalist ideology requires domination of the state by one ethnic group, then ethnic conflict is likely. Such illiberal values are not compatible with liberal democracy in ethnically mixed societies. The politics of East-Central Europe are relatively liberal (in East European terms), while the Romanian political system allows the Hungarians in Transylvania a great deal of autonomy. Second, where ethnic minorities are large, there is greater scope for ethnic conflict: the minority is more of a threat to the majority and more able to defend itself. Obviously, this is not a necessary condition for ethnic conflict, merely one which makes it more likely. Third, ethnic conflict is more likely if the groups have negative perceptions of each other's identity and historical relations. Serbs, Croats and Muslims have extremely negative and one-sided mutual perceptions; Bulgaria patronisingly denies the existence of a Macedonian nation; and Serbs and Macedonians have memories of Albanian atrocities during the Second World War. The mutual perceptions of Hungarians, Czechs, Slovaks and Romanians are not free of grudges but lack the same intense hostility. Fourth, ethnic conflict is greatly magnified when political actors try to or feel forced to exploit nationalist fears or ambitions for electoral gain. This has become the norm in the former Yugoslavia and plays a limited but still significant role in Hungary and Romania. Bulgarian politicians have been willing to improve relations with ethnic Turks after the extreme repression of the Communist years. Finally, as will be discussed below, ethnic conflict and the military security dilemma can be mutually reinforcing in a spiral of hostility.

Military security and democratisation

The basic theme of this section is that liberal democracy is reducing military insecurity in East-Central Europe and in Romania and Bulgaria, whereas illiberal values have combined with societal and military security dilemmas in the former Yugoslavia to undermine democratisation and to produce war or the potential for war. International organisations have been significant in encouraging reassurance and cooperation on security matters in most of Eastern Europe. The exception is the case of the former Yugoslavia, where international organisations have unintentionally exacerbated the military security dilemma and made the poor prospects for liberal democracy even worse. Before these contrasting patterns are explained, the general arguments about the relationship between liberal democracy and military security will be discussed.

Peace among liberal democracies

It is increasingly believed that liberal democracies very rarely, if ever, go to war with each other.[10] The two main counter arguments require modification rather than rejection of this claim. First, one might argue that those who say that democracies have never fought each other may have arrived at their conclusion tautologically – specifically, that they have adjusted their definitions of war or democracy to ensure that the argument cannot be disproven. In the last few years, Serbia has gone to war with Croatia and Slovenia, and yet the leaders and parliaments of all three states were elected. However (aside from the fact that the elections took place before they were sovereign states), Croatia and Serbia have proven to be very illiberal democracies. The conclusion to draw is that the hypothesis should be couched in terms of degree. Second, one might argue that, even if democracies have rarely, if ever, gone to war with each other, it may have nothing to do with the fact that they have been democracies. Democracies have only been around for a short time and in small numbers, and the rarity of wars between them may be explained by the fact that wars are not very common between any kind of state (Mearsheimer, 1990; Krasner, 1992, p. 48). However, there are good theoretical arguments for the hypothesis. Liberal democracies are part of a security community in which war is not seen as an acceptable or useful instrument of policy and in which the expectation of reciprocity minimises the military security dilemma. Jack Snyder suggests that leaders of liberal democracies are more likely to avoid external adventurism in order to avoid losing votes, although some may gamble on it to maintain or increase their support (Snyder, 1991). Mature liberal democratic states – i.e., well-entrenched ones with reasonably efficient mixed economies – are extremely unlikely to go to war with each other. Such a war would generally clash both with their values and with their economic self-interest.

Democratisation, ethnic conflict and the incentives for war

The previous section of this chapter discussed the factors which cause ethnic conflict. The next question to answer is: when does ethnic conflict take the form of war? There has been war between Serbia, Croatia and Bosnia, but not between Macedonia and Albania, the Albanian Kosovars and Serbia, the Czech Republic and Slovakia, Hungary and Slovakia, Hungary and Romania, or Hungary and Serbia. Barry Posen (1993) argues that war took place between Serbia and Croatia because the degree of ethnic hostility was particularly intense; Serbia perceived itself to have clear but probably temporary military superiority; and Serbia believed that the Croatian Serbs could only be protected by rapid offensive military action. The Croatian Serbs lacked the military capability to defend themselves, and the existence of uncontrolled Croatian army gangs terrorising and killing increased the urgency for action. This explanation must be supplemented by two other factors, namely, the extent to which decision-makers are influenced by the political and economic costs of war. Serbia has accepted political ostracism and economic chaos as a tolerable cost for establishing a greater Serbia. The cost of the economic sanctions imposed by the international community has certainly been immense: even the state news agency of rump Yugoslavia admitted in April 1993 that 'under these conditions there can be no economic activity'. Output fell 35.3 per cent in February 1993 alone; most workers were on 'compulsory leave', i.e., effectively unemployed; inflation was running at around 4 per cent every day; and the UN Food and Agriculture Organisation (FAO) said that 15 per cent of children in Yugoslavia were undernourished.[11] A liberal democracy would be unlikely to embark upon, never mind sustain, such a military campaign due to the potential political opposition (Snyder, 1991).

In none of the other cases have the incentives for war been so powerful. Albanian military intervention in Macedonia would meet with Serbian and Greek opposition, and Albanians in Macedonia are in any case relatively well treated. Albania cannot afford such a war: it is concentrating on its economy and on developing good relations with the West. In the case of Kosovo, hostility between Albanian Kosovars and Serbs is intense but Serbian military superiority is assured and the Serb minority is in control of the government of Kosovo. The Serbs may use force but they can do so at their leisure. The mildness of ethnic tension between the Czech Republic and Slovakia makes military calculations unnecessary, and the Hungarian minority in Slovakia is reasonably secure, although there is a degree of touchiness, as evidenced by a rumour in July 1992 of unusually large Hungarian military manoeuvres on the Hungarian-Slovak border (*SWB*, EE/1441 A2/1, 24 July 1992). The Hungarian community in Transylvania is well organised and is not yet seriously vulnerable. Nor does Hungary feel that it is under time pressure to use a window of military opportunity to protect it. The Vojvodina Hungarians are under much greater pressure but it is unlikely that Hungary would be a military match for Serbia. A central factor in Hungary's restraint is that it is determined that Hungary be integrated with Western Europe: it has no stomach for the economic or political costs of war. When Hungarian politicians bang the drum about Hungarian minorities abroad, they tend to be doing so for domestic electoral consumption.

International institutions – which may take the form of established practices, treaties or the activities of international organisations – can play an important role in making cooperation more likely and reducing the incentives for war by providing stable expectations about behaviour (Keohane, 1984, 1993; Keohane and Nye, 1989; Snyder, 1990). Slovak Prime Minister Měciar has argued that operating through international organisations is the best way for Hungary to deal with fears for its minority in Slovakia. The Conference on Security and Cooperation in Europe (CSCE) – in which all the states of Europe and of the former Soviet Union plus Canada and the United States participate – is the main forum for such reassurance. For conflict prevention, the CSCE has established the post of High Commissioner for National Minorities and a Centre for Prevention of Conflict in Prague, and there are plans for new arbitration and conciliation procedures. It has also set up an Office of Free

Elections (to become the Office of Democratic Institutions and Human Rights with a wider remit) in Warsaw and a Forum for Security Cooperation (*The Economist*, 18 July 1992, p. 41; Farrell, forthcoming; Latawski, forthcoming). Of course, calculations can change and international institutions have their limits. In particular, Hungary could find itself dragged reluctantly into a war to protect Hungarians in Vojvodina or Transylvania. In Romania, a large neo-Fascist paramilitary organisation with up to 700,000 paying members, called Ion Antonescu (after the Second World War Fascist dictator in Romania who had about 100,000 Gypsies killed in concentration camps), has been set up to coordinate anti-Gypsy violence. The Gypsies have threatened to set up their own police force and army if the state does not protect them (*SWB*, EE/1651 B/8, 31 March 1993). It is likely that the friendless Gypsies will be abandoned to their fate, but Hungarians in Transylvania would be unlikely to be immune in such an intolerant atmosphere.

The roles of international organisations in the Yugoslav conflict

Where the parties wish to pursue cooperative outcomes, international organisations can be facilitators. However, they do not always make cooperation and peace more likely. In some respects, the EC, NATO and UN have magnified the worst dimensions of the Yugoslav conflict. International recognition was extended to Croatia and Bosnia without adequate guarantees for minority rights. Then the arms embargo imposed by the international community on the region effectively left the Bosnian state at the mercy (or rather mercilessness) of Serbian and Croatian forces. The arms embargo deprived the Bosnian state of any ability to impose its authority over its own territory. In this situation of total anarchy, trust between neighbours of different ethnic groups was replaced by fear, suspicion and violence. Armed thugs of all ethnic groups have been allowed to roam freely, with no Bosnian state apparatus to deal with them: hence the arms embargo has contributed to ethnic cleansing.

If the international community had backed Bosnia from the outset in return for guarantees for minority rights, there is a reasonable possibility that most of the slaughter in Bosnia could have been prevented. There was no need for vast outside military intervention with ground troops: the Bosnian state had plenty of people willing and able to do their own fighting, and the military operations could have been monitored by the EC, NATO and UN to discourage revenge attacks. These international organisations failed to act because the member states did not see their interests at stake, did not want to risk military involvement of their own and expressed vague fears of escalation into a wider Balkan war if the Bosnian state was given arms. As a result, they decided to tolerate the establishment of a greater Serbia and to concentrate on humanitarian aid, and hoped that the war would be over quickly.

The simple characterisation of the role of international organisations as being willing to endorse gains made through military aggression as the price of peace (Posen, 1993, pp. 33–4) is a partial exaggeration. In order to stop the fighting, international organisations and their mediators have proposed peace plans which would require the victors to give up many of their gains. The carrot has been international legitimation for some of the gains made and the stick has been the possibility of the use of force as the reluctant response to total intransigence. Hence each round of peace talks in the former Yugoslavia has been accompanied by intense fighting as the factions jockey to improve their position. Before the war, the population of Bosnia was 33 per cent Serb, 44 percent Muslim and 17 per cent Croat. The Carrington plan of March 1992 proposed to award 44 per cent of the territory each to the Bosnian Serbs and the Bosnian state and 10 per cent to the Bosnian Croats (*The Economist*, 31 July 1993). The Bosnian government rejected the plan and hoped for international assistance but the arms embargo ensured that the war went badly.

By early 1993, the Serbs held 70 per cent of Bosnia, the Bosnian state a mere 10 per cent and the Bosnian Croats 20 per cent. The Vance-Owen peace plan of January 1993 envisaged an extremely decentralised Bosnia divided into ten provinces with multi-ethnic governments reflecting ethnic numerical balances and administrations with (belated) guarantees for each ethnic group. The Bosnian Serbs were awarded 43 per cent of the territory in the peace plan, which represented very substantial but not complete rollback. The Bosnian Croats agreed to the plan enthusiastically because they were awarded a substantial amount of territory while the Bosnian state acquiesced out of desperation. Milošević, who had vigorously backed the Bosnian Serbs, pressed them hard for a short period in May 1993 to comply with the peace plan. The temporary switch in policy was caused by two factors. First, the Yugoslav economy was in deep trouble due to the sanctions imposed in May 1992. Second, and most important, air strikes and arming of the Bosnian state by NATO or at least by the United States looked, for a very short while, more likely. In spite of this pressure, the Bosnian Serbs, who had already unilaterally proclaimed the independent state of Herceg-Bosna as the first step to joining with Serbia, voted almost unanimously to reject the Vance-Owen peace plan in a referendum on 15–16 May 1993. In a parallel process, the territory held by the Bosnian Croats continued to be absorbed into Croatia (*Guardian*, 22 May 1993).

Rather than enforce the Vance-Owen plan, Britain, France, Spain, Russia and the United States came up with the Washington plan on 23 May 1993 which backed away from the threat of air strikes. Instead, it concentrated on totally misnamed UN 'safe areas' occupied by 1.1 million Muslims and non-Muslims loyal to the Bosnian government in enclaves around Sarajevo, Bihac in north-western Bosnia, and Srebrenica, Zepa, Gorazde and Tuzla in the east (*Guardian*, 24 May 1993, 2 June 1993; *The Economist*, 29 May 1993). In spite of their military vulnerability and (with the exceptions of Sarajevo and Tuzla) their complete isolation, there were no provisions for military action against those who attacked them. The Bosnian government instantly rejected the plan. Subsequently, like shooting fish in a barrel, the 'safe areas' have been ghettos which have been shelled with impunity.

Any pretence that hope remained for the Vance-Owen plan was cast aside in June 1993 when the EC and UN began to lean hard on the Bosnian government to accept a partition of Bosnia into three loosely-connected units. The Geneva plan which emerged in August 1993 offered the Bosnian Serbs 52.5 per cent, the Bosnian state 30 per cent and the Bosnian Croats 17.5 per cent. NATO promised 50,000 troops to police the implementation of the Geneva plan if it is implemented in some form (*Guardian*, 28 August 1993). The talks stalled at the beginning of September when the Bosnian government demanded another 4 per cent in order to regain land which had a Muslim majority before ethnic cleansing (*Guardian*, 3 September 1993). Even if the Geneva plan is implemented, it will not stop the ethnic cleansing in Croatian and Serbian areas of the proposed new union. Nor will it stop the expected rapid absorption of those areas into a Greater Croatia and Greater Serbia respectively.

In contrast to the Croatian-held and Serbian-held areas, the extent to which the multi-ethnic nature of the Bosnian state has survived the war (and the arms embargo which prevents it from controlling militant militias) is truly impressive. Serbs and Croats continue to fight against other Serbs and Croats to defend Bosnia (*SWB*, EE/1574 C1/13, 30 December 1992). As Mirko Pejanovic, an ethnic Serb member of the Bosnian Presidency, pointed out, the territory in the Geneva plan would also be home to around 500,000 Croats, Serbs and other nationalities (*SWB*, EE/1577 C1/1 4 January 1993). This represents about 18 per cent of the population of the Bosnian state (*Guardian*, 31 August 1993). Pejanovic also pointed out that this means that the Muslims would in effect be receiving far less than 30 per cent of the territory (*SWB*, EE/1778 C/3, 27 August 1993). Inevitably, in some cases tolerance has been broken down. For example, a 2,000-strong militia offshoot which has broken away from the Bosnian army and which calls itself the Muslim Armed Forces (MOS) has been accused of terrorising Bosnian Croats and Serbs in the central Bosnian city of Zenica (*Guardian*, 26 August 1993; *The Economist*, 4 September 1993). In spite of this kind of serious problem, support for the Bosnian multi-ethnic state remains strong.

The EC negotiator Lord David Owen invited members of the Bosnian parliamentary opposition to Geneva to try to obtain their support for the Geneva plan. However, they have been just as unwillling as the government to endorse the ethnic partition of Bosnia (*SWB*, EE/1572 C1/7–8, 24 December 1992). According to *The Economist*: 'They were expelled from the conference room because they constantly objected to Lord Owen's reference to them as the "Muslim side", (*The Economist*, 4 September 1993). Why is the Bosnian conflict portrayed almost exclusively as a war between three ethnic groups? Aside from ignorance or the inconvenience of a more complex picture, the main reason is that it is a politically convenient fiction: the policy pursued by the international community of containing the war and not taking sides becomes much easier to justify.

Democratisation and the building of security regimes

Outside of the territory of the former Yugoslavia, the relatively liberal form which democratisation has taken has created benign conditions for the building of military security regimes with the potential in East-Central Europe to become security communities in the not too distant future. Decision-makers are seeking to reassure each other and the West on military security issues. In a diffuse manner, the continuing implementation of the 1990 Conventional Forces in Europe (CFE) treaty contributes to confidence-building by reducing perceptions of external threats. These external threats may be perceived as being short term or long term, and they may be viewed as involving invasion or intimidation, or be based on a more vague fear of proximity to a greater power. The CFE treaty was a product of the Cold War era: it was aimed at eliminating the prospect of Europe-wide coalition warfare between the states of NATO and the Warsaw Treaty Organisation (WTO). Under the CFE treaty, ceilings in various weapon categories were agreed so that, if all states deployed their full permitted capabilites, no single country could have more than 30 per cent of the conventional forces between the Atlantic to the Urals area (Herring, 1992, pp. 359, 372). In June 1992, NATO, Eastern Europe and the former Soviet Union reconfirmed their commitment to the CFE treaty. The treaty represents an important corrective to fears of resurgent Russian imperialism, and any attempt by Russia (or any other state) to breach the limits of the treaty would be an alarming signal. However, if other countries deploy many fewer forces than they are permitted (as seems likely), then Russia could end up with more than 50 per cent of the forces in the region. Another point to note is that the CFE limits are of no value with regard to the fighting in former Yugoslavia. To enhance confidence further the foreign ministers of NATO, Bulgaria, Czechoslovakia, Belorussia, Georgia, Poland, Hungary, Romania and Ukraine signed on 24 March 1992 an Open Skies agreement which allows reconnaissance overflights on the basis of proportionate options discussed annually (*SWB*, EE/1655 B/3–4, 5 April 1993).

The process of demilitarisation which is widespread in East-Central Europe (IISS, 1992, pp. 66–7) has had a positive effect on military security. The Hungarian army (which still requires one year of national service) shrank from 155,000 (a figure which includes civilian employees) in 1989 to 100,000 in mid-1992, of whom 70,000 were military personnel (*SWB*, EE/1464 B/8–9, 20 August 1992). Although the Hungarian army is relatively weak, the Hungarian National Security Adviser Csaba Ferencz indicated in an interview in August 1992 that he was relaxed about his country's position. He argued that the countries of the region were mainly concerned with trying to become members of the EC; that they were bound by the CFE agreement to limits on their armed forces; that there was no evidence of any country wishing to break those limits; and that the small size of the Hungarian army would reassure other countries that it was not a threat. Substantial demilitarisation is also under way in parts of the Balkans. Bulgaria is sufficiently insulated from the Balkan troubles to allow it to take the same road. In order to demonstrate symbolically its commitment to democracy and European integration, the Bulgarian Ministry of Defence now publishes the quarterly journal *Bulgarian Military Review* in English, German and French – the first foreign-language Bulgarian military journal (*SWB*, EE/1460 B/2–3, 15 August 1992). President Zhelyu Zhelev stressed that he wanted the armed forces to be apolitical and argued optimistically that, due to its cooperation on military matters, it was 'practically a member of NATO' (*SWB*, EE/1441 B/1, 24 July 1992).

Mutual confidence-building is also being assisted by the development of a network of bilateral military cooperation. Bulgaria is exploring, in cooperation with the Belgian armed forces, how to make the transition from conscription to a smaller professional force (*SWB*, EE/1460 A1/1, 15 August 1992). Similarly, Hungary has developed military contacts with the United States, Germany and Poland; Britain has established military links with the Czech Lands and Slovakia; and Slovakia has done the same with Austria.[12] In spite of its delicate position, Albania is also reforming and reducing the size of its armed forces, with the objective of, as the Minister of Defence Safet Xhulali put it, 'adhering [to] and participating in the UN, CSCE, and NATO structures' (*SWB*, EE/1427 B/1, 8 July 1992). In particular, it values its increasing military ties with NATO-member Turkey.

NATO membership and democratisation

The key institution for European military security is NATO, and the key question about NATO's future is whether it should allow the new democracies to join.[13] The new democracies (excluding the Yugoslav republic, which is prepared to accept the costs involved in establishing a greater Serbia) certainly want to join NATO as well as the EC (*SWB*, EE/1651 A1/1–2, 31 March 1993). They understand that both are medium-term objectives and in the interim want as close relations with both as possible. The North Atlantic Cooperation Council (NACC) was established at the Rome summit of November 1991 as an institutional link between NATO and the former Warsaw Pact states. Hungarian Foreign Minister Jeszensky made it clear that a visit in July 1992 by the NATO Secretary-General Manfred Wörner symbolised the support of the West, NATO and the European democracies for Hungary. This support, he argued, would allow Hungary to concentrate on economic issues rather than worrying about military threats (*SWB*, EE/1439 A1/2, 22 July 1992). NATO does not want its cohesion threatened by disputes or even wars between new member states, or between new member states and non-member states. However, integration into Western institutions will help democratisation by refocusing the armed forces of Eastern Europe away from politics; NATO does not have to involve itself in disputes between its members (as shown by the conflict between Greece and Turkey over Cyprus); and increasing numbers of NATO voices are arguing for contingency planning against the possibility of a Russian military threat to Europe. Of course, the pacifying and democratising effects of NATO membership should not be exaggerated – as indicated by the Greco-Turkish dispute and the brutality of governments in Turkey. In September 1993 NATO decided to convene a heads of state meeting for January 1994 to take the momentous step of agreeing in principle that all 22 NACC states should be allowed to join NATO (*Guardian*, 8 September 1993). However, NATO watered down the proposal subsequently and offered a less committing, more vague 'Partnership for Peace'. NATO membership if it is offered will probably be tied to EC membership, which means that Eastern Europe (except the former Yugoslav states) can be expected to join first. NATO membership, as Paul Latawski points out, need not be an all-or-nothing choice: France and Spain are signatories to the North Atlantic Treaty but are not part of the integrated military command structure, while Denmark and Norway do not have foreign troops or nuclear weapons deployed on their territory in peacetime. This graduated approach makes sense in that it balances the need to reward and help consolidate democratisation with the need to minimise threats to NATO cohesion.

Conclusion

To a substantial degree there is a benign circle of democratisation and security. Democratisation can improve environmental security by increasing controls on potential polluters. It can improve economic security by encouraging cooperative and complementary economic policies rather than protectionism, and by reducing perceptions of the need for military spending. It can improve military security through the reassurance and openness that exists between democracies. And it can play a particularly important role in increasing societal security though its code of values involving a minimum of respect for the rights of minorities. In turn, security can free the resources and build the confidence, tolerance and trust necessary for democratisation.

Liberal democracy and security

Of course, greater security does not necessarily lead to democratisation, and democratic procedures do not guarantee liberal political outcomes that may enhance security – people are free to vote for intolerant policies such as ethnic cleansing or to vote for environmentally-damaging consumerism – and liberal principles may be applied only half-heartedly or selectively. Hence the degree to which democratisation is liberal has a powerful impact on international security. The case of East-Central Europe shows that liberal democracy is conducive to the development of military and societal security regimes and, eventually, security communities. NATO, the EC, the CSCE, arms control treaties, demilitarisation and military cooperation are reinforced by and are reinforcing democratisation in that region and to a lesser extent in Bulgaria and Romania. However, liberal democracy is usually associated with consumerist market economies. Market efficiency rests to a great degree on competition and hence on an element of economic insecurity, and consumerism represents a long-term threat to environmental security. However, too much economic insecurity can threaten democracy, because it generates societal insecurity as extremist nationalists make scapegoats of minorities. A broad concept of security is valuable because different aspects of insecurity interact with each other, and because liberal democracy can be jeopardised by non-military threats.

Economic threats to liberal democracy

The main threat to liberal democracy in Eastern Europe apart from the former Yugoslavia is economic insecurity. In spite of economic cooperation, the pain of marketisation, made worse by the costs of demilitarisation and EC trade barriers, is generating popular support for former Communists and for the extreme right. Within the moderate ruling Hungarian Democratic Forum a vocal neo-Nazi faction emerged, led by István Csurka who rails against Jews, Communists, liberals and Western companies, and calls for living space for Hungarians. Csurka and three other members of Parliament were expelled from the party in June 1993 (*The Economist*, 30 January 1993; *Guardian*, 4 June 1993, 7 June 1993). Hungarian politicians and academics are generally convinced that Hungarian democracy is secure in spite of West European fears. As evidence of West European double standards they point to the fact that there are equivalent neo-Nazi groups in established democracies such as Germany, France and Austria. However, the economic insecurity in East-Central Europe is much more pronounced and has much greater potential to produce support for an authoritarian leader who will sweep aside the squabbling party politicians.

The former Yugoslavia; illiberal democracy and insecurity

Although the Bosnian state is still multi-ethnic, liberal democracy has for the most part been subordinated to intolerant majoritarianism in the former Yugoslavia. This intolerance, combined with the existence of large minorities, mutually negative perceptions among ethnic groups and the exploitation of those perceptions for electoral gain, has created a high degree of societal insecurity. Mutual intolerance has entrapped the various ethnic groups in the societal security dilemma. Ethnic conflict has resulted in war in cases where the ethnic conflict has been particularly intense, where one side has clear but possibly temporary military superiority, where use of that military superiority is the only way to protect that state's minority abroad from violence, and when the economic and political costs of using force are tolerable (even if they are high). Although ethnic groups in the former Yugoslavia have been concerned about economic security, their main preoccupation has been with threats to identity and self-expression. Hungary has protested over the treatment of ethnic Hungarians in Slovakia and especially in Transylvania and Vojvodina, but the factors making for ethnic conflict and war have not been so powerful – at least thus far.

The impact of the external environment on Eastern Europe

The external environment presents Eastern Europe with a complex mix of security threats and opportunities. In the near future, Russia is unlikely to pose a military threat to any East European state and, for most states, NATO is seen as an allliance which can guarantee their military security. The exception is Serbia which was threatened (briefly) with air bombardment over the conflict in Bosnia. Romania, Hungary and Bulgaria have all paid a heavy economic price for cutting off their trade with Yugoslavia in support of international economic sanctions. Western recognition of Slovenia, Croatia, Bosnia and Macedonia without guarantees for minority rights exacerbated societal insecurity, and the arms embargo which followed resulted in extreme military insecurity for the Bosnian Muslims and non-Muslims loyal to the Bosnian government and to a lesser extent the Bosnian Croats. Instability in the Balkans and former Soviet Union are seen as indirect economic threats by the Hungarian Prime Minister (*SWB*, EE/1463 A2/2, 19 August 1992). The EC is seen primarily as an economic opportunity, but if the EC dumps cheap exports on East European markets and if the IMF imposes excessively stringent conditions on loans, that perception will change, and forces of economic nationalism will be unleashed. West European companies pose an environmental threat because there is a booming business of dumping West European toxic waste in Eastern Europe: East European states tend to say nothing because of the profits involved. In addition, Russia's industries and dangerous nuclear power stations pose a further environmental threat. However, eventually these states may be protected from West European hazardous exports by EC environmental standards.

The limited commitment of the West to the building of democracy in Eastern Europe

There are three main reasons why Western Europe and the United States have made only very limited efforts to assist in the building of democracy in Eastern Europe. The first is that they believe that they can insulate themselves from the troubles of Eastern Europe without great cost. In other words, their sense of security has reduced their willingness to do anything about East European insecurities. Although John Mearsheimer (1990) has argued that Europe is heading for a dangerous era of multipolarity, the more persuasive analysis is that the democratic values and conflict-resolving institutions of the main European states mean that the present and future will not resemble Europe's nineteenth and early twentieth-century past (Snyder, 1990; Ullman, 1991; van Evera, 1991). Democratisatioin has removed the military threat of the Warsaw Pact, reduced the environmental threat from East European industries and opened up substantial economic opportunities. Second, the West is preoccupied with problems of its own. The transitional economic costs of demilitarisation in the West are proving to be so great that analysts tend to refer to the peace tax rather than the peace dividend. In particular, Germany is spending vast sums on absorbing former East Germany. The population movements caused by conflict in former Yugoslavia and by the economic magnetism of the EC are fuelling anti-democratic forces in Western Europe. There are even those who are nostalgic for what they perceived as the ideological certainties and military simplicities of 'the Soviet threat' during the Cold War. Finally, helping East Europeans to build democracy is often a subordinate objective for Western policy-makers. Economic protectionism often comes first and economic assistance to Eastern Europe is a vote loser. Once the war broke out in Bosnia, the primary objective was containment of the war and peace at virtually any cost to the Bosnian state. Decision-makers in organisations such as the IMF pay too much attention to narrow economic calculations and not enough attention to the consequences for the stability of democracy (Nelson, 1993; Pereira, Maravall and Przeworski, 1993; Snyder, 1993), while, on occasion, those who work for international organisations can be more concerned with their own prestige and profit than with helping Eastern Europe. The most stark example of the gravy train is the European Bank for Reconstruction and Development (EBRD) which spent £200 million on itself (for equipment, lavish furnishings, marble floors, artwork, travel and corporate credit cards) and only £100 million on its programmes for Eastern Europe (*Guardian*, 17 July 1993).[14] Most significantly, the liberal democratic values of politicians and electorates in the West have distinct limits. If building democracy at home is not a top priority, it is unlikely to be a top priority in foreign policy.

Acknowledgements

The author would like to thank Theo Farrell, Paul Latawski, Margot Light, John Pinder, Geoffrey Pridham, Helen Redmond-Cooper, Susanna Reid, George Sanford and Laurence Whitehead for their valuable comments on earlier drafts of this chapter.

Notes

1. In this chapter, 'East-Central Europe' refers to Poland, Hungary, the Czech Republic and Slovakia; 'the Balkans' refers to Bulgaria, Romania, Croatia, Slovenia, Bosnia, Macedonia, Yugoslavia (i.e. Serbia and Montenegro),

Albania and Greece; and 'Eastern Europe' refers to East-Central Europe and the Balkans together. Other categorisations are, of course, possible. For example, the Hexagonal Group, which has been renamed the Central European Initiative, includes the Czech Republic, Slovakia, Poland, Hungary, Bosnia, Slovenia and Croatia, with non-member participation by Bulgaria, Romania, Ukraine and Belorussia. Officially, members are only to be states which meet Council of Europe standards of human rights (*SWB*, EE/1438 C2/1–4, 21 July 1992).

2. A favourable military security environment was clearly a crucial precondition for the initial transition to democracy in Eastern Europe. There was a powerful (but by no means universal) politico-cultural desire for democracy in one form or another and the economic benefits expected to accompany it, but that desire could only be realised once the Soviet military veto on democratisation was lifted. For analysis of this see the chapter by Margot Light in this volume.
3. Buzan, 1991, pp. 176–7. The British literature on international society has important similarities to the US literature on regimes, although the connection between the two is rarely made. For explicit comparisons see especially Evans and Wilson, 1992, and also Cutler, 1991.
4. The concept has mostly been used until now with reference only to military security and only to states. See Herz, 1950, 1951; Butterfield, 1951; Deutsch *et al.*, 1957; Wolfers, 1962; Jervis, 1978; Waltz, 1979; Wheeler and Booth, 1992. The exception is Buzan, who develops the notion of the societal security dilemma. The book of which Buzan's chapter is a part is the first full-length study of societal security (Waever *et al.*, 1993). If we adopt a broader and non-state-centric notion of security, then it follows that we ought to take the same approach to the concepts of security dilemma, security community and security regime.
5. Indeed there are some signs of strain in their cooperation – see the chapter by Judy Batt in this volume.
6. Glenny, 1993, pp. 31–2, 94, 104. The damage in the former Soviet Union far exceeds that in Eastern Europe. According to Russian government scientists, 15 per cent of the territory of the Russian Federation (one million square miles) is unfit for human habitation; 1.3 million Russian people are registered with hospitals as being ill due to radiation exposure from the Chernobyl nuclear disaster of 1986; 75 per cent of all Russian 16-year-olds are unhealthy; and 85 per cent of city dwellers breathe heavily polluted air (*Guardian*, 8 October 1992).
7. Societal security should not be equated with the question of ethnicity. For example, the issue of societal security and its relationship with democratisation can be explored from the perspective of gender. The societal insecurity of women rests on the existence of a world of male-dominated societies, and Eastern Europe before and after the fall of Communism has been no exception. Indeed, the salience of the ethnicity issue and the virtual invisibility of the gender issue shows how thoroughly patriarchy is entrenched. Perhaps it can be otherwise, but at present, and regardless of their own attitudes, men benefit from their institutionalised supremacy: hence the societal security of men is based in part on the insecurity of women. Furthermore, the societal insecurity of women increases their vulnerability to other threats. As a result, attempts at democratisation and struggles for security in Eastern Europe have affected men and women differently. Bosnian Serbs have been running rape camps and have raped up to 50,000 non-Serb women as part of a campaign to intimidate

and humiliate the victims and their families and communities, to make them unattractive as marriage (and thus breeding) partners and to dilute the genes of the other ethnic groups. Democratisation is reinforcing the insecurity of women in some respects in Eastern Europe because the limited gains made by women under Communism are being rolled back. In Poland, state subsidies for child care have declined dramatically and women are usually sacked before men when redundancies have to be made (*The Economist*, 12 December 1992). Hence women are suffering increased economic insecurity in order to shore up the economic security of men in the wake of the collapse of Communism. Democratisation has also allowed the Roman Catholic church in Poland to press successfully for legislation to restrict abortion rights (*The Economist*, 12 December 1993; *Guardian*, 8 January 1993; French, 1992, pp. 100–1).

8. *The Economist*, 1 August 1992; p. 31; *SWB*, EE/1666 C1/18–19, 19 April 1993. The situation in Montenegro is very similar: ethnic Albanians are leaving in their thousands due to discrimination (*SWB*, EE/1660 C1/7, 12 April 1993).
9. *SWB*, EE/1655 B/7–10, 5 April 1993; *SWB*, EE/1657 B/1–2, 7 April 1993; *SWB*, EE/1660 B/11, 12 April 1993; *SWB*, EE/1661 A2/4–5, 13 April 1993.
10. Doyle, 1983a, b; 1986; 1991; Chan, 1984; Russett, 1990; Ember, Ember and Russett, 1992; Maoz and Russett, 1992; Schweller, 1992.
11. *The New York Times*, 6 September 1992; *The Economist*, 20 March 1993; *SWB*, EE/1653 C1/11, 5 April 1993; *SWB*, EE/1660 C1/5, 12 April 1993.
12. *SWB*, EE/1655 A2/1, 5 April 1993; *SWB*, EE/1657 A1/2–3, 7 April 1993; *SWB*, EE/1658 A1/1–2, 8 April 1993; *SWB* EE/1661 B/1, 13 April 1993.
13. For useful discussions of the future of NATO and the arguments for and against expansion of its membership, see Farrell (forthcoming) and Latawski (forthcoming). The Western European Union (WEU) is expanding its membership and has a minor role as an institutional link between the EC and NATO. France has always been keen on the WEU rather than NATO because the United States is not a member. However, the WEU remains marginal.
14. In Britain, it has been commonplace for ministers in the Conservative government immediately upon leaving office to become directors of major companies which they have played an important role in privatising. This has been condemned by many but is at least legal. In Eastern Europe, corruption is extreme, both as a legacy of the Communist system of patronage and bribery and as a product of the opportunities provided by the poorly regulated privatisation of tens of thousands of enterprises. In Hungary alone at the beginning of 1993 there were around 27,000 companies still to be privatised (Hungarian News Agency, *Daily News*, 30 December 1992 - 7 January 1993).

References

BASIC, 1992, *BASIC Reports on European Arms Control*, British American Security Information Council, London, 19 February 1992, No. 20.

Brown, Chris, 1992, '"Really existing liberalism" and international order', *Millennium: Journal of International Studies*, Vol. 21, No. 3, pp. 313–28.

Bull, Hedley, 1977, *The Anarchical Society. A study of order in world politics*, Macmillan, London.

Butterfield, Herbert, 1951, *History and Human Relations*, Collins, London.

Buzan, Barry, 1991, *People, States and Fear. An agenda for international security studies in the post-Cold War era*, 2nd edn., Harvester Wheatsheaf, London.

Buzan, Barry, Little, Richard and Jones, Charles, 1993, *The Logic of Anarchy. Neorealism to structural Realism*, Columbia University Press, New York.

Chan, Steven, 1984, 'Mirror, mirror on the wall . . . Are the democratic states more pacific?', *Journal of Conflict Resolution*, Vol. 28, No. 4, pp. 617–48.

Chomsky, Noam, 1989, *Necessary Illusions. Thought control in democratic societies*, Pluto Press, London.

Chomsky, Noam, 1992, *Deterring Democracy*, Vintage, London.

Chomsky, Noam, 1993, *Year 501: the conquest continues*, Verso, London.

Crampton, Richard, 1990, 'The intelligentsia, the ecology and the opposition in Bulgaria', *The World Today*, Vol. 46, No. 2, pp. 23–6.

Cutler, A. Claire, 1991, 'The "Grotian tradition" in international relations', *Review of International Studies*, Vol. 17, No. 1, pp. 41–65.

Deutsch, Karl W. *et al.*, 1957, *Political Community and the North Atlantic Area*, Princeton University Press, Princeton, NJ.

de Nevers, Renée, 1993, 'Democratisation and ethnic conflict', *Survival*, Vol. 35, No. 2, pp. 31–48.

Doyle, Michael W., 1983a, 'Kant, liberal legacies and foreign affairs', Part 1, *Philosophy and Public Affairs*, Vol. 12, No. 3, pp. 205–35.

Doyle, Michael W., 1983b, 'Kant, liberal legacies and foreign affairs', Part 2, *Philosophy and Public Affairs*, Vol. 12, No. 4, pp. 323–53

Doyle, Michael W., 1986, 'Liberalism and world politics', *American Political Science Review*, Vol. 80, No. 4, pp. 1151–69.

Doyle, Michael W., 1991, 'An international liberal community' in Graham Allison and Gregory F. Treverton (eds), *Rethinking America's Security. Beyond Cold War to new world order*, W.W. Norton, New York, pp. 573–93.

Ember, Carol R., Ember, Melvin and Russett, Bruce, 1992, 'Peace between participatory polities: a cross-cultural test of the "Democracies rarely fight each other" hypothesis', *World Politics*, Vol. 44, No. 4, pp. 573–99.

Evans, Tony and Wilson, Peter, 1992, 'Regime theory and the English school of International Relations: a comparison', *Millennium: Journal of International Studies*, Vol. 21, No. 3, pp. 329–51.

Farrell, Theo, forthcoming, 'Can a leopard change its spots? The rhetoric and reality of NATO's transformation' in Bogdan Szajkowski and Mette Skak (eds), *Response of Western European Institutions to Changes in the Former Soviet Union and Central and Eastern Europe*, Routledge, London.

French, Marilyn, 1992, *The War Against Women*, Penguin, London.

Gilbert, Alan, 1992, 'Must global politics constrain democracy? Realism, regimes, and democratic internationalism', *Political Theory*, Vol. 20, No. 1, pp. 8–37.

Glenny, Misha, 1992, *The Fall of Yugoslavia: the third Balkan War*, Penguin, London.

Glenny, Misha, 1993, *The Rebirth of History: Eastern Europe in the age of democracy*, 2nd edn., Penguin, London.

Herman, Edward S. and Chomsky, Noam, 1988, *Manufacturing Consent: the political economy of the mass media*, Pantheon, New York.

Herring, Eric, 1992, 'The collapse of the Soviet Union: the implications for world politics' in John Baylis and N.J. Rengger (eds), *Dilemmas of World Politics. International issues in a changing world*, Clarendon Press, Oxford, pp. 354–83.

Herz, John, 1950, 'Idealist internationalism and the security dilemma', *World Politics*, Vol. 2, No. 2, pp. 157–80.

Herz, John, 1951, *Political Realism and Political Idealism*, University of Chicago Press, Chicago.

IISS (International Institute for Strategic Studies), 1992, *The Military Balance 1992–93*, Brassey's for the International Institute for Strategic Studies, London.

Jervis, Robert, 1978, 'Cooperation under the security dilemma', *World Politics*, Vol. 30, No. 2, pp. 167–214.

Jervis, Robert, 1983, 'Security regimes' in Stephen D. Krasner (ed.), *International Regimes*, Cornell University Press, Ithaca, NY, pp. 173–94.

Johansen, Robert C., 1992, 'Military policies and the state system as impediments to democracy', *Political Studies*, Vol. 40, No. 5, pp. 99–115.

Keohane, Robert O., 1983, *After Hegemony: cooperatiion and discord in the world political economy*, Princeton University Press, Princeton, NJ.

Keohane, Robert O., 1989, *International Institutions and State Power*, Westview, Boulder, Colo.

Keohane, Robert O., 1993, 'Institutionalist theory and the realist challenge after the Cold War' in David Baldwin (ed.), *Neorealism and Neoliberalism: the contemporary debate*, Columbia University Press, New York.

Keohane, Robert O. and Nye, Joseph S., Jr., 1989, *Power and Interdependence: world politics in transition*, 2nd edn., Little-Brown, Boston, Mass.

Krasner, Stephen D., 1992, 'Realism, imperialism, and democracy. A response to Gilbert', *Political Theory*, Vol. 20, No. 1, pp. 38–52.

Lake, David A., 1992, 'Powerful pacifists: democratic states and war', *American Political Science Review*, Vol. 86, No. 1, pp. 24–37.

Latawski, Paul, forthcoming, 'NATO and East Central Europe: the case of Poland' in Andrew Williams (ed.), *Reorganizing Eastern Europe: European institutions and the refashioning of Europe's security architecture*, Dartmouth, London.

Maoz, Zeev and Russett, Bruce, 1992, 'Alliance, contiguity, weath, and political stability: is the lack of conflict among democracies a statistical artifact?', *International Interactions*, Vol. 17, No. 3, pp. 245–67.

Mearsheimer, John J., 1990, 'Back to the future: instability in Europe after the Cold War', *International Security*, Vol. 15, No. 1, pp. 5–57.

Milner, Helen V., 1991, 'The assumption of anarchy in international relations theory: a critique', *Review of International Studies*, Vol. 17, No. 1, pp. 67–85.

Mortimer, Edward, 1992, *European Security after the Cold War*, Adelphi Paper, No. 271,. Brassey's for the International Institute for Stategic Studies, London.

Nelson, Joan M., 1993, 'The politics of economic transformation: is Third World experience relevant in Eastern Europe?', *World Politics*, Vol. 45, No. 3, pp. 433–63.

Parenti, Michael, 1988, *Democracy for the Few*, 5th edn., St. Martin's Press, New York.

Pereira, Carlos Ruiz Bresser, Maravall, José Maria and Przeworski, Adam, 1993, *Economic Reforms in New Democracies. A social-democratic approach*, Cambridge University Press, Cambridge.

Posen, Barry, 1993, 'The security dilemma and ethnic conflict', *Survival*, Vol. 35, No. 1, pp. 27–47.

Rengger, N.J., 1992a, 'Culture, society and order in world politics' in John Baylis and N.J. Rengger (eds), *Dilemmas of World Politics. International issues in a changing world*, Clarendon Press, Oxford, pp. 85–103.

Rengger, N.J., 1992b, 'No longer a tournament of distinctive knights: systemic transition and the priority of international order' in Robin Brown and Mike Bowker (eds), *Theory and World Politics in the 1980s*, Cambridge University Press, Cambridge, pp. 145–74.

Rich, Vera, 1991, 'The future of the Danube', *The World Today*, Vol. 47, Nos. 8–9, pp. 142–4.

Russett, Bruce, 1990, 'Politics and alternative security: towards a more democratic, therefore more peaceful, world' in Burns H. Weston (ed), *Alternative Security. Living without nuclear deterrence*, Westview, Boulder, Colo, pp. 107–36.

Schweller, Randall, 1992, 'Domestic structure and preventive war: are democracies more pacific?', *World Politics*, Vol. 44, No. 2, pp. 235–69.

Snyder, Jack L., 1990, 'Averting anarchy in the new Europe', *International Security*, Vol. 14, No. 4, pp. 5–41.

Snyder, Jack L., 1991, *Myths of Empire*, Cornell University Press, Ithaca, NY.

Snyder, Jack L., 1993, 'Nationalism and the crisis of the post-Soviet state', *Survival*, Vol. 35, No. 1, pp. 5–26.

SWB (BBC *Summary of World Broadcasts*).

Thompson, Mark, 1992, *A Paper House. The ending of Yugoslavia*, Vintage, London.

Ullman, Richard H., 1991, *Securing Europe*, Princeton University Press, Princeton, NJ.

van Evera, Stephen, 1991, 'Primed for peace: Europe after the Cold War', *International Security*, Vol. 15, No. 3, pp. 7–57.

Waever, Ole, Buzan, Barry, Kelstrup, Morton and Lemaitre, Pierre, 1993, *Identity, Migration and the New Security Agenda in Europe*, Pinter, London.

Waltz, Kenneth N., 1979, *Theory of International Politics*, Addison-Wesley, Reading, Mass.

Wheeler, Nicholas J. and Booth, Ken, 1992, 'The security dilemma' in John Baylis and N.J. Rengger (eds), *Dilemmas of World Politics. International issues in a changing world*, Clarendon Press, Oxford, pp. 29–60.

Wolfers, Arnold, 1962, *Discord and Collaboration*, Johns Hopkins University Press, Baltimore, Md.

Zametica, John, 1992, *The Yugoslav Conflict*, Adelphi Paper No. 270, Brassey's for the International Institute for Strategic Studies, London.

Zielonka, Jan, 1992, *Security in Central Europe*, Adelphi Paper No. 272, Brassey's for the International Institute for Strategic Studies, London.

5

The European Community and democracy in Central and Eastern Europe

John Pinder

Since the watershed of 1989, the European Community has acted to support pluralist democracy in Central and Eastern Europe. Before that year, the Community's influence on its eastern neighbours had been almost entirely a result of what it was, rather than of what it did in its relationship with them. As with the previous transition to democracy in Southern Europe, there was a 'demonstration effect' of the prosperity and security among the Community's member states (Whitehead, 1991, p. 52). It was identified with liberal democratic values (Pridham, 1991c, p. 223) and with its economic superiority over the East which grew steadily more evident from the 1970s onwards.

The Soviet attempt to impose integration on the East had followed the integration initiatives in the West. Stalin founded the Council of Mutual Economic Assistance (CMEA) in 1949 in response to Marshall Aid, which was the starting-point for unification in Western Europe. Khrushchev tried to imitate the establishment of the European Economic Community (EEC) by proposing, in 1962, a supranational structure for CMEA, which was thwarted by Romania's defence of its sovereignty (Kaser, 1967, pp. 9–12, 106 ff). The success of the Community in the 1960s, together with the agreement to accept Britain, Denmark and Ireland as members after the departure of President de Gaulle, stimulated Brezhnev's push for further integration through the CMEA's Comprehensive Programme in the early 1970s. Economists in the Soviet Union saw integration as an objective tendency responding to 'scientific-technological' progress and the need for a wider market (Maximova, 1971; Shishkov, 1972). But the CMEA Programme was flawed. The command economies with their rigid centralisation were not amenable to integration; and politically, the Programme was a reaction to the Prague Spring of 1968. It was, beyond the economic justifications, an instrument of Soviet domination: an example of imperial integration, as against the Community's liberal and federal form.

The attempts at integration in the CMEA failed to overcome the incapacity of the command economies to provide a framework for the development of the new technologies. Their growth rates declined and they became less and less competitive. The Community, on the contrary, after weathering the storms of the 1970s, recovered its political and economic dynamism with the single market programme and the Single European Act. It presented an impressive contrast to the failure in the East.

The character of the Community

The Community is identified with democratic values because its member states are pluralist democracies. The transition to democracy in Germany and Italy after the Second World War was consolidated within the Community, initiated with the European Coal and Steel Community and extended to a more general economic integration through the EC: and the experience was repeated with the southern enlargement in the 1980s (Pridham, 1991a). The replacement of power relationships among the member states by the rule of law in fields of Community competence has been a key in establishing the framework within which democracy could thrive. Other federal elements have been progressively added (Pinder, 1991a; 1992a). The Community has by now substantially federal powers with respect to trade, the environment, the budget and, stipulated by the Maastricht Treaty, currency. It has a broadly federal judiciary and significant federal elements in its political institutions, with majority voting applicable in the Council of Ministers, a fair amount of executive independence for the Commission and much influence together with some power for the European Parliament. Citizens of the Community have equal rights under Community law, irrespective of their nationality – a crucial principle in preventing nationalist conflicts of the kind that are now so dangerous in Central and Eastern Europe (Heltai and Rau, 1991).

Successive steps in the Community's development have brought good results: Franco-German reconciliation in the 1950s, prosperity in the 1960s, enlargement in the 1970s, further enlargement and the regeneration following the Single European Act in the 1980s. It is reasonable to suppose that the Community, with its federal elements, has managed the growing interdependence among its members states better than a simply intergovernmental system would have done. There will surely be further efforts to develop, or 'deepen', the Community in the 1990s, as well as to widen it to include not just the remaining West European countries that want to join, but also later the Central and East Europeans, many of whom are likely to be more attracted by a deeper Community.

EC policies towards Central and Eastern Europe before 1989

Before the change of regime in Russia, East-West relations were dominated by questions of security: the province of NATO not the Community. The Community's policies towards the East were quite modest. But it did make a significant impact with its policies towards the CMEA, its assertion of linkages between economics and politics, and its promotion of human rights.

The Community resisted Soviet attempts to get it to negotiate with the CMEA on trade. The grounds included the long-standing Soviet efforts to undermine the Community, with the refusal to recognise it and to accept the Commission's role in trade policy. But more fundamental was the Community's reluctance to contribute to Soviet domination over the other CMEA members by enhancing the role of the CMEA in their trade relations. The Community stood its ground until Mikhail Gorbachev accepted that the individual Central and East European countries could conduct trade negotiations with it. Thus the Community showed itself ready, within its field of competence, to resist an abuse of Soviet power, preserving this element of autonomy for the Central and East Europeans and meriting the respect of those who were to succeed the Soviet-backed regimes.

At the same time, the Community saw political merit in encouraging trade with the Soviet Union, giving Soviet leaders an interest in stable relations and establishing links between Soviet people and the world outside. This attitude attained particular prominence in the early 1980s in the quarrel between the Community and the USA over the gas pipeline that the Community was helping to build in order to convey gas from the Soviet Union to Western Europe. The US administration felt that the large flow of natural gas, which was to reach a value of $10 billion a year, would make the Community dependent on the Soviet Union, and sought to impede the project by forbidding the use of US technologies that were important for the equipment. The Europeans argued that the Soviet Union would become at least as dependent on the Community and would thus have more interest in good relations. The Europeans went ahead with the project and can still argue, though not prove, that trade relations contributed to the process of change in Central and Eastern Europe.

The Community's espousal of human rights in the Helsinki negotiations in the mid-1970s appears, with hindsight, to have been its most significant contribution, apart from the demonstration effect, to the ferment that led to the changes of regime. The security basket in the negotiations was clearly an American responsibility; and for the rest, the USA showed 'benign neglect' and let the Community play the leading role (Regelsberger, 1988, pp. 6, 13). In the economic basket, the Community pursued its quest for more openness on the Eastern side; and with respect to the remaining basket, it introduced, apparently somewhat quixotically, the subject of human rights, which turned out to be the most important element in the Helsinki process.

Human rights and civil society

The Chronicle of Current Events was founded in Moscow in 1968 with, on its masthead, an extract on freedom of opinion and expression taken from the UN Declaration of Human Rights. In August 1975 the Soviet Union signed the Helsinki Final Act, including the clauses on human rights and the free contact of peoples on which the Community had insisted. One consequence was to provide 'an international validation' for the concerns of the people producing *The Chronicle* and thus to impart 'new influence to their work' (Hosking, 1990, p. 41). The Helsinki clauses gave a lift to independent organisations in other countries too. In 1976, Poles founded The Movement for the Defence of Human Rights and The Committee for the Defence of the Workers (KOR), initiating the chain of actions that led to the foundation of Solidarity and the first breakthrough towards democracy in Central and Eastern Europe. In 1977, Czechs founded Charter 77, likewise inspired by the human rights principles, and likewise playing a momentous part in securing the change of regime. The Community's initiative at Helsinki surely helped to stimulate this development of a politically active civil society in these countries which provided an essential basis for the transition to democracy.

The totalitarian regimes installed by Stalin in Central and Eastern Europe had sought to extirpate civil society by suppressing or taking over all autonomous institutions. The Soviet Communist Party decided in December 1919 that it should 'effect party supervision over the work of all organisations and institutions' (cited in Hosking, 1990, p. 14); and it carried through this policy with obsessive thoroughness, determined to monopolise not only political but also economic and 'ideological' power, denying the citizens the capacity to express their own values through their own institutions (Rau, 1987, p. 587). It was through organisations such as KOR and Charter 77 that citizens strengthened their 'ideological power' to the point where they could instigate the radical changes of regime. The shift from totalitarian to authoritarian government had begun earlier in most of the Central and East European countries, with greater latitude for social and cultural organisations, allowing more scope for some of the institutions that can generate ideological power. But the regimes continued not only to make this difficult, but also to restrict or suppress the development of autonomous institutions in the economy and the polity: the elements of civil society that are indispensable for the market economy and for constitutional democracy. If the transition to democracy is to be successful, the civil society must not only be strong in the cultural and social fields but must also predominate in the economy and control the government. Private firms have to become a foundation for an effective market economy, and non-state political institutions, such as parties and the media, are essential to the conduct of effective democratic government.

Institutions with the necessary capacities are not easy to create. People have to acquire the skills and behaviour needed in competitive firms in a market economy. Constitutional government requires the rule of law and representative government. Courts and the legal profession must be competent and independent. Elected representatives must comprise an effective legislature based on parties with viable programmes and the capacity to relate properly to citizens and interest groups; and the representatives should also be capable of keeping sufficient control over the government, which itself has to include ministers with enough ability. The public administration too has to be competent; and it should be able to work with whatever government is democratically appointed. Most of these characteristics were undermined by the previous regimes; and support for democratisation has to take account of the need to build them up.

Liberal democracy may come in different mixes of individualism, participation and social provision (Parekh, 1992, p. 169). Their preferred mix is for the Central and East Europeans to determine. The interest of the Community is that they apply the principles of constitutional democracy, that is the rule of law and representative government, as the best guarantee of peaceful behaviour. Since constitutional democracy has to be based on civil society and the market economy, the Community's interest reaches to the latter as well. Pluralism being 'a condition in which political power is diffused among a wide variety of social groups' (Jordan, 1987, p. 426), it is legitimate to use the term pluralist democracy for the combination of constitutional democracy, civil society and market economy. This term is often employed in discussion of the aims of Community policy in Central and Eastern Europe. It is a valid one, so long as it does not conceal the fact that an effective civil society is comprised together with the market economy and constitutional democracy.

If this point may appear laboured, it is because Community and Western policies tend to ignore it. Yet the building up of civil society is a critical element in democratisation in Central and Eastern Europe and it is a big problem in all these countries, even if the Hungarians, Poles and Czechs for example are considerably less disadvantaged than the Albanians and Romanians. The magnitude of the problem is reflected in the use of the word 'transformation' rather than 'transition' in much of the literature about the process of democratisation and marketisation in Central and Eastern Europe. Several years of consolidation will be necessary before the transformation can be regarded as secure. Until then, the process may at any time be reversed; and the mobilisation of public support to support the new system has to be regarded as a continuous effort (Stevens and Kennan, 1992, p. 16). The demonstration effect of the Community and the West should continue to provide substantial encouragement. But it may not be enough. Community and Western policies towards Central and Eastern Europe may also have an essential part to play.

EC policies towards Central and Eastern Europe since 1989

The Community was quick to respond to the events of 1989 (see Pelkmans and Murphy, 1991), with trade liberalisation, aid and the negotiation of trade and cooperation agreements. Much of the literature that has appeared so far on the subject[1] concludes that this was a good start, but that what has followed has not been enough to ensure the transformation to competitive market economies and to provide the conditions for pluralist democracy. Among the measures that would help are, it is argued, reduced protection, increased aid and a more explicit policy to prepare the

Eastern countries to achieve membership of the Community. Some telling expressions give a flavour of what is suggested: 'creative interdependence' (Rood, 1991, pp. 15, 24–6); 'combined structure of partnership' (Skak, 1991, p. 58); 'a transformation partnership' (Weidenfeld and Huterer, 1992, p. 334). The writer finds this perspective congenial; and what follows considers not only existing policies, but also how they might be developed in order to support democratisation more effectively.

EC aims

The Community has three main aims in its policies towards Central and Eastern Europe: to support their movement towards market economy, pluralist democracy and international integration. These aims have been made explicit in some of the principal Community documents relating to the PHARE programme and the Europe Agreements (Commission, 1990a,b; *Official Journal*, 1992) as well as in the statutes of the European Bank for Reconstruction and Development (EBRD).

The PHARE programme was launched in July 1989 to aid Poland and Hungary in the first instance, then other Central and East European countries. The initial decision was taken by the Group of seven large industrial countries (G-7), then adopted by the twenty-four countries that are members of the OECD (G-24); and the G-7 asked the EC Commission to coordinate the aid for the G-24 as a whole. The Community together with its member states is by far the largest contributor of both grants and loans. The Commission underlined, in a policy statement, the importance of the 'basic legislation needed to move towards democratic and competitive market-oriented systems' and held that by May 1990, 'the infrastructure of political and reform programmes' in Bulgaria, Czechoslovakia, the GDR, Romania and Yugoslavia as well as Poland and Hungary, had 'largely satisfied the conditions for the extension of coordinated assistance' (Commission, 1990a). The statutes of the EBRD, agreed in May 1990 after both Western and Eastern countries had accepted a Community initiative for its establishment, expressed similar aims: 'to foster the transition towards open-market oriented economies and to promote private and entrepreneurial initiatives in the Central and East European countries committed to and applying the principles of multi-party democracy, pluralism and market economies'. In proposing the association with, at first, Hungary, Poland and the Czech and Slovak Federal Republic under what came to be called Europe Agreements, the Commission envisaged such a relationship with 'those countries giving practical evidence of their commitment to the rule of law, respect for human rights, the establishment of multi-party systems, free and fair elections and economic liberalisation with a view to introducing market economies' (Commission, 1990b). The Agreements accordingly commit the parties to 'strengthening the political and economic freedoms which constitute the very basis of this association' and express the readiness of the Community 'to contribute to the strengthening of this new democratic order', specifying the same elements as the Commission had done, as well as supporting the creation of free market economies. The Agreements aim, in addition, to provide a framework for the associates' 'gradual integration into the Community' and to facilitate their 'full integration into the community of democratic nations' (*Official Journal*, 1992).

Thus the aims of market economy and of European and international integration were stated in very general terms, whereas the elements of democracy were variously specified, to include the rule of law, human rights, pluralism, a multi-party system, and free and fair elections. The fundamental principles of representative government, that the elected representatives should enact legislation and control the executive, which must be accountable either to them or to the citizens direct, were not mentioned. It seems to have been taken too much for granted that, given elections and parties, the civil society would become effective in controlling the state. But the danger that this may not occur has been pointed out in, for example, Poland, where the government has been 'operating democratically' while 'pluralist structures in politics and economics are slow in forming' (Wesolowski, 1992, p. 131). Community policies may have taken too little account of this deficiency, which could frustrate its other aims.

These aims are not just altruistic. Their fulfilment will provide the Community with much better neighbours. Security was obviously enhanced when the changes of regime extracted the Community's immediate neighbours from Soviet domination and the Warsaw Pact. But once that had been accomplished, security came to depend on peaceful behaviour on the part of the new regimes in Central and Eastern Europe; and there is evidence that pluralist democracies seldom if ever go to war with each other (see Herring, 1994 in this volume). Security must, therefore, be defined in broader terms than in the past, 'to include the stability and democratisation' of Central and Eastern Europe (Wallace, 1992a, p. 429). The Community's prosperity will likewise benefit from pluralism in the East. It has been noted that the Community's exports to Sweden have been on a par with its exports to the whole area of the CMEA, with fifty times the population; and a significant part of this discrepancy can be attributed to the fact that Sweden has throughout been a market economy, which made it both more prosperous and more open to trade. Before the depression of the 1930s, 17 per cent of German exports went to Eastern Europe and the Soviet Union; in 1989, the proportion was only 4 per cent (Storf, 1990, p. 4). Trade could expand enormously with successful market economies.

Security can be more solidly guaranteed by the integration of Central and East Europeans in the European and international system of democracies. Nationalist conflicts among or within these states are dangerous for those in the West; and integration can channel the peoples' energies in more constructive directions. But the Community will also benefit from the wider participation in the fostering and management of interdependence, not only because it will bring closer trade relations, but also because the Eastern economies, as they grow and become more active in the international arena, could have a destabilising effect unless they take full part in the European and international organisations that manage the international economy. The eventual membership of Eastern countries in the Community is the firmest guarantee of such cooperation, provided that the Community is not weakened by such enlargement; the means by which any such weakening can be avoided are considered later.

Relations between market economy, pluralist democracy and international integration

It is important to evaluate the relationship between market economy and pluralist democracy. The Community and Western policies in support of market economy in Central and Eastern Europe are much stronger than its policies that aim to help democracy directly, and we need to know how much the former can contribute to the latter. Conversely, we should consider how far market economy deserves support even if it is accompanied by authoritarian government.

There is no example of a constitutional democracy without a market economy. The market economy is such a major element in the civil society that a civil society without it will scarcely be strong enough to control the state. The market economy is therefore a necessary aim, not only because it offers more scope for trade and for prosperity among the trading partners, but also because it is an essential basis for the form of government that is most favourable to security. But the transition to market economy is far from being without risk. If the economy in transition fails to deliver the goods to improve welfare, it can undermine a fragile new constitutional democracy. The authoritarian government that ensues may be better able to push through the economic transition. But experience suggests that it is more likely to threaten security. This risk may be thought worth taking, and the market economy of an authoritarian state therefore worth supporting, if the market economy is likely to lead eventually to constitutional democracy. Is the market economy not only a condition of such democracy, but also a force that promotes it?

There is reason to suppose that market economy does conduce to democracy, even if the effect may take quite a time. The example of Southern Europe, as well as of some newly industrialising countries, shows that the growth of a middle class brings pressures to accompany the economic autonomy that they enjoy in the market economy with the political and ideological autonomy of pluralist democracy (see Pridham, 1991b, p. 24; Segal, 1991, p. 42). The risk that an authoritarian regime with a thriving market economy may have too great a capacity to destabilise the international system meanwhile may be thought worth taking, particularly as the international linkages inherent in the market economy will give such a regime a motive for keeping any disruptive proclivities within bounds.

A successful market economy without a tendency towards international integration is, indeed, hard to conceive given the wide market and international interdependence required for success with new technologies.

The autarkic economy no longer works; and the world is so interdependent that the transformation process too 'needs a strong international context' (Gabrisch, 1992, p. 247). Nor will democracy be effective if it lacks the means to deal with the many forces that cross frontiers, in the fields of economy, ecology and security. It was pointed out that democracy in Poland would be 'extremely fragile' without 'organic association,' through economic relations, of Poland with the uniting Europe (Perczynski, 1990, p. 25). Nor, it may be added, are the economic links in themselves sufficient, unless they are accompanied by political association strong enough to manage the problems of ecology and security as well as of the economy.

Policies to promote market economy, pluralist democracy and international integration are, then, mutually reinforcing and are considered in turn below. The policies to support the transformation to market economy are analysed first, in the three components of macro-economic stabilisation, the institutions of the market economy and the restructuring to create a competitive market economy.

Macro-economic stabilisation: the policies and the problems

The starting-point for Western policies to help the economic transition is that a competitive market economy will require sound monetary and fiscal policies; and along with this go liberalisation of prices, without which inflation will remain suppressed in the economy, and of international monetary and trade relations, without which the economy will remain isolated and distorted. The Community and the G-24, including the IMF, have helped the Central and East Europeans to devise and implement stabilisation programmes to carry through this aspect of the transition. Central European countries, Bulgaria and Romania have been supported to the tune of $1 billion or so each in launching such programmes. Some $16 billion, or half, of Poland's debt to official lenders have been written off, on condition that Poland respects the stabilisation programme which it agreed with the IMF on receiving its loan. The IMF has, indeed, been given the leading role in negotiating loans for stabilisation and convertibility programmes, as the institution with the greatest experience in such matters.

The conditions for the loans have been stabilisation programmes that the IMF deems adequate to control inflation and to lead towards convertibility. In addition to control of the money supply, reduction of budget deficits and moves towards a stable and liberal exchange rate regime, there has been enough price liberalisation to ensure progress towards the market economy, and a programme for privatisation and demonopolisation so that competition can begin to work against inflation. These measures cause deflation. How suddenly and how much has become a matter of controversy.

When East Germany became the five new *Länder* of the Federal Republic, stabilisation, liberalisation and the institutions of the market economy were introduced in one very big bang. But this was possible only through incorporating the new *Länder* in a strong state which already had all the institutions of a successful market economy and of welfare provision that could cope with the unemployment caused by a halving of the region's industrial production. Even such a state clearly has difficulty in dealing with the consequent economic and political stress.

Poland and Yugoslavia engendered hyperinflation, which can be stopped only by a powerful stabilisation programme. As far as the control of money and of budget deficits is concerned, a big bang is necessary if the hyperinflation is not to continue. But full adoption of the institutions of a market economy is necessarily a more gradual process. For the Hungarians, Czechs and Slovaks, the process of stabilisation itself could be less abrupt, because inflation was less acute. But suppressed inflation existed, so stabilisation programmes had to be agreed with the IMF. It has been justly observed that, whether a big bang or a stepwise stabilisation is adopted, all these countries need a 'critical mass' of reforms, if the process of transformation is to get under way (Rosati, 1992, p. 5); and such a critical mass has to include enough price liberalisation and deflation to ensure an approach to stability over the short term, a programme for privatisation and demonopolisation to reinforce the stability and inject some dynamism over the medium term, and a start to the restructuring that is the long-term requirement for a competitive market economy.

The process is, however, highly problematic. In an economy still dominated by monopolies, firms may respond to price freedom by continuously raising prices rather than production, so that deflation cuts output without stopping inflation. The consequent pain for employees and consumers undermines support for the transformation to market economy and democracy, unless the emergence of a dynamic economy within a reasonable time is expected.

The pain caused by the demand shock of stabilisation, together with the collapse of trade among the former CMEA countries, has been very sharp. The fall of GDP in 1990 and 1991 was severe: Hungary, with a decline of 11 per cent, was the least hard hit; Bulgaria and Yugoslavia suffered reductions by as much as a third, with the others at various points between (Gabrisch, 1992, p. 230). Industrial production in Central and Eastern Europe fell by a quarter (Portes, 1992b, p. 18). Nothing like this has been seen in Europe since the slump of 1929–32 and the Second World War; and it is raising the question of support for the transformation in an acute form.

The Community and the G-24 have provided humanitarian aid of food and medical supplies where there has been a need; but beyond that, little help has been given to alleviate the rapid erosion of welfare. Wage-earners and low-income groups have been hurt the most, leading to a 'crisis of disillusion', especially in Poland and Romania and this opens up the danger of entrenching a cleavage, since the gainers are property-owners, entrepreneurs and often the former nomenclature who have the means to organise satisfactory positions for themselves (Rosati, 1992, pp. 13–15, citation from p. 14). More immediately, the patience of the citizens will run out unless the need for the political and social changes involved in the transformation continues to be accepted (Perczynski, 1990, p. 23). The remedy must lie in enough support for the welfare of those who are hard hit and in giving people cause to expect that the economy will become sufficiently dynamic before too long.

The hard evidence of dynamic elements in the Central and East European economies lies in the upsurge of small businesses, mostly in the service sector, and the rapid growth of exports to the West from Hungary and Poland and also, though more modestly, from the former Czechoslovakia, but not from most of the other countries. Optimists have been confident that the dynamic sectors are outweighing the dead wood (for example, Sachs, 1991, p. 77). Sceptics have pointed out that, two years after the reforms in Poland began, inflation remained as high as 75 per cent, that it has been stubbornly persistent in other countries, and that the fall in output and incomes has become increasingly acceptable (Richter, 1992, *passim*). Until reforms of institutions and structures have proceeded far enough, they contend, the economy will lack the capacity to adjust in response to the stabilisation programmes that have been adopted so far. Such programmes are necessary but not sufficient, because in the absence of other forms of support the institutional and structural transformation takes too long to produce acceptable results. Privatisation has, probably inevitably, been slow; and 'state desertion', or governments' inability to take decisive action towards the state enterprises, has left the large part of the economy in which they predominate stagnant (Portes, 1992a, pp. 11–12). A sufficiently dynamic impulse would come, rather, from more active policies to stimulate growth and the expanding economy they would make possible. The 'IMF model' is not enough, because it 'assumes away the key issues of what mechanism brings about the resumption of investment' (Dornbush, 1990, pp. 12–13). Community policy has to look beyond that model for an answer to the key question: how to promote investment and inject enough dynamism into the economy.

EC policies on market institutions and restructuring

The market economy requires much by way of legislation, financial institutions, regulatory bodies, statistics and public administrative capabilities that have been absent in the Central and East European countries. The Community and the G-24 have, through the PHARE programme, provided advice, training, information and the like to help rectify these deficiencies. Grants for such purposes have amounted to some $3 billion a year for Central and Eastern Europe. The capacity to absorb such aid varies from country to country and it is doubtful whether much more could usefully be applied at present for these purposes. A legislative and institutional framework is being established which should become adequate for market economies over the medium term. That is good; but it is not enough (Portes, 1992a, pp. 9–10). The response from economic agents is inadequate.

This brings us to the subject of restructuring to create a competitive and dynamic market economy: a huge task that will take a long time to complete. The conversion of monopolistic state enterprises into competitive private companies is uphill work, given the lack of efficient capital markets, investors and managers. Throughout the economy, indeed, there is a great need of skills applicable to the competitive modern economy; and the allocation of labour as well as capital has to be drastically altered to meet the economy's needs. Community policies that are relevant to this process include trade, private investment, aid for investment and labour movement.

The growth of exports to the West is the most effective means to expand the competitive parts of the Eastern economies, while their imports from the West may be the quickest way to insert competition into the sectors dominated by state monopolies. Trade in both directions is the royal road to integration in the international economy. When the changes of regime began in 1989, the Community and the G-24 moved quickly to liberalise quotas and grant tariff advantages through the Generalised System of Preferences. Combined with the new exchange rates and economic liberalisation on the Eastern side, this lifted exports rapidly from those countries with a readily available capacity to export. Exports from Hungary and Poland to the Western industrialised countries rose by about a half from 1989 to the first half of 1991, from Czechoslovakia by 18 per cent, though from Bulgaria and Romania, where the economies were in very poor shape, the exports fell by half or more (Gabrisch, 1992, p. 231). But the performance of Central Europeans could have been yet more spectacular had the Community and other G-24 countries not retained their protection of 'sensitive' products. For agricultural products, the Community offered only modest quotas. Tight quotas against textiles remained, pending an international agreement in the GATT. Preferential entry on many other products was limited by tariff quotas. In the background, 'safeguard' quotas and anti-dumping duties are still potential deterrents. Even with the Europe Agreements associating Poland, Hungary and the Czech and Slovak Republics with the Community, a degree of protection is retained, particularly for the next few years when the process of restructuring has to acquire a strong momentum. Its remaining protection is a black spot in the Community's policies. Further liberalisation would be very significant for the prospects of economic dynamism and for encouraging what should be one of its crucial elements: private foreign investment.

Private foreign investment is a key to the Eastern countries' success. It is the most effective way to transfer technology, management ability, skills and capital, as well as to open up access to export markets; and it is the clearest evidence of confidence in the prospects for the economy. Open access to the Community's market encourages such investment; and here the Europe Agreements, with the prospect of fairly complete free entry into the Community for industrial products within five years, should be a considerable help. These agreements also provide an encouraging environment as regards investment protection and freedom of capital movements. But for all that, private foreign investment still does not flow in in any decisive quantity. Public investment, reflecting the overriding public interest in a successful transformation, may be necessary to prepare the way.

There is need for massive investments in infrastructure such as transport and telecommunications, which would both stimulate the economy and provide facilities required by private investors; and the same goes for investment in cleaning up the environment, which is closely linked with modernisation of the presently polluting industrial equipment (Hughes, 1990). There is also a need to fund financial restructuring, with over half the bank loans in some countries non-performing – a major obstruction to a healthy capital market (*The Financial Times*, 1990). The Community and the G-24 do provide some public funds for investment in the East. But the EBRD is mainly to support private investment rather than for path-breaking public investment; and the World Bank, European Investment Bank and ECSC loans are useful but far from sufficient. The PHARE programme does too little for public investment. The same can be said, more forcefully, about the Community's readiness to accept workers from the Central and East European countries.

Despite the good start that the Community and G-24 made with trade liberalisation, then, and with the provision of funds for technical assistance and for stabilisation programmes, it appears that the policy-makers have not done enough to ensure that the transition to a dynamic and competitive market economy will get under way before the people lose patience and reject the process of economic and political transformation. There are growing doubts that this process will be maintained, against the temptation to revert to authoritarian, and probably nationalist, government or to degenerate into unstable democracy and an enduring economic mess.

A faster and more radical removal of protection is therefore indicated; and there are calls for an aid programme of a scope that could be compared with Marshall Aid (*The Financial Times*, 1989; Mortimer, 1990; Richter, 1992; Weidenfeld and Huterer, 1992). This would help to support welfare until the people gain enough confidence in the prospects for a dynamic economy; and it would support investment in order to stimulate the necessary dynamism. The Alexis de Tocqueville Institution has recently suggested an annual budget of $50 billion a year for Russia alone (*The Financial Times*, 1992a). It may well be that a similar budget could usefully be absorbed in Central Europe and would do much to ensure a successful transformation; and while the absorption capacity in South-East Europe is at present less, such a perspective might make a critical difference in that region too.

The feasibility of such suppositions will be considered later. Meanwhile, a need for greater coordination of the Western aid effort has been asserted (Portes, 1992a, pp. 15–16); and a special agency such as that which administered Marshall Aid, with a staff including businessmen, has also been proposed (*The Financial Times*, 1992a). All such proposals assume that the IMF, while well equipped for its responsibilities for stabilisation programmes, is not suited to a leading role with respect to the transformation process as a whole.

Along with the calls for more aid come proposals for a more active policy to encourage restructuring and investment. The economic dynamism in France, Germany and Japan, we are reminded, did not spring from the more *laissez-faire* version of liberalism that was the mode in a number of countries in the 1980s. The kind of industrial policy that is advocated has nothing to do with crude statist interventionism. It is, on the contrary, envisaged as supporting private investment, emphasising exports and penetration into foreign markets (Bhaduri, 1992, p. 29). The advice from the Japanese Ministry for International Trade and Industry (MITI) has been to concentrate official assistance on key sectors, such as energy in the case of Russia (*The Financial Times*, 1992b). It has been suggested that industrial regeneration should be an aim not only of financial restructuring, privatisation and commercialisation of state enterprises, deconcentration, exchange rate and tariff policies, but also of other forms of industrial policy (Portes, 1992a, p. 12).

All these ideas are stimulated by growing unease about the state of the Eastern economies and the prospects for them if Western policies remain limited to their existing scope. There is also some unease about economists in general as well as about Eastern economies, on the grounds that they are not qualified to tackle the intellectual problem of economic transformation since this depends not only on economic but also on social and political factors (Etzioni, 1992, p. 41). Whatever the merits of that criticism, it is certain that attention needs to be paid to the building up of civil society and constitutional democracy.

EC policies regarding civil society and constitutional democracy

The transformation in Central and Eastern Europe will not succeed unless these countries establish the institutions and skills required for effective constitutional democracy and civil society; parliament, parties, judiciary, public administration, media and educational, scientific, cultural and religious bodies. But too little thought has been given to the question of how the West can contribute to this. The attention paid to the economic transformation has been impressive in comparison.

The Community has imposed sanctions against states responsible for flagrant abuses of human rights. Negotiations for a trade and cooperation agreement were suspended for nearly a year following the former Bulgarian regime's abuse of the rights of the Turkish minority in 1989. Similar negotiations and PHARE technical assistance were likewise suspended after the violent repression in Romania in June 1990. The Soviet action against the Baltic republics was followed by suspension of the Community's aid programme and of meetings of the joint committee that oversees the trade and cooperation agreement. Trade and aid sanctions were imposed on Yugoslavia as a result of the violence against the newly independent former Yugoslav states. But these are disincentives for outrageous behaviour. Help for the strengthening of constitutional democracy and civil society is more important.

The Europe Agreements may be regarded as a reward for progress in establishing democracy. They provide favours for trade and, implicitly, for aid, although the assistance for associates is part of the more general

PHARE programme; and they establish a framework of institutions, cooperation and to some extent of law, which should be some help to the consolidation of democracy. But the PHARE programme itself, and hence the main potential channel for helping democratisation in the associates as well as in the other Eastern countries, has done little to help the process, except indirectly through the assistance for economic transformation. The PHARE programmes for Hungary and Poland, to take two examples, do mention civil society, aiming to involve 'intermediate non-state bodies, associations and organisations', such as trade unions, employers' associations, professional associations, consumer bodies and environmental non-governmental organisations, in the development of civil society and to help them to contribute to shaping policy proposals; the development of local government is also placed under the heading of civil society (Commission, 1990c). But the resources allocated for this are very small; and the same can be said of the support for such things as the training of parliamentary staff under the British Know-How Fund. Much more is required.

Effective political parties are a basic need for constitutional democracy. Most of the more important ones belong to transnational party organisations. Through these can be channelled organisational and technical support, political training, financial and other material support (Kohler, 1982). The major German parties have foundations funded with public money, which have done a great deal in such ways to help parties in emergent democracies (Pinto-Duschinsky, 1991); and this is in line with that aspect of German public policy which made the Federal Republic 'perhaps the only West European state with a systematic strategy' for promoting liberal democracy in Southern Europe (Pridham, 1991c, p. 238). With respect to Central and Eastern Europe, the Community should follow the German example. Competent interest groups are another feature of civil society, and here again the Community can, and to a small extent does, help with various forms of support. This can both promote 'decentralised activities in a society' (Sidjnaksi, 1991a, p. 200) and also provide an element in the unofficial texture of integration.

There have been proposals for advice, technical help, training and education for building up the institutions and skills over a wide range of the fields of constitutional democracy and civil society (Weidenfeld and Huterer, 1992, p. 330). So far, the Community has relied largely on its demonstration effect in these fields. But this may not be enough especially at a time when it is hardly demonstrating itself in the best possible light.

EC policies and Eastern countries' integration

The third main aim of the Community policy towards Central and Eastern Europe is the integration of these countries in the European and international systems, thus favouring prosperity and democracy as well as security, including the damping down of nationalist conflicts. The policies of trade and aid tend in this direction, even if they are not sufficient to ensure dynamism in the Eastern economies. Politically, the Community has established formal relations through the trade and cooperation agreements and, more importantly, the Europe Agreements. The latter offer something more on the economic side, though still not enough; but they also begin to introduce the rule of Community law into the relationship, for example with respect to the competition policy which the associates have undertaken to apply; and they establish institutions of cooperation, including Association Councils, for ministers and Commissioners, Asssociation Committees for high officials and Parliamentary Association Committees. These institutions are not only to supervise the economic aspects of the Agreements but also to engage in 'political dialogue' concerning both domestic and external matters: domestically, the dialogue is to 'support the political and economic changes under way'; externally, to contribute to the establishment of 'lasting links of solidarity and new forms of cooperation', and to lead to a convergence of positions on international and security issues. The most important political aspect of the Europe Agreements is, however, the perspective they offer of future membership of the Community.

The Community at first resisted the idea of linking the Agreements with future membership, which was 'not among the objectives' of the agreements when the Community originally proposed them (Commission, 1990b). But Hungary, Poland and Czechoslovakia pressed hard for an explicit link; and the EC Council eventually agreed to a statement in the preambles of the Agreements, 'recognising the fact' that the associate's ultimate objective is to accede to the Community, and that this association, in the view of the parties, will help (the associate) to achieve this objective' (*Official Journal*, 1992). The European Council of heads of EC governments decided in December 1992 that it would, at its meeting in June 1993, sets out a path towards membership for the Central and East-European countries (Commission, 1992). Membership of the Community, when it becomes possible, is indeed the best way to underpin democracy. The Europe Agreements already begin the process of 'close and progressive interweaving of national economies and regular and routine political relations as well as a variety of transnational links' (Pridham, 1991b, p. 14). But the most active elements in the emergent market economies, the business and middle classes, look beyond that to membership, which they see as guaranteeing business freedoms and the protection of private property, as well as establishing links that enhance prosperity (Whitehead, 1991, p. 52). This ensures the support of these people for democracy, which they know to be a condition of membership.

There are practical reasons why member states must be constitutional democracies. They must respect the rule of law, because they have to accept the authority of the Court of Justice in matters of Community law and to cooperate effectively in the application of that law, as most cases under it are tried in member states' courts. These states must also apply the principles of representative government, because the ministers they send to the Council must be democratically appointed and controlled and their Members of the European Parliament must be properly elected. The governmental aspect of representative government also requires that they have competent public administrations, to which much of the execution of Community policy is delegated. The Maastricht Treaty states that the member states' 'systems of government are founded on the principles of democracy' (art. F). But this is, without that treaty, already implicit in the Community's constitution.

Membership is the end of a road of integrating steps: from trade and cooperation agreements to association, and from association towards accession. Between such formal staging posts, the relationship may be strengthened through cuts in protection and increases in aid and private investment; and the Commissioner for External Relations, Frans Andriessen, suggested a form of affiliated membership would allow, for certain purposes, Central and East European ministers to sit in the Council and parliamentarians in the European Parliament (*Agence Europe*, 1991b).

Some European countries may never become members of the Community and for several it may take a long time. Meanwhile, their integration into the European system can be effected in wider organisations, such as the CSCE, the Council of Europe and the North Atlantic Association Council; and the same goes for wider international integration through organisations such as the IMF, the World Bank and the OECD. More locally, regional organisations for parts of Europe can promote economic cooperation and discourage nationalist conflicts – especially desirable in, for example, the Balkans, but also useful elsewhere (Skak, 1991, pp. 65–76). Particular regional projects could include a free trade area among Central European countries and a payments system for the CIS (Portes, 1992a, p. 14; 1992b, p. 21).

The Community can further its aims in Central and Eastern Europe by working to develop such multilateral relationships as well as its bilateral links with these countries. In this, as in other aspects of its policy towards them, it has to take account of the differences among them. Only a rough indication of such differentiation can be given here, with some suggestions as to the principal points of emphasis in the policies towards the major regions of Central and Eastern Europe.

Central Europe: democratisation through incorporation and through convergence

The concepts of democratisation through incorporation and democratisation through convergence (Whitehead, 1991, pp. 48–9) may both be applicable to the relationship between the Community and Central European countries.

The former East Germany was accepted into the Community through incorporation in an existing member state, the Federal Republic. This was done before East Germany had attained 'a high standard of democratic practice' (Whitehead, 1991, p. 49), or indeed any standard at all; and this, together with economic and psychological divergences, and the burden on

West Germans of aid transfers amounting to 3 per cent of their GDP, has caused much stress. But German democracy is expected to stand the strain.

The Community responded very positively to the opportunity of incorporation. President Delors and the Commission, immediately the Wall came down, expressed their welcome for East Germany into the Community, whether as part of the Federal Republic or as a separate member state (*Agence Europe*, 1989). The vast amount of legislation required for incorporation into the Community was enacted in a short time; and some support was provided from the Community's structural funds. The arrival of the five new *Länder* also had a powerful impact on the Community itself. The French government's desire to anchor the larger Germany yet more firmly in the Community added impetus to the drive for agreement on economic and monetary union, to which the German government, also wishing a secure anchorage within the Community, responded with the demand for political union, that is to say power for the European Parliament and a common foreign and security policy. The result was the Maastricht Treaty, for which difficulties were caused partly by the effect on the European economy of another repercussion of German unification: the deflationary effect of the high interest rates imposed by the Bundesbank in order to counter the unification's inflationary effects.

The enlargement of a 'democratic community of sovereign states' has been said to lead to democratisation-through-convergence (Whitehead, 1991, p. 49). This process may, perhaps, start before accession, when the Community's influence on democratisation is being felt during a previous relationship, such as association. Accession itself may bring with it elements of incorporation, depending on how much sovereignty the member states retain and how much they share in the Community's institutions.

The principles of the rule of law and representative government are, as we saw, obligatory for members of the Community. The Community has less ability than a state has to intervene in order to enforce these principles, because it does not have an armed force with which to do so. But it could employ sanctions, ranging from the loss of financial benefits, through the reversal of trade liberalisation, up to suspension or even expulsion. Such measures are not foreseen by the treaties. But nor was the right to secede, and Greenland's secession was accepted. Departure by a member state from the principles of constitutional democracy would present the Community with such a crisis that it would certainly devise new measures in response. With the degree of interdependence attained among the member states, one which was excluded from the existing integration with all the others would suffer severe disruption: enough, perhaps, to cause those who would wish to depart from democracy to pause. It may be questionable whether the threat of the use of armed force, which pluralist democracies are anyway reluctant to employ, would have greater influence than the probability of economic and political isolation. The 'convergence of international and domestic political processes' (Hanrieder, 1978, p. 1280) has reached a point in the Community where the concept of incorporation may be as relevant as that of convergence, once a candidate for membership has reached, as East Germany had not, a standard of democracy that makes its membership justifiable.

The element of incorporation will become the greater, the farther the Community moves towards federal institutions and powers. There are strong arguments for contending that the Community will have to become 'deeper', or more federal, as it widens to include new members (Pinder, 1992b). Unanimity among the increasing number and diversity of member states will be ever harder to achieve, so majority voting will be a growing necessity. With majority voting, which removes the blocking power from member states' governments and parliaments, the case for the European Parliament to have equal power with the Council is strengthened. It becomes less and less practicable to conceive the Council as a many-headed executive, and more necessary to give that role clearly to the Commission. Accession of each new member state has to be approved by all the existing member states and the European Parliament; and accession is not likely to be accepted until all are satisfied that the Community is at the same time being strengthened enough to counteract the centrifugal dangers.

Strengthening of the Community applies to both its institutions and its powers. The principal remaining reforms to the institutions would be the general use of majority voting in the Council, codecision of the European Parliament with the Council and fuller executive competences for the Commission, leading to a two-house legislature and a government responsible to the Parliament, that is to say adding, for the Community's affairs, the principle of representative government to that of the rule of law. The Community already having federal powers over internal and external trade, its economic powers would be completed by realisation of the economic and monetary union set out in the Maastricht Treaty. A widening membership would point towards further development of the common foreign and security policy. With enlargement to as many as 25–30 member states or more, it seems likely that integration of armed forces would be required if the Community's coherence is to be retained. It would then become a federal state; and new member states would certainly be fully incorporated, in so far as armed force can make this more sure.

As well as taking steps to strengthen itself *pari passu* with enlargement, the Community will probably wish to accept new members in successive waves at intervals of five years or more, in order to enable each wave of them to become socialised in the Community's ways of doing things before the next wave comes, and thus to avoid overwhelming the Community with too many members that are not yet adapted to its nature at any one time. After the members of the European Free Trade Association (EFTA) that are likely to enter in the mid-1990s, and will present few problems save, in some cases, tension between their tradition of neutrality and the common foreign and security policy, the Central Europeans that already have Europe Agreements are likely to follow, provided that their democracies and market economies are in sufficiently good shape. The next wave could include other Central Europeans and, perhaps, those countries of South-East Europe that have made the most effective transformation. Any other Central or South-East Europeans could follow them; and consideration would have to be given to European members of the CIS that may apply to join. For Central Europeans, membership within a decade may be possible. For most of South-East Europe, a longer time-scale has to be envisaged. For these countries and for the CIS, the Community's policy to help democratisation cannot rely on the influence of a perspective of membership in the medium term.

Eastern Europe: nationalism against the democratisation effect

The development of an effective civil society faces greater difficulties in most countries of South-East Europe than in Central Europe; and if the values of the civil society tend to be more nationalist than liberal throughout Central and Eastern Europe (Heltai and Rau, 1991, p. 141), this is more pronounced in the South-East. The consequences are painfully apparent in former Yugoslavia.

Yugoslavia was among the most advanced of the Central and East European countries with respect to the market economy and civil society. The Community responded to its economic reforms, as well as to its refusal to remain aligned with the Soviet Union, by negotiating a trade agreement in 1970, a trade and cooperation agreement in 1980 and granting the benefits of the Generalised System of Preferences in 1974. By the 1980s, Yugoslavia had most of the advantages that the others acquired through the liberalisation associated with the PHARE programme ten years later. To varying degrees, however, the nations of which Yugoslavia was composed adhered to the belief that 'the nation is . . . the fundamental ethical category' which overrules private rights, and demonstrated the consequential principle that 'in asserting its historic rights, a nation rejects the rights of other nations living in the same territory' (Heltai and Rau, 1991, pp. 134, 137). This is the converse of the principle maintained by the Community within its field of competence and by its member states, that all are equal before the law. We saw that the Community was firm in reacting against contraventions of this principle when it applied sanctions to Bulgaria, Romania and the Soviet Union. But the Community's response to the disregard of rights and then the escalating violence in Yugoslavia was slow and inadequate, meriting the criticism of its 'reluctance either to define a policy towards Yugoslavia or to use the Community's very considerable economic leverage until fighting had broken out' (Wallace, 1992b, p. 51).

One reason why the Community was so dilatory was the unanimity procedure that applies to its cooperation in foreign policy. Differences between member states, which have been pronounced in this matter, prolong indecision for longer than they would if there were majority voting and a source of policy and contingency planning independent of the several member governments. The foreign policy cooperation, moreover, even in the stronger form foreseen by the Maastricht Treaty, is separate from the formation of external economic policy which is embedded in the

Community's normal institutions, with majority voting and full competences for the Commission. To apply an effective policy against violations of individual and minority rights, the Community would need in cases such as this a strong policy-planning capacity located in the Commission, where the use of its powerful external economic instruments is planned; and it will need to develop a defence capacity alongside that, beyond the tentative measures indicated in the Maastricht Treaty. Meanwhile, the proper use of its economic instruments for the ends of foreign policy would enable it to make a better contribution to the promotion of democratic values in South-East Europe. Beyond resisting unacceptable behaviour, constructive policies that the Community could pursue in countering nationalism and encouraging democracy could include the establishment of an organisation for regional cooperation based on a very substantial aid programme. Meanwhile, Europe Agreements are being negotiated with Bulgaria and Romania, which will affirm their commitments to the rule of law and human rights. If the Community is to contribute to the containment of nationalist conflicts and the development of democracy, its policy in support of rights, the rule of law and civil society as well as representative government needs to be clear and strong.

Nationalism is also a critical problem in the former Soviet Union. Instability in that region is a grave danger for the rest of Europe. The Community has a powerful interest in democratisation and the market economy in Russia and its neighbours, which would justify a massive programme of aid and an agreement along the lines of the Europe Agreements, though without the perspective of membership. Russia being too big to join the Community without unbalancing it, the suitable response to a successful Russian transformation would be a partnership along the lines of that between the Community and the Unites States. It would also be in the Community's interest to assist the creation of a satisfactory regional relationship between Russia and other republics of the CIS, making for peaceful relations among them and offering an alternative to unrealistic expectations of accession to the Community.

Democracy and the federal process: an *idée force*

After their good start in 1989–90, the Community and the West have been disappointingly inadequate in their support for democratisation in Central and Eastern Europe. They have had no clear idea of how to assist the consolidation of pluralist democracy and they have been too protectionist and too ungenerous with their aid to stimulate the necessary dynamism in the new market economies. Is it unrealistic to consider whether they might do more?

The example of Marshall Aid is often cited, when the Americans were generous enough in their interpretation of self-interest to provide 1.3 per cent of their GDP for four years to assist the regeneration of Western Europe. The West Germans have been transferring some 3 per cent of their GDP to the five new *Länder* in the East; if the West as a whole were to make an equivalent effort, it could supply three aid programmes of $50 billion each for Central Europe, South-East Europe and the CIS. The Americans were seized by the idea that they had to defend democracy in Western Europe against undermining by Soviet Communism and the Germans were inspired by the idea of uniting themselves in a free political system. Is there any idea that could evoke equivalent inspiration in the Community or the West as a whole?

Western Europe was stirred by the peaceful changes of regime and the prospect of democracy in the East. But the difficulties of the transformation have caused some disillusion in both East and West. People need a clearer idea of the future of democracy if they are to have the confidence to overcome the difficulties and do what is needed to see the transformation through. This future cannot be confined to democracy within the existing European states, for they will not severally be able to deal with the increasingly predominant problems of interdependence. With a European as well as state democracies, however, these problems can be managed. The idea which might stir Europeans to act on a more generous scale, then, is that of the development of democracy both within the newly democratic states of Central and Eastern Europe and at the European level where many of the problems of interdependence can be mastered. In this perspective, aid for Central and Eastern Europe is aid for a part of our European body politic, hence for constructing a framework that should assure our own security and prosperity as well as theirs. Properly grasped, the idea of this federal process of developing democracy both through the transformation in Central and Eastern Europe and through stengthening the democratic elements in the Community might evoke the energies required to accomplish both of these complementary projects.

Note

1. Literature on the relationship between the Community and the new democracies of Central and Eastern Europe includes Bonvicini *et al.*, 1991; Pelkmans and Murphy, 1991, Pinder, 1991b; Portes, 1990, 1992a, 1992b; Senior Nello, 1991; Sidjanski, 1991b; Skak, 1991; Weidenfeld and Huterer, 1992.

References

Agence Europe, 1989, 15 November.

Agence Europe, 1991a, 19 April

Agence Europe, 1991b, 10/11 June.

Bhaduri, Amit, 1992, 'Conventional stabilisation and the East European transition' in S. Richter (ed.), *The Transition from Command to Market Economies in East-Central Europe*, The Vienna institute for Comparative Economic Studies Yearbook IV, Westview Press, Boulder, Colo.

Bonvicini, Gianni *et al.*, 1991, *The Community and the Emerging European Democracies: a Joint Policy Report*, Royal Institute of International Affairs, London.

Commission of the EC, 1990a, *Action Plan: coordinated assistance from the Group of 24 to Bulgaria, Czechoslovakia, the German Democratic Republic, Romania and Yugoslavia*, SEC (90) 843 final, Brussels, 2 May.

Commission of the EC, 1990b, *Association Agreements with the Countries of Central and Eastern Europe: a general outline*, Communication from the Commission to the Council and Parliament, COM/90/398 final, Brussels, 27 August.

Commission of the EC, 1990c, Directorate General for External Relations, *Indicative Programme for European Community Assistance to Hungary*, 14 December; *Indicative Programme for European Community Assistance to Poland*, 18 December.

Commission of the EC, 1992, *Conclusions of the European Council*, Edinburgh 11/12 1992, Brussels, December.

Dornbush, Rudiger, 1990, *From Stabilisation to Growth*, National Bureau for Economic Research Working Paper No. 3302, New York, cited in Laski, 1992, pp. 46–7.

Etzioni, Amitai, 1992, 'How is Russia bearing up?', *Challenge*, May/June.

The Financial Times, 1989, leading article, 28 December.

The Financial Times, 1990, 18 January.

The Financial Times, 1992a, 'G7 passes the future of Russia to the IMF', 14 July.

The Financial Times, 1992b, 'A Japanese lesson for all', 20 July.

Gabrisch, Hubert, 1992, 'International aspects of the economic transformation in Central and Eastern Europe' in S. Richter (ed.), *The Transition from Command to Market Economies in East-Central Europe*, The Vienna Institute for Comparative Economic Studies, Yearbook IV, Westview Press, Boulder, Colo.

Hanrieder, W., 1978, 'Dissolving international politics: reflections on the nation-state', *American Political Science Review*, December, pp. 1276–87, cited in G. Pridham, 1991a, *Encouraging Democracy*, Leicester University Press, Leicester, p. 10.

Heltai, Peter Andras and Rau, Zbigniew, 1991, 'From nationalism to civil society and tolerance, in Z. Rau (ed.), *The Reemergence of Civil Society*, Westview Press, Boulder, Colo.

Herring, Eric, forthcoming, 'International security and democratisation in Eastern Europe', in G. Pridham, E. Herring and G. Sanford (eds), *Building Democracy?*, Leicester University Press, Leicester.

Hosking, Geoffrey, 1990, *The Awakening of the Soviet Union*, William Heinemann Ltd., London.

Hughes, Gordon, 1990, *Are the Costs of Cleaning up Eastern Europe Exaggerated? Economic reform and the environment*, Discussion Paper No. 482, Centre for Economic Policy Research, London.

Jordan, A. Grant, 1987, 'Pluralism', in Vernon Bogdanor (ed.) *The Blackwell Encyclopaedia of Political Institutions*, Basil Blackwell, Oxford.

Kaser, Michael, 1967 (1st edn. 1965), *Comecon; Integration problems of the planned economies*, Oxford University Press, London.

Kohler, Beate, 1982, *Political Forces in Spain, Greece and Portugal*, Butterworth, London, cited in G. Pridham, 1991a, *Encouraging Democracy*, Leicester University Press, Leicester, p. 244.

Laski, Kazimierz, 1992, 'Transition from command to market economies in Central and Eastern Europe: first experiences and questions', in S. Richter (ed.), *The Transition from Command to Market Economies in East-Central Europe*, The Vienna Institute of Comparative Economic Studies, Yearbook IV, Westview Press, Boulder, Colo.

Maximova, M.M., 1971, *Osnovnye Problemy Imperialisticheskoy Integratsii*, Mysl, Moscow.

Mortimer, Edward, 1990, 'Where are you, Marshall and Monnet?, *The Financial Times*, 10 July.

Official Journal of European Community, 1992, 92/228EC in *OJ* L114; 92/229, EEC in *OJ* L115; 92/230 EEC in *OJ* L116, 30 April.

Parekh, Bhiku, 1992, 'The cultural particularity of liberal democracy', in David Held (ed.), *Prospects for Democracy*, Special Issue of *Political Studies*, Vol. XL.

Pelkmans, Jacques and Murphy, Anna, 1991, *Catapulted into Leadership: the Community's trade and aid policies vis-à-vis Eastern Europe*, CEPS Working Document No. 56, Centre for European Policy Studies, Brussels.

Perczynski, Maciej, 1990, 'Democratisation of the economy as a precondition for the emergence of a democratic society in Poland', in *Eastern Europe and Democracy: The Case of Poland*, Special Report, Institute for East-West Security Studies, Westview Press, Boulder, Colorado.

Pinder, John, 1991a, *The European Community: the building of a union*, Oxford University Press, Oxford.

Pinder, John, 1991b, *The European Community and Eastern Europe*, Pinter Publishers for Royal Institute of International Affairs, London.

Pinder, John , 1992a, *The European Community after Maastricht: how federal?*, Special Issue, *New European Quarterly Review*, Vol. 5, No. 3, MCB University Press, Bradford.

Pinder, John, 1992b, 'The future of the European Community: a strategy for enlargement', *Government and Opposition*, Vol. 27, No. 4, Autumn.

Pinto-Duschinsky, Michael, 1991, 'Foreign political aid: the German political foundations and their US counterparts', *International Affairs*, Vol. 67, No. 1.

Portes, Richard, 1990, *The European Community and Eastern Europe after 1992*, CEPR Occasional Paper No. 3, Centre for Economic Policy Research, London.

Portes, Richard, 1992a, 'The European Community's response to Eastern Europe' in *The Economic Consequences of the East*, Centre for Economic Policy Research, London.

Portes, Richard, 1992b, 'Is there a better way?', *International Economic Insights*, Vol III, No. 3, May/June.

Pridham, Geoffrey (ed.), 1991a, *Encouraging Democracy: the international context of regime transition in Southern Europe*, Leicester University Press, Leicester.

Pridham, Geoffrey, 1991b, 'International influences and democratic transition: problems of theory and practice in linkage politics' in G. Pridham, (ed.), *Encouraging Democracy*, Leicester University Press, Leicester, pp. 1–30.

Pridham, Geoffrey, 1991c, 'The politics of the European Community, transnational networks and democratic transition in Southern Europe' in G. Pridham (ed.), *Encouraging Democracy*, Leicester University Press, Leicester, pp. 212–45.

Rau, Zbigniew, 1987, 'Some thoughts on civil society in Eastern Europe and the Lockean Contractarian approach', *Political Studies*, Vol XXXV, December.

Rau, Zbigniew (ed.), 1991, *The Reemergence of Civil Society in Eastern Europe and the Soviet Union*, Westview Press, Boulder, Colorado.

Regelsberger, Elfriede, 1988, 'EPC in the 1980s: reaching another plateau?' in Alfred Pijpers, Elfriede Reglsberger, Wolfgang Wessels, in collaboration with Geoffrey Edwards (eds), *European Political Cooperation in the 1980s: a common foreign policy for Western Europe?*, Martinus Nijhoff, Dordrecht.

Richter, Sándor (ed.), 1992, *The Transition from Command to Market Economies in East-Central Europe*, The Vienna Institute for Comparative Economic Studies Yearbook IV, Westview Press, Boulder, Colorado.

Rood, Jan Q. Th., 1991, 'The EC and Eastern Europe over the longer term', in G. Bonvicini *et al.*, *The Community and the Emerging European Democracies*, Royal Institute of International Affairs, London.

Rosati, Dariusz K., 1992, *The Politics of Economic Reform in Central and Eastern Europe*, CEPR Occasional Paper No. 6, Centre for Economic Policy Research, London.

Sachs, Jeffrey, 1991, *The Economist*, 19 January.

Segal, Gerald, 1991, 'International relations and democratic transition', in G. Pridham (ed.), *Encouraging Democracy*, Leicester University Press, Leicester, pp. 31–44.

Senior Nello, Susan, 1991, *The New Europe: changing economic relations between East and West*, Harvester Wheatsheaf, Hemel Hempstead, Hertfordshire.

Shishkov, Y.V., 1972, *Obshchiy Rynok: Nadezhdy i Deistvitelnost*, Mysl, Moscow.

Sidjanski, Dusan, 1991a, 'Transition to democracy and European integration: the role of interest groups in Southern Europe' in G. Pridham (ed.), *Encouraging Democracy*, Leicester University Press, Leicester, pp. 195–211.

Sidjanski, Dusan, 1991b, *Union ou désunion de l'Europe? La Communauté européenne à l'épreuve de la crise yougoslave et des mutations en Europe de l'Est*, Institut universitaire d'études européennes, Geneva, September.

Skak, Mette, 1991, *East Europe, the Soviet Union and Europeanisation: a challenge for the European Community*, Institute of Political Science, Aarhus University.

Stevens, Christopher and Kennan, Jane, (eds), 1992, *Reform in Eastern Europe and the Developing Country Dimension*, Overseas Development Institute, London.

Storf, Otto, 1990, *Business Risks and Opportunities in Eastern Europe and the Soviet Union*, paper for Seventh Annual Conference of the Centre for European Policy Studies, Brussels, 14–16 November.

Wallace, William, 1992a, 'British foreign policy after the Cold War', *International Affairs*, Vol. 68, No. 3.

Wallace, William, 1992b, 'From Twelve to Twenty-Four? The challenges to the EC posed by the revolutions in Eastern Europe' in Colin Crouch and David Marquand (eds), *Towards Greater Europe? A continent without an Iron Curtain*, Special Issue, *The Political Quarterly*, Blackwell Publishers, Oxford.

Weidenfeld, Werner and Huterer, Manfred, 1992, 'Der Westen und die Stabilisierung der Demokratien in Osteuropa', *Europa-Archiv*, Folge 12, 25 June.

Wesolowski, Wlodzimierz, 1992, 'Poland's transition to democracy: how much pluralism?' in Colin Crouch and David Marquand (eds), *Towards Greater Europe? a continent without an Iron Curtain*, Special Issue, *The Political Quarterly*, Blackwell Publishers,Oxford.

Whitehead, Laurence, 1991, 'Democracy by convergence and Southern Europe: a comparative politics perspective' in G. Pridham (ed.), *Encouraging Democracy*, Leicester University Press, Leicester, pp. 45–61.

6

The USSR/CIS and democratisation in Eastern Europe

Margot Light

Introduction

Of all the influences on the domestic events which preceded the transition to democracy in Eastern Europe in 1989, none was more important than the changes which occurred in the USSR after 1985. In the pre-transition phase of democratisation the events which occurred in individual Eastern European countries were primarily, although perhaps not solely, dependent upon the transformation which had occurred in the Soviet Union. In other words, Soviet *perestroika* was a necessary but not a sufficient condition for East European democratisation. Domestic political influences within individual countries clearly played an indispensable role in making the transition possible. Moreover, given the speed with which the Eastern European Communist regimes toppled as transformation spread from country to country, it is not difficult to detect the operation of demonstration effects. *Perestroika* was the first in a sequence of events which set into reverse operation the domino theory so long feared by the West in other regions of the world. But the democratisation of Eastern Europe also required changes in the international political and economic environment and this paper will argue that the USSR brought them about.

Notwithstanding the importance of domestic, transnational and other international influences, however, the crucial variable in the pre-transition phase was undoubtedly the reform process in the Soviet Union and Soviet encouragement of similar reforms in Eastern Europe. Because of the relationship that existed between Eastern European governments and Communist parties on the one hand, and the Soviet government and the Communist Party of the Soviet Union (CPSU) on the other, the Soviet Union exerted a direct influence on events in this phase of democratisation. Although the Soviet leadership no longer insisted that East European governments mirror every Soviet policy after 1956, the limits to East European pluralism had been demonstrated in 1968. The Brezhnev doctrine made explicit Soviet hegemonic control over the pace and type of change in Eastern Europe. To use Rosenau's term, until 1989 the countries of Eastern Europe were penetrated systems (Rosenau, 1966, p. 65).

Once East European democratisation was under way, however, a reverse linkage went into operation. Indeed, it can be argued that the Soviet Union became the penetrated system, at least in terms of indirect influence. At first Mikhail Gorbachev had been a powerful symbol of change to East European dissidents. Now Eastern Europe became the catalyst. The democratisation of Eastern Europe served as an impetus, for example, for further and faster democratic changes within the Soviet Union itself. Moreover, the failure of the Soviet government to prevent the *de facto* defection of East European countries from the Soviet alliance system spurred the secessionist drive of the Baltic republics which, like the countries of Eastern Europe, had only entered the Soviet sphere of influence as a result of the Second World War.[1] It is not surprising, therefore, that Soviet policy in Eastern Europe became one of the focal points for opponents of the *perestroika* project. By then, however, the Soviet government could no longer control the course and speed of events in Eastern Europe. The new East European governments were no longer permeable to Soviet influence since the initial political changes had interrupted the channels of control which the USSR had previously enjoyed. They were thus increasingly impervious to political pressure. On the other hand, coercion was out of the question since the use of force would have discredited Soviet reform and adversely affected relations with the West. In the second phase of East European democratisation, therefore, the Soviet Union did not influence events directly. However, it continued to exert an important indirect influence.

In 1990 and 1991 Eduard Shevardnadze claimed that the Soviet withdrawal from Eastern Europe was the result of rational calculation, a policy that had been actively adopted early in the process of *perestroika* and then acted upon when conditions allowed (Shevardnadze, *Pravda*, 8 February 1990; Shevardnadze, 1991, pp. 112–27; and see Batt, 1991, pp. 23–7 for a discussion about the timing of the decision). In other words, the Soviet Union did not lose Eastern Europe but consciously abandoned it. An analysis of Soviet goals in Eastern Europe from 1945 onwards, however, and of the changes in Soviet attitudes towards its European allies in the 1980s, casts doubt on Shevardnadze's assertion. The Soviet government certainly promoted change in Eastern Europe from 1987 onwards, but it is unlikely that it either envisaged or desired that those changes would lead to the loss of its allies and a diminution of the geopolitical influence that had contributed largely to Soviet superpower status after the Second World War.

It is far more probable that Soviet leaders hoped that East European governments would reform and then, as a result of a rational calculation of national interest, remain economically and politically allied with an equally reformed Soviet Union (Herring, 1992, p. 366). In fact, however, the new foreign policy which the Soviet Union had adopted as a counterpart to domestic reform had opened Eastern Europe to other international influences which were more relevant to democratisation. In the second phase of

East European democratisation, therefore, the Soviet Union exerted an indirect and largely inadvertent influence by changing East-West relations in such a way that the implicit rules of international conduct which had been in existence throughout the Cold War were radically transformed. Thus even after the revolutionary events of 1989, Soviet influence on the democratisation of Eastern Europe remained important.

When the USSR itself disintegrated on 25 December 1991, it seemed doubtful that the amorphous Commonwealth of Independent States (CIS) which replaced it would survive. The new government in Russia was preoccupied with domestic affairs, the urgent need for Western assistance and relations within the CIS. As for the opponents of the new regime, both the Communist old guard and the Russian nationalists were more concerned with the possibility of reinstating the inner empire (the Soviet Union) than with attempts to reconstitute the Soviet zone of influence in Eastern Europe.

Let us expand these arguments by looking first at the direct impact of the Soviet Union on the pre-transition phase of democratisation in Eastern Europe. The next section of this chapter begins by considering previous attempts at democratisation in Eastern Europe in order to examine the historical evidence that change in the Soviet Union was a necessary precondition for the transition to democracy in Eastern Europe. It then turns to the nature of, and reasons for, the transformation in Soviet attitudes towards Eastern Europe in the period between 1985 and 1989.

The focus of the following section is the indirect influence of the Soviet Union on Eastern European democratisation which extended well beyond the pre-transition phase. It considers how the new political thinking in the Soviet Union changed East-West relations and brought an end to the Cold War. The argument here is that the changes that Soviet foreign policy produced in the international environment between 1985 and 1991 made it impossible to return to the *status quo ante*. Thus even if the attempted coup in August 1991 had been successful, for example, and even if the Soviet economy had made a miraculous recovery, the Soviet Union would have been unable to regain its pre-eminent position *vis-à-vis* Eastern Europe.

The pre-transition phase of Eastern European democratisation

Soviet intolerance of previous attempts at Eastern European democratisation has been thoroughly documented and the examples are well known. Indeed, the shift in 1948 from satellisation, that is 'the binding of the region's states to the Soviet Union' at the end of the Second World War, to Sovietisation, or the final 'transformation of the region's domestic political, economic and social structures, institutions, and patterns according to Soviet norms and values' (Gati, 1990, p. 9) was caused precisely because Joseph Stalin was afraid that diversity (which, in the case of Czechoslovakia, might include a continuing coalition government) would loosen the links that tied Eastern Europe to the Soviet Union, open those countries to Western influence and turn them into unreliable allies in the inevitable (to his mind) struggle between socialism and imperialism (Brzezinski, 1967, pp. 41–64).

In one sense, of course, this was a self-fulfilling prophecy, both because the Sovietisation of Eastern Europe was one of the primary causes of that struggle and because the Soviet Union's veto over appointments and over policies deprived the Eastern European Communist leaders of the opportunity of establishing their own domestic legitimacy. In the long run, this made the East European countries unreliable allies. But Stalin's primary concern was Soviet security which seemed under more immediate threat. Given the interest expressed by Czechoslovakia and Poland in participating in the Marshall Plan in 1947, Stalin's suspicion that the Truman Doctrine might be applied to Eastern Europe, his fear that the Western allies intended building up a strong German state in their zones of occupation and the defection of Yugoslavia from the Soviet bloc in 1948, it seemed self-evident to him that security could only be ensured by uniformity within the region under tight Soviet control (Gati, 1990, pp. 9–28). There were important secondary political, economic and ideological advantages that accrued to the Soviet Union from the Sovietisation of Eastern Europe, but what is important for the subject matter of this chapter is that the system that was imposed in 1948 established channels of control which enabled the CPSU to exert a direct influence on future political and economic events, turning Eastern Europe into a totally penetrated system. The Communist parties which governed the countries of Eastern Europe were subject to Moscow's control. The security forces were responsible to the KGB. Economic dependence on the Soviet Union increased and, with the establishment of the Warsaw Treaty Organisation in 1955, East European military forces were directed by the Soviet High Command.

Although Nikita Khrushchev loosened Soviet control over Eastern Europe after Stalin's death in 1953 and implied, in his doctrinal revisions in 1956, that there were different paths to socialism (Khrushchev, 1956, p. 38), the CPSU did not renounce its right to approve the selection of East European leaders and Khrushchev's 'many roads' to socialism soon turned out to be limited to those approved by Moscow. The Soviet response to events in Poland in October 1956 and the invasion of Hungary less than two weeks later gave some indication of the kinds of diversity that would be countenanced. In the case of Poland, the initial Soviet veto over the appointment of Władysław Gomułka as First Secretary was withdrawn when the Soviet Presidium was reassured that Poland would remain a one-party state with firm Communist Party control over domestic and foreign policy (Brzezinski, 1967, pp. 239–68). In Hungary, however, Soviet fear of a multi-party system led to the violent repression of the revolution. The announcement (made after Soviet troops had invaded the country) that Hungary would withdraw from the newly established Warsaw Treaty Organisation (WTO) seemed to confirm that democratisation would undermine the reliability of the Soviet alliance (Gati, 1990, pp. 39–43).

The suppression of the Hungarian revolution was brutal but it did not represent a return to Stalinism within the Soviet bloc. Limited forms of economic and cultural diversity became possible and, in Hungary, for example, after initial repression János Kádá introduced economic reform and a relatively liberal cultural policy without incurring further censure. Within a decade, however, there was further evidence that Moscow would not tolerate East European democratisation.

In August 1968 Soviet troops intervened to curtail Czechoslovakia's attempt to create 'socialism with a human face'. Although the initial drive for change came from within the Czechoslovak Communist Party, Soviet leaders feared that the abolition of censorship and the secret election of party officials would lead, sooner rather than later, to the loss of Communist Party control of Czechoslovakia.[2] By now their fears were shared by other bloc leaders and this time Soviet troops were aided by token forces from four other member states of the Warsaw Pact (Dawisha, 1984). The intervention was rationalised after the event by the enunciation of the Brezhnev Doctrine (Kovalev, in Remington, 1969, pp. 412–16), which explicitly limited the sovereignty of socialist countries. In fact, however, it had been obvious from 1948 onwards that the countries of Eastern Europe did not enjoy full sovereignty. Moreover, although the West protested against Soviet intervention in 1956 and 1968, there seemed to be implicit acceptance that Hungary and Czechoslovakia were in the Soviet sphere of influence.

The suppression of the Prague Spring had severe and long-lasting consequences in Czechoslovakia and Brezhnev took an increasingly hard line against dissidents in the Soviet Union. Within the Soviet bloc, however, he tried to give a greater voice to Eastern Europe. A joint command structure was established in the Warsaw Treaty Organisation in 1969, for example, and a Commission of Foreign Ministers and a Joint Secretariat were added in 1976. Pact meetings increasingly became a forum in which East European members could lobby the Soviet leadership (Holloway and Sharp, 1984, p. 250). East European leaders successfully blocked moves from Moscow to increase economic integration within the Council for Mutual Economic Assistance (CMEA). Moreover, Brezhnev permitted them more leeway in their dealings with the West. East European trade with the West expanded rapidly in the 1970s, for example, and Poland, Romania and Hungary joined GATT (Czechoslovakia was already a member) without incurring Soviet objections. Throughout these years, Romania openly opposed many Soviet policies without provoking an invasion or expulsion from the bloc.

East-West detente provided the context in which the countries of Eastern Europe expanded their independent relations with the West. The Helsinki Final Act in 1975 represented the climax of detente, in that Soviet relations with the West began to deteriorate soon after it was signed. But the Helsinki process, as it became known, continued to have a profound impact on the domestic and foreign policies of the Soviet Union and Eastern Europe. For one thing, the civil rights provisions of the Helsinki Act let to the formation of human rights watchdog groups in the Soviet Union and Eastern Europe which encouraged and supported one another and enjoyed Western support.[3] More importantly, although it was not binding in international law, the provisions of the Act and the biennial conferences which it established, made it far more difficult for the Soviet leadership to use military coercion in its relations with Eastern Europe. Thus although East European Communist parties retained their leading role and the CPSU continued to supervise them, Soviet hegemonic control over Eastern Europe was undermined in the 1970s (Larrabee in Laird and Hoffmann, 1986, pp. 543–6).

The Soviet response to the rise of Solidarity in Poland in 1980 indicated, however, that there were still limits to Soviet tolerance. In many ways Solidarity represented the most alarming challenge that had occurred in the bloc. In the first place, it was a grass roots working-class movement and the possibility that it might be emulated in other socialist countries was extremely alarming (Teague, 1988). Secondly, it was a mass movement supported by the Catholic Church, which had remained a powerful social force in Poland. The response to outside intervention, therefore, would almost certainly have been prolonged fighting. Thirdly, it was doubtful that military intervention could put an end to the strikes that were paralysing the Polish economy (and affecting other East European economies as well). Fourth, the Soviet army was already tied down in Afghanistan and the prospect of a second military involvement could not have been attractive. Furthermore, the unexpectedly harsh Western response to the invasion of Afghanistan must have instilled some doubt about whether the implicit recognition of spheres of influence could still be taken for granted. In the event, martial law was declared in December 1981 and active Soviet intervention was avoided (Sanford, 1986, pp. 94–115).

It could be argued that in any of the above cases, a firm stand on the part of a popular East European leader combined with unambiguous Western support might have led, as in the case of Yugoslavia in 1948, to a different outcome with the possibility of an earlier transition to democracy. But few East European leaders enjoyed Tito's popularity and the Western response was ambivalent. Thus the evidence suggests that a precondition for East European democratisation was the transformation of Soviet-East European relations which, in turn, required radical change within the Soviet Union itself. When Soviet *perestroika* was launched in 1985, however, there was no immediate indication that East European democratisation was a necessary corollary of Soviet reform

Looking back at the period between 1985 and the end of 1989, three distinct periods can be distinguished in Soviet leadership attitudes towards Eastern Europe, ranging from the apparent perpetuation of traditional attitudes in 1985–6, through attempts to reform Soviet-East European relations and encouragement of East European domestic reform in 1987–8, to disavowal of responsibility for events in Eastern Europe in 1989. The reason why nothing seemed to have changed at first was that the new leadership was silent about inter-socialist relations. Gorbachev spoke often and extensively about Soviet reform plans and he urged his East European allies to follow suit. He also began to publicise the 'new political thinking' and its implications for Soviet foreign policy. He launched a series of foreign policy initiatives towards Western Europe, Asia and the United

States. But his initial policy towards Eastern Europe was little different from that of his predecessors. Indeed, it seemed feasible that the Gorbachev leadership had learnt from the history of the Soviet bloc that it would be dangerous to extend *perestroika* to Eastern Europe because domestic reform there would probably be uncontrollable.

The renewal of the Warsaw Treaty for a further twenty years in April 1985 and the adoption of a CMEA programme for scientific and technological cooperation up to the year 2000, together with general exhortations to increase the speed and extent of economic integration seemed to suggest that the new Soviet leadership wanted to strengthen alliance ties (Brown, 1991, p. 65). In fact, however, there were some subtle changes in the Soviet approach to Eastern Europe. Despite Gorbachev's open disapproval of Todor Zhivkov, for example, he remained the leader of the Bulgarian party. Hungary was not prevented from seeking a cooperation agreement with the European Community. Gorbachev's explanation of the Polish crisis was quite reasonable and bore little resemblance to Brezhnev's pronouncements (TASS, 30 June 1986, cited in Teague, 1988, p. 316). Gorbachev began to brief his allies about East-West relations far more frequently than his predecessors had. And even if the political leadership was silent on the question of relations with the countries of Eastern Europe, an active debate had been in progress among academics for some time about the nature of inter-socialist relations and the correct balance between national interests and internationalism (Light, 1988, pp. 305–8). Furthermore, throughout this period, as Dawisha points out (1990, pp. 198–201), Gorbachev was consolidating his power base and surrounding himself with colleagues who would design and support his new policies in Eastern Europe.

In 1987 the Soviet reform programme changed gear. By then it had become clear that economic reconstruction required a degree of political democratisation as well as a less confrontational foreign policy (Light, 1989, pp. 172–4). It was equally obvious that because of the interdependence of the East European and Soviet economies, effective economic reform would be difficult without parallel changes in Eastern Europe. Since they were economically more developed than the Soviet Union, the East European countries did not at first appear to be performing as poorly as the stagnant Soviet economy. None the less, their economic performance had deteriorated in the 1970s and 1980s (Batt, 1991, pp. 3–21). Moreover, the Soviet leadership wanted to move towards charging its East European allies the full world market price for energy. At the same time, a better trade balance was necessary and the Soviet leadership wanted an improvement in the quality and variety of goods it bought from Eastern Europe (Dawisha, 1990, pp. 117–21). As far as the CMEA was concerned, a plan to reform the intra-bloc trading system was adopted in October 1987 but it was inconceivable that it could work unless member states undertook domestic economic reform (Gati, 1990, pp. 128–35).

Just as effective *perestroika* within the Soviet Union required domestic democratisation, East European economic reform had political implications. In any case, political stability in Eastern Europe must have been an important goal to the Soviet leadership, not only because it would facilitate economic reform but also because instability would undoubtedly, as it had in the past, have repercussions on East-West relations. And political stability, it was thought, would be assisted if reformist (but still pro-Soviet) leaders could build up their domestic legitimacy by introducing official accountability (which was the initial aim behind the Soviet policy of *glasnost*), and by democratising their political systems. In fact, in retrospect it seems clear that the Gorbachev leadership misunderstood the nature and sources of political legitimacy and assumed (both at home and abroad) that gratitude for reform and the benefits of a more efficient economy would ensure the election of reformist Communist leaders (similar to Gorbachev in outlook and aims) even if there were free elections. Throughout this period there was talk of the deepening sympathy and understanding between socialist states that *perestroika* was promoting (see, for example, Gorbachev, 1987, Chapter 4) which suggests that there was no thought then that democratisation might threaten the viability of the alliance.

Gorbachev maintained that the international precondition for Soviet reform was the elimination of East-West confrontation and the integration of the Soviet Union into Europe and into the international system. His call for a 'common European home' shared by both the Soviet bloc and the West (Gorbachev, 1987) was one attempt to achieve this.[4] Another means to diminish confrontation was to step up the pace and extent of arms control. The West had been particularly alarmed by the vast increase in Soviet conventional forces in Europe in the 1970s and Gorbachev decided to reduce them unilaterally to demonstrate his commitment to arms control. In his speech to the United Nations in December 1988 he promised that Soviet armed forces would be reduced by 500,000 men, 50,000 of them to be removed from Eastern Europe. He also pledged that 'the Soviet divisions which still remain on the territory of our allies will be reorganised . . . they will become strictly defensive' (Gorbachev, 1988, p. 203).[5] Of course, this was part of Gorbachev's wider international strategy: after the Second World War Eastern Europe had served both as a defence glacis against the West and as a forward springboard for Soviet troops. Thus this gesture was an important token of the improvement in East-West relations. In fact, however, Soviet forces in Eastern Europe had also (some would argue primarily) served to police the region and to provide the Soviet Union with the ability to intervene quickly should the need arise (Jones, 1981). The announcement of the reduction was, therefore, a powerful symbol of the way in which the Soviet alliance was changing.

A decision with equally powerful symbolic resonance had been taken two months before Gorbachev's United Nations speech. At the end of September 1988 there was an unexpected plenary meeting of the CPSU Central Committee (CC) during which Andrei Gromyko finally retired and Gorbachev became the President of the USSR. But the decision that particularly affected Soviet-East European relations was the fusion of the Department for Liaison with Ruling Communist and Workers' Parties (which had responsibility for Soviet relations with socialist states) with the International Department which dealt with the rest of Soviet foreign policy and with relations with non-ruling Communist parties (Rahr, 1988). On the one hand, this reflected the fact that foreign policy decision-making had shifted away from the Party apparatus to the Ministry of Foreign Affairs. But it was also a sign that in future the same rules might pertain to Soviet policy towards socialist states, as those that had always applied to relations with states with different social and economic systems. If one is looking for a particular moment at which the Brezhnev Doctrine ceased to be the basis of inter-socialist relations, this is an appropriate event, although the explicit repudiation only came a year later.

The CC changes were only one aspect of a wide range of political reforms which occurred within the Soviet Union in this period. A number of informal movements were established, some of them overtly political. A new electoral law adopted in December 1988 made multi-candidate elections universal. At the same time, the Soviet constitution was amended to create a new elected legislative body, the Congress of People's Deputies, which would elect a Supreme Soviet which, unlike the previous Supreme Soviet, would have real legislative power. When the Congress held its first session in May 1989, Soviet television broadcast the proceedings.[6] The new Supreme Soviet was charged with approving the new government and, as if to affirm its independence of action, it rejected several nominations made by the Prime Minister (White, 1990, Chapter 2). The most significant political change, the abolition of clause 6 of the constitution which guaranteed to the CPSU the leading role in society, occurred in February 1990, after the East European revolutions and a full year after Hungary had introduced a multi-party system. As Dawisha points out, however, Soviet democratisation influenced events in Eastern Europe by encouraging similar debates there and by making it possible for reformist leaders to introduce their own changes (Dawisha, 1990, pp. 208–10).

Although Gorbachev and his colleagues publicly (and, presumably, privately too) advised their East European allies to follow the Soviet lead in reforming their own economic and political systems and introducing *glasnost*, there is little evidence that they interfered directly in East European domestic affairs during this period. There were enormous variations in the way that the East European leaders reacted. While there was a positive response in Poland and, after a shaky start, in Hungary, in Bulgaria Zhivkov constantly praised *perestroika* and proposed plans for restructuring the Bulgarian economy but very little changed on the ground. There was certainly no *glasnost* and the position of the Turkish minority deteriorated seriously. The leaders of Czechoslovakia were resistant to reform although they did not criticise Soviet policy. Both Erich Honecker and Nicolae Ceauşescu, on the other hand, were openly critical and frank in their rejection of similar policies for East Germany and Romania.

In terms of demonstrating the extent to which political relations within the bloc had changed what is important here is both the variety of responses and the absence of pressure from Moscow, particularly given how important *perestroika* was to Gorbachev and how keen the Soviet leadership was that it should be extended to other socialist countries.

Moscow was no longer using its veto over policies and appointments. In fact, democratic centralism – the system under which a decision taken in Moscow was binding on all members of the bloc – had ceased to be the *modus operandi* of the Soviet alliance and it was by no means clear that socialist internationalism – the term used to define the relations between socialist states – retained any meaning. Whether this demonstrated that Gorbachev had repudiated Soviet interference in East European domestic affairs, or whether it was evidence that East European Communist elites had simply extended the range of the relative policy independence they had long enjoyed, the fact is that there was little Gorbachev could do. For the irony is that it is easier to call up domestic forces of repression or to encourage the revolutionary overthrow of existing authority than to force a measured and controlled programme of change.

The academic debate about inter-socialist relations had continued, particularly at the influential Institute of the Economy of the World Socialist System (IEMSS) in Moscow (Valdez, forthcoming). Regular symposia were held with East European academics which resulted in the publication of articles which were astonishing both in the openness of their criticism of the past and in their proposals for the future structure of relations between the countries of Eastern Europe. It should be stressed, however, they were based on the assumption that what was required was the renovation and reform of the present distorted form of socialism, rather than its abandonment. Although they appeared in books which were published in very small editions of 200-300 (Novopashin, 1986; Novopashin, 1987; Shentov, 1987; Shentov, 1989), Gorbachev's reformist advisers were almost certainly well aware of their contents. In 1988 *Problems of Communism* published an article under the collective authorship of a number of scholars from IEMSS which suggests something of the tenor of the discussions at the symposia and of Soviet expectations for Eastern Europe.[7]

According to the authors of the *Problems of Communism* article, *perestroika* implied 'the delegation of considerable responsibility to the local level, to labor and territorial collectives; the expansion of pluralism in public life; and the democratisation of all institutions, including the vanguard party' (Dashichev, 1988, p. 211). This, they maintained, would make East European political decision-making more efficient and more effective. It would also democratise the foreign policy process and prevent the hegemony of any one socialist country. They prescribed economic and legal reform within individual countries and claimed that the division of labour had already begun to change within CMEA where 'the main imperative . . . is to shift from interstate barter to direct commercial links between enterprises' and to allow 'the unimpeded movement across borders of all factors of production' (Dashichev, 1988, p. 213). With regard to Soviet-East European relations, the Soviet Union had adopted 'a relationship free from dictate, pressure, and interference in . . . the internal affairs [of other states]; and toward strict observance of the principles of equal partnership, independence, and attentive respect for the national interests and the national forms of socialist development of each country' (Dashichev, 1988, p. 210).

Ironically there was rather more direct Soviet interference in the domestic affairs of some East European countries *after* this article was published than there had been in the preceding two years. In the fateful year of 1989, the third period of the pre-transition phase under review here, there were several instances in which the Soviet leadership either committed, or refused to commit, actions and, paradoxically, thereby contributed to the rapid downfall of Communism. It should be stressed, however, that Gorbachev was essentially reacting to events rather than initiating them. After the Polish elections in June 1989, for example, he urged the leader of the Polish United Workers' Party to join a non-Communist government (Dawisha, 1990, p. 155). In August the Soviet government made it abundantly clear that it did not support the unrepentantly orthodox Czech leader, Miloš Jakeš (Gati, 1990, pp. 178–81). While this did not cause the velvet revolution in Czechoslovakia, it weakened the leadership since Civic Union knew it had little reason to fear a repeat of August 1968. When Hungarians began to dismantle the 'Iron Curtain' along the Austro-Hungarian border in May, there was no public protest from Moscow. And when East German refugees were allowed to leave Hungary via Austria for West Germany in September, Moscow remained silent (Ash, 1990, p. 66). In Budapest this may have been interpreted as quite proper restraint from interference in Hungary's domestic affairs. To Honecker, however, Gorbachev appeared to be colluding in Hungary's infringement of the bilateral Hungarian-East German consular agreement and undermining the East German government.

Gorbachev's antipathy for Zhivkov seems to have been quite open and he had warned him publicly in 1987 to speed up reform (Tass, 16 October 1987, cited in Brown, 1991, p. 187). Although Petar Mladenov, Zhivkov's successor, visited Moscow immediately before Zhivkov was forced to resign in November 1989, there is no evidence that Gorbachev engineered his removal. Nor is there any reason to believe that Moscow had a hand in Ceauşescu's violent end in December, despite the numerous rumours during the Romanian uprising that his opponents had requested Soviet aid. Visiting Berlin in October 1989, Gorbachev is said to have urged Honecker to make political concessions and to have rejected the use of Soviet troops to suppress the increasingly massive popular demonstrations (Dawisha, 1990, pp. 95–6). Again, this does not make the Soviet Union directly culpable for Honecker's fall from power. But in the case of both East Germany and Czechoslovakia it can be argued that if Gorbachev had insisted earlier on the appointment of reformist leaders, democratisation might have occurred without the total collapse of Communism. By waiting until the situation had already become unstable and then withdrawing his support from Honecker and Jakeš, he fatally undermined not only them, but reform Communism as well. For Gorbachev certainly *was* responsible for removing the threat of Soviet intervention which had been the prop that had previously made it unnecessary for East European Communist leaders to consolidate their own legitimacy by building up popular support.

There are two further ways in which Gorbachev influenced the future course of events in Eastern Europe. First, by relinquishing Soviet approval of the appointment of the successors to East European leaders after 1985 and, in effect, abolishing the principle of socialist internationalism, he cut off the CPSU's direct channel of supervision of the European socialist states. Eastern Europe ceased to be a penetrated system, at least with regard to the Soviet Union. Second, Moscow's acceptance of the opening of the Berlin Wall on 9 November 1989 presaged not only the final collapse of East Germany's Communist government but also the point at which all the countries of Eastern Europe became more open to influences from the West than to Soviet influence. Ever since Gorbachev had begun calling for a 'common European home', the Berlin Wall had seemed an anachronism. In 1989, when demands for freedom to travel to the West had precipitated Honecker's resignation, opening the Wall seemed to be the only way to alleviate the tension in the GDR and shore up the authority of Egon Krenz, his replacement. But once the Wall was down, it was inevitable that Germany would be reunified. It was also more or less certain that in Eastern Europe the reform of socialism would be replaced by an attempt to establish market democracies.

The international influence of the Soviet Union on East European democratisation

Many of the changes in Soviet attitudes and policies towards Eastern Europe described in the previous section arose from the logic of Gorbachev's broader foreign policy aims which, in turn, were directed towards creating favourable international conditions for his domestic reform programme. But the new Soviet foreign policy changed the whole international political system, as a result of which the constraints that had operated during the Cold War began to disappear and Eastern Europe became open to Western influence and to Western models of democracy. Thus quite apart from the direct effect of Soviet *perestroika* on East European democratisation, the Soviet Union also played a vital indirect role. These indirect effects only really became apparent after the Soviet Union had lost its power and ability to intervene directly in East European affairs. To examine them we need to begin by looking at the connection between domestic reform and foreign policy.

In the same way that democratisation and *glasnost*, the political aspects of Soviet domestic reform, were introduced because of the perceived needs of economic transformation, the origins of Soviet foreign policy reform are also to be found in the economy. The aim of diplomacy, according to Shevardnadze and others, was to create a favourable environment for internal development (see, for example, Shevardnadze, 1987, p. 31). In other words, at the most basic level, a peaceful international climate would allow attention to be concentrated on domestic issues. But the potential economic advantages were even more important. If Soviet military expenditure could be reduced, for example, more of the budget could be used to develop the civilian economy. Moreover, unless sanctions were removed, Soviet foreign trade could not expand.[8] The removal of sanctions might also encourage Western firms to invest in new joint ventures which would introduce much needed foreign capital and expertise into the Soviet economy. Finally, if East-West relations improved, it might become possible to import the advanced technology required for the modernisation of the Soviet economy.[9] In sum, the economic benefits of a new foreign policy would be invaluable to the reform process in the Soviet Union.

There were also urgent external reasons for adopting new policies: Soviet foreign policy seemed far less successful in 1985 than it had in the 1970s, when Brezhnev's claim that the correlation of forces was changing in favour of the Soviet Union reflected the achievement of military parity between the superpowers and the adoption of socialist forms of development by a number of Third World states. The second Cold War at the beginning of the 1980s indicated just how successful Brezhnev's foreign policy had become. One of its causes – Soviet policy in the Third World – had involved the Soviet Union in prolonged regional conflicts and civil wars. Military parity was threatened by the American intention to develop strategic defence. The socialist states had never achieved the economic integration planned since the 1960s. In fact, there were few areas of foreign policy which the new leadership could regard with equanimity (Light, 1989, p. 175). The Gorbachev leadership decided that the principles on which its foreign policy was based needed rethinking. The result was called the 'new political thinking' and it presaged the foreign policy reform which eventually brought the Cold War to an end.

As far as the transformation of the international political system was concerned, three important aspects of the new political thinking affected East-West relations and, therefore, democratisation in Eastern Europe: the redefinition of security, a new approach to conflict and the realisation that perceptions were vitally important in international relations, and that political rhetoric affected them and made it difficult to establish trust.

The redefinition of security arose from a belated understanding that attempts to ensure Soviet security by building up ever more military power had, in the end, produced the reverse effect and undermined it. Soviet theorists now recognised that security was essentially a political problem and that the zero-sum calculations that had lain behind the effort to achieve unilateral military security were self-defeating, since they instigated arms races. Both theorists and officials began to talk in positive-sum terms about the indivisibility and interdependence of security, and the urgency of reducing the nuclear balance to lower levels (Petrovsky, 1986).[10] The arms controls proposals which were an early and prominent feature of Gorbachev's foreign policy were the result of this aspect of the new political thinking. To the consternation of much of the Soviet military establishment, the new definitions of security also led to the formulation of strategies of 'reasonable sufficiency' and 'defensive defence' which, as MccGwire (1991, p. 332) points out, rendered Soviet forces in Eastern Europe redundant. New thinking about security, therefore, soon began to affect Soviet-East European relations and, indirectly, the process of democratisation.

The second important aspect of the new political thinking took rather longer to translate into policy. Prompted by the intractable conflicts in which many of their Third World clients were involved, Soviet theorists became concerned about the propensity of local conflict to spread from one issue to others, and from one region to contiguous areas. They pointed out that in a bipolar world in which the superpowers invariably supported opposing sides in regional conflicts, it was all too easy for a local conflict to escalate into superpower military confrontation. They proposed new methods of resolving conflict through reconciliation, political negotiation and superpower cooperation (Kovalev, 1988). From the point of view of the international political system, what was important was the implied intention to withdraw from Third World conflicts, thus alleviating one of the sources of tension in superpower relations and breaching global bipolarity.

The new political thinking included a number of other important and interesting features[11] but the third aspect which is particularly relevant to change in the international political system relates to perceptions and the problem of trust in international relations. Rather more vague than new theories about security and conflict, the effects of this aspect of the new thinking were quite dramatic, particularly if one compares the East-West discourse of the Gorbachev years with that of the Brezhnev era. Since they assumed that the West was implacably hostile to socialist states and that there was a constant danger of aggression, previous Soviet leaders had believed that socialists should be vigilant at all times. The perception of an external enemy was also useful, of course, because it encouraged internal cohesion. One way of promoting vigilance was to warn people constantly about the hostile intentions of imperialism. Public statements, newspaper articles and academic analyses of international relations, therefore, usually carried a compulsory warning about imperialist aggression. Once the policy of *glasnost* was introduced, however, the Gorbachev leadership suddenly realised that this kind of belligerent propaganda often served to undermine security rather than to enhance it. On the one hand, it did not necessarily persuade its domestic audience. On the other hand, it often succeeded in convincing foreign audiences, including policy-makers, that the Soviet Union was implacably hostile. As a result, it sometimes became a self-fulfilling prophecy, causing the international tension it was intended to avert.

Arms control verification had also raised the question of the nature of trust in international relations. Hostile propaganda and 'enemy images', Soviet theorists maintained, should be eschewed by both sides in East-West relations because it undermined the trust on which arms control relied. Moreover, since policy-makers often became the victims of the enemy images they used and began to believe their own rhetoric, hostile propaganda had an adverse affect on perceptions, and hence on the quality of foreign policy decisions (Petrovsky, 1987). At first this aspect of new thinking primarily affected the tone of foreign policy statements and analyses. But when Gorbachev began to urge his foreign policy specialists to 'fill in the blank spots' of Soviet international relations (*Pravda*, 15 February 1987), it was this aspect of the new political thinking that made it possible for scholars to re-examine the past.[12] Finally, and more directly related to Eastern Europe, the depiction of a 'common European home' raised the question of the future of the two Cold War alliances and the status of Eastern Europe within that common home.

It should be stressed that the translation of the new political thinking into policy after 1985 required a considerable degree of new thinking from the West as well – zero-sum thinking and 'enemy images' were by no means the sole prerogative of the Soviet Union. An unprecedented number of bilateral superpower summits, a dozen or more meetings between Gorbachev and other Western leaders, innumerable rendezvous between Shevardnadze and American Secretaries of State, George Shultz and James Baker, produced, in a period of five years, increasingly far-reaching arms control agreements, an ever broadening agenda of matters of mutual interest and Soviet withdrawal from a number of regional conflicts (see, for example, Fleron, Hoffmann and Laird, 1991; Bochkarev and Mansfield, 1992). The climax of East-West *rapprochement* was the Paris Agreement in November 1990 which declared the Cold War over.

As we will see in relation to German reunification, it was not all plain sailing. But the atmosphere of East-West relations improved radically,[13] and the contention here is that the change in Soviet foreign policy transformed the implicit rules of international conduct which characterised the bipolarity of the Cold War. These rules had evolved gradually as a means to impose and maintain order in a highly dangerous international system. Gaddis (in Bochkarev and Mansfield, 1992, p. 14) points out that the stability of the Cold War system arose partly from the existence of nuclear weapons: both sides of the Cold War ideological divide soon recognised that the costs of a war between them would far outweigh any gains that could be achieved. But it also reflected a shared commitment to preserve the existing system. The result was a paradox. While both sides based their political and strategic reasoning in relation to one another on zero-sum calculations, there was an area of shared interest – the avoidance of nuclear war and the preservation of the existing international system – which allowed for positive-sum behaviour from which an implicit set of rules evolved.

What were these rules? There was agreement, for example, that whereas vertical proliferation of nuclear weapons was permissible (although agreements on ceilings were desirable), states that possessed nuclear weapons should cooperate to prevent horizontal proliferation. A second rule resulted from the extreme tension caused by the crises in Berlin in 1961 and in Cuba in 1962: the two superpowers should avoid direct confrontation and conflict. With regard to Europe, there was implicit respect for each side's sphere of influence. This meant that Moscow could limit the freedom of action of its allies without great risk of interference from the West. There was also agreement (made explicit but ambiguous in the Helsinki Final Act in 1975) that the European borders that had resulted from the Second World War were inviolable. This referred particularly to the borders between the two spheres of influence in Europe. In fact, the division of Germany – the concrete symbol of bipolarity – was sacrosanct.

German reunification could be used in rhetoric as a long-term goal, therefore, but neither side would actively attempt to attain it.[14]

When these rules were followed, the Cold War was an extremely stable system. Moreover, detente (which, in effect, meant translating some of the rules into explicit agreements) was possible. When they were violated, on the other hand, international tension became acute (for example, in 1962 or during the Second Cold War). When Soviet foreign policy began to change after 1985 the first two rules, the prohibition on horizontal proliferation of nuclear weapons and the avoidance of direct conflict, became stronger as a result of more active cooperation between the two superpowers. But the other rules gradually eroded, making East European democratisation and marketisation possible.

In a situation where Gorbachev and his colleagues were pleading for Western aid, for example, and trying to entice Western direct investment and applying for membership of the international economic institutions which their predecessors had despised as agents of international capitalism, the implicit rules about respecting spheres of influence became untenable. There were no conceivable objections that could be raised to Western aid for Eastern Europe or East European membership of international economic organisations. Even after the revolutions of 1989, when it became clear that the new governments would abandon socialism, there could be no reversion to the Brezhnev doctrine of ‘defending the aims of socialism’ and no reimposition of Soviet control over East European policy choices. The new Soviet policy of non-interference in Eastern Europe had been widely articulated and any attempt to invoke the old rules would have had repercussions on the relationship that the Soviet Union was forging with the West. In essence, the relationship with the West was considered so important to *Soviet* transformation that it could not be risked, even if this meant losing the USSR’s European sphere of influence. As a result, it became possible for Western governments, Western academic economists and officials of international economic institutions to influence the democratisation process and the introduction of market reforms in Eastern Europe in a way that had previously been impossible.

As far as security was concerned, Soviet policy in Eastern Europe had previously been based on the assumption that a reliable security system required that Eastern Europe should serve as a defence glacis for the Soviet Union. Moreover, Soviet control over the political and economic systems of Eastern Europe, ensured by the leading role accorded to local Communist parties, was deemed essential to Soviet security. When Soviet policy and strategy began to change, however, the territorial defence of Eastern Europe ceased to be important, at least to reformist politicians, and there seemed to be better ways to ensure Soviet security than to dictate East European policy from Moscow (Deudney and Ikenberry, 1991/92). Soviet policy-makers called, for example, for the reinvigoration of the United Nations (Gorbachev, 1988) and for formalised institutional provisions for European security under the aegis of the Conference on Security and Cooperation in Europe (CSCE) (Shevardnadze, *Pravda*, 26 June 1990). There was a presumption in Moscow that both NATO and the WTO would continue to exist, albeit as looser organisations with higher political profiles and fewer military functions, until both alliances were submerged and dissolved within a continent-wide security system (Karaganov, in Bochkarev and Mansfield, 1992, pp. 255–66). Both the new governments of Eastern Europe and Western governments shared this assumption at least until the middle of 1990 (Brzezinski, in Bochkarev and Mansfield, 1992, p. 55). It was also taken for granted that the economic ties between the European CMEA members would continue to be important (Larrabee, in Bochkarev and Mansfield, 1992, p. 253).

The implicit Cold War rule that proved most difficult to change concerned the inviolability of borders and, specifically, the reunification of Germany. In fact, since the division of Germany had initially reflected a shared determination to prevent a re-emergence of German hegemony over Europe, the Western powers at first shared Soviet disquiet at the speed of German reunification. Although there was no rational reason for the existence of two German states once the Communists had lost power in the German Democratic Republic, it was generally thought that unification would be a gradual and prolonged process. But whereas the West came round quite quickly to the idea of a reunified Germany within NATO, for the Soviet government German membership of NATO was a major problem. Old security perceptions and fears were rekindled and Soviet objections 'were clearly based on the potential . . . for the reconstitution and growth of the military threat directed against the Soviet Union by a more powerful NATO' (Wallander, 1992, p. 58). It should be stressed that it was not just the old guard conservatives who were perturbed about German unification and NATO membership. For many Soviet people the events of July 1990 made a mockery of their sacrifices in the Second World War (Larrabee, in Fleron, Hoffmann and Laird, 1991, p. 649).

In the end, of course, the Soviet Union capitulated. In July 1990 the Soviet Union agreed to German reunification and membership of NATO in return for limitations on the size of German forces, financial assistance towards the withdrawal of Soviet troops from East Germany and a prolonged timetable to accomplish the withdrawal (*Guardian*, 17 July 1990). According to Shevardnadze, 'the security of the Soviet Union was not lessened but in fact was enhanced' by German reunification and membership of NATO (Shevardnadze, 1991, p. 147). This view was not shared, however, by Soviet conservatives. Criticism of the Gorbachev government for losing Eastern Europe had already been voiced publicly at the February 1990 Plenum of the CC (*Pravda*, 7 February 1990). The attacks, particularly against Shevardnadze, increased in ferocity in July and they contributed to his resignation in December 1990.

When German reunification was first mooted, there was a brief period when it seemed that East European security fears might save the WTO. Although Czechoslovakia, Hungary and Poland had demanded the withdrawal of Soviet troops from their territory,[15] the Czech and Polish governments were both concerned about Chancellor Kohl's delay in guaranteeing Poland's western border (*Guardian*, 6 March 1990). In May a Pact summit agreed to a review of its structures and functions, although by then Prime

Minister József Antall had announced that Hungary would leave the Pact. But the efforts to find a new role for the WTO were futile and Moscow finally accepted that it had outlived its usefulness. In February 1991 members agreed to dissolve its military structures and, when its political organs were dissolved on 1 July 1991, the WTO formally ceased to exist (Dunay, 1992, p. 3). Although some argue that Moscow wanted to retain the Pact so that it could influence events in Eastern Europe (Eyal, in Pravda, 1992, p. 208), a far stronger motive was probably fear that its abolition would create a security void which would result in the absorption of Eastern Europe into NATO and the isolation of the USSR from Europe. The attempt to persuade East European governments to sign treaties which included a clause preventing membership of hostile alliances reflected Soviet concern.[16] The retention of the WTO would also have served Gorbachev well in the domestic struggle between reformists and conservatives which had become acute by 1991.

Economic cooperation within CMEA proved equally difficult to sustain. Even before trade in convertible currencies at world prices was introduced in January 1991, Soviet oil deliveries to Eastern Europe had fallen by a third (*Guardian*, 3 August 1990). Although it has been suggested that the reason might partly have been Soviet reluctance to support Western-oriented democraticising regimes (Smith in Pravda, 1992, p. 90), the economic chaos in the Soviet Union is a more convincing explanation. A Western economic report published at the beginning of 1991, for example, blamed the fall in the production of oil on 'inadequate maintenance of plant and equipment as well as insufficient efforts at exploration and development' (Deutsche Bank, 1991, p. 94). Although oil shortfalls and price rises complicated the economic situation in Eastern Europe, those countries which were embarking on rapid marketisation were more interested in expanding their trade with Western Europe than in the survival of CMEA. The Soviet Union itself was far less concerned about the future of CMEA than about the WTO. Thus there was scarcely a lament in February 1991 when the CMEA was converted into the Organisation for International Economic Cooperation tasked simply with providing information and consultation (Eyal, in Pravda, 1992, pp. 222–7).

In retrospect, it is remarkable not that the conservative opposition to Gorbachev's reforms objected to the loss of Eastern Europe but that they made so little of it. In fact, the power struggle between Soviet conservatives and reformists revolved far more around economic reform, ethnic conflict and the potential secession of the Baltic republics than around the future of Eastern Europe. And when the Union disintegrated and the republics of the CIS began formulating independent foreign policies, they concentrated on the 'near abroad' (their own interrelations) and on Western Europe and the United States rather than on the countries of East-Central Europe. As for the latter, fear that the conservatives in Moscow might win the power struggle in 1991 and that the disintegration of the Soviet Union would cause instability on their eastern borders made them even more determined to seek security from association with NATO. There was little sign, however, that the Soviet Union or the CIS intended to influence East European democratisation and market reforms. Indeed, Poland served as the model for the economic reform introduced by Boris Yeltsin in January 1992.

A few Russian journalists bemoaned the absence of economic and political ties with East-Central Europe which could mutually shore up their frail democracies and struggling economies (see, for example, *Nezavisimaya gazeta*, 14 May 1992). Others worried about the eagerness of Hungary, Poland and Czechoslovakia to join NATO (see, for example, *Moskovskie novosti*, 29 March 1992). In fact, however, the complaint that 'the baby had been thrown out with the bathwater' and that there were virtually no policies towards or serious analyses of Eastern Europe (Kaznacheyev, 1991) accurately reflected the situation in the academic and policy fields. By the middle of 1992 there was more concern about Russia's future, and about the fact that the republics of Belorussia and Ukraine 'distanced Russia from Europe' and threatened to turn it into an Asian power, than there was about domestic developments in East Central Europe (Zagorsky, 1992, p. 17). To rally support against them, Russian reformists found it useful to warn that conservatives yearned for their former 'big brother' role in Eastern Europe (*Nezavisimaya gazeta* 14 May 1992). By then, however, the CIS had ceased to be an important international influence on East European democratisation.

Conclusion

It is possible, of course, that East European democratisation would eventually have taken place even if there had been no change in the Soviet Union. Past history suggests, however, that the revolutions would probably not have been 'velvet' without the change in Soviet attitudes and policies that took place after Gorbachev became General Secretary of the CPSU in 1985. Given the extraordinary control that the Soviet Union exerted in Eastern Europe – primarily through its penetration of the political systems of Eastern Europe but also via the WTO and CMEA – there can be little doubt that the Soviet Union was the most important and most direct international influence on the pre-transition phase of East European democratisation.

As far as the direction of the reforms beyond 1989 are concerned (in other words whether Eastern Europe would stop at democratic socialism or progress to liberal democracy and market economies), the Soviet Union continued to be an important influence, but by then its influence was indirect. By adopting a new foreign policy, and continuing it even though it cost it its European sphere of influence, the Soviet Union effectively created the conditions in which democratic forces within Eastern Europe could come to the fore, and Western democratic and market influences could penetrate the region.

It is true, however, that even if the Soviet leadership had changed its mind and had wanted to prevent East European democratisation, it would probably have failed. The level of popular support for democratisation within Eastern Europe was very high and there was no guarantee that the West would act with the restraint that it had shown in 1956 and 1968. Moreover, the evidence of the August 1991 coup suggests that the Soviet Union no longer had a reliable army. Despite the diminution of its power, however, the Soviet Union still possessed sufficient force, including nuclear power, to pose a credible threat. Had it threatened to prevent democratically elected governments taking power in Eastern Europe (or stopped the fall of the Berlin Wall or refused to accept the unification of Germany), an extremely acute international crisis would have occurred. Since it had always been considered axiomatic in the West that Moscow would not countenance the loss of its security zone in Eastern Europe, fear of the Soviet response tempered Western policy towards East European democratisation until it was clear that there was little risk (Brzezinski, in Bochkarev and Mansfield, 1992). The importance of the USSR's indirect influence on East European democratisation should not, therefore, be underestimated.

Lenin believed that revolutions occurred when the oppressed classes no longer *wanted to* and the ruling classes no longer *could* live in the old way (Lenin, 1915, pp. 213–14). In 1989 Eastern Europe no longer wanted Moscow's tutelage and Soviet power had greatly diminished so that it could no longer control Eastern Europe in the old way. But the revolutions might still have been violent. After all, peaceful revolutions can only occur if *neither* oppressed *nor* rulers want to live in the old way. What made the revolutions of 1989 virtually non-violent (except in Romania) was Moscow's rejection of its previous use of force. The system that follows a peaceful revolution, however, depends only partly on external factors. In the final analysis, therefore, the Soviet Union may have created the necessary conditions for East European democratisation, but only the East Europeans themselves can ensure that what follows is democracy.

Notes

1. There were secessionist movements in Moldava, Ukraine and Georgia as well. Large parts of the former two republics had also only been incorporated into the Soviet Union after the Second World War, while Eastern Ukraine and Georgia had unwillingly joined the Union in 1922.
2. Pravda (1992, p. 3) points out that 1968 was a formative influence on many of Gorbachev's aides and advisors who saw 'socialism with a human face' as the forerunner to *perestroika*.
3. These groups were, in effect, the beginning of civil society in Eastern Europe and the Soviet Union. Many of their members later became the leaders of the 1989 revolutions.
4. Dawisha (1990, p. 198) believes that Gorbachev's desire that Russia should become part of Europe was one reason why he abandoned Eastern Europe, since 'the Europeanisation of the Soviet Union could not proceed without the de-Sovietisation of Eastern Europe'. Rubinstein (1991, p. 70–1) agrees but accuses Gorbachev of wanting to reduce the American role in Europe.
5. By this time Gorbachev had urged a new strategy of 'defensive defence' on his military, and Eastern Europe was less strategically important than it had been

under the old military doctrine. Keeping troops in Eastern Europe had also become a heavy financial burden. None the less, the unilateral cuts and the eventual withdrawal of Soviet troops were strenuously opposed by the military as well as by the political old guard who still saw Eastern Europe as a vital defence glacis (see Eyal, in Pravda, 1992, pp. 33–72).

6. Television had a powerful effect on the transition to democracy in the Soviet Union. Millions of Soviet citizens followed the Congress, Supreme Soviet and the Moscow and Leningrad Soviet debates for hours on end. Curiously, however, their intense interest in local and national politics tended to make them rather parochial. There seemed to be far less interest among the Moscow intelligentsia about the 1989 revolutions in Eastern Europe, for example, than there had been about Czechoslovakia in 1968 or Poland in 1980.
7. Although the article in *Problems of Communism* was written by *academics* and does not, therefore, represent an official view, it is reasonable to presume that the politicians advised by these scholars were influenced by their views. In fact, a number of IEMSS scholars stood for election for the Congress of People's Deputies and became politicians.
8. Sanctions had been imposed by the West after the intervention in Afghanistan and again when martial law was declared in Poland.
9. An informal Coordinating Committee had, since the beginning of the Cold War, maintained a list of goods with potential military application which advanced capitalist states were prohibited from exporting to Communist countries.
10. There are literally hundreds of articles by Soviet scholars on the new political thinking and, since pluralism was now the order of the day, they by no means all expressed the same views. There are also many excellent Western analyses of the ideas embodied by the new political thinking. Since I am concerned here to establish views which affected East-West relations and, therefore, the nature of international relations, the articles I have cited were written by what one might call 'theorist-practitioners' – the authors were high-ranking members of the Ministry of Foreign Affairs.
11. The debate about inter-socialist relations discussed in the previous section was an important aspect of the new political thinking. Soviet analyses of Third World economic development also changed dramatically (Light, 1989).
12. 'Filling in the blank spots' of the history of Soviet-East European relations proved far more difficult than telling the truth about domestic events. In May 1987, for example, a joint Polish-Soviet History Commission was established to fill in the blank spots of Soviet-Polish relations. Two years later the Soviet side was still not prepared to admit responsibility for the Katyn massacre although it had, after much delay, accepted that there had been secret protocols attached to the German-Soviet pact of 1939 (Valkenier, 1989). Similarly, the invasion of Czechoslovakia was only formally condemned as illegal in December 1989.
13. Even if one allows for their different personalities and generations, the different circumstances in which they wrote their books and the different purposes for which they were written, an eloquent indication of the way in which the climate of East-West relations changed can be obtained by comparing Gromyko's memoirs (Gromyko, 1989) with Shevardnadze's autobiography (Schevardnadze, 1991).
14. John Lewis Gaddis (in Bochkarev and Mansfield, 1992, pp. 10–37) also argues that there were implicit rules of conduct during the Cold War. His five rules differ somewhat from those offered here. He does not have a rule about nuclear proliferation, for example, but suggests instead that there was tacit

acceptance that nuclear weapons would only be used as an ultimate resort. He maintains that each side accepted that it should not undermine the other side's leadership but he relates that not to restricting the freedom of action of allies, but to the domestic position of Khrushchev after the Cuban missile crisis and of Nixon after Watergate. He does not mention European borders but has a more general rule: both sides preferred 'predictable anomaly over impredictable [*sic*] rationality' (p. 32) and this allowed them to tolerate awkward regional arrangements like the division of Germany.

15. Troops began leaving Czechoslovakia at the end of February and Hungary in March. Soviet troops in Poland remained a contentious issue, since their presence was tied up with the withdrawal of soldiers from Germany (Sanford, in Pravda, 1992, pp. 115–16).
16. Only Romania agreed to include the clause. The treaties with Hungary in December 1991 (*Izvestiya*, 6 December 1991), between Czechoslovakia and Russia in April 1992 (*Nezavisimaya gazeta*, 14 April 1992) and Poland and Russia in June 1992 (*Nezavisimaya gazeta*, 30 June 1992) contained no mention of alliance membership.

References

Ash, T. Garton, 1990, *We the People: the revolution of 89*, Granta Books, Cambridge.

Batt, J., 1991, *East-Central Europe from Reform to Transformation*, Royal Institute of International Affairs and Pinter Publishers, London.

Bochkarev, A.G. and Mansfield, D.L. (eds), 1992, *The United States and the USSR in a Changing World: Soviet and American perspectives*, Westview, Boulder, Colo.

Brown, J.F., 1991, *Surge to Freedom: the end of Communist rule in Eastern Europe*, Adamantine Press, Twickenham, Middlesex.

Brzezinski, Z., 1967, *The Soviet Bloc: unity and conflict*, Harvard University Press, Cambridge, Mass.

Dashichev, V., *et al.*, 1988, 'East-West relations and Eastern Europe . . . the Soviet perspective', *Problems of Communism*, (3–4), May-August, pp. 60–70, reprinted in C. Gati, 1990, pp. 205–22.

Dawisha, K., 1984 *The Kremlin and the Prague Spring*, University of California Press, Berkeley.

Dawisha, K., 1990, *Eastern Europe, Gorbachev and Reform: the great challenge*, Second edition, Cambridge University Press, Cambridge.

Deudney, D. and Ikenberry, G.J., 1991/92, 'The international sources of Soviet change', *International Security*, 16 (3), Winter, pp. 74–118.

Deutsche Bank, Economics Department, 1991, *Rebuilding Eastern Europe*, Deutsche Bank, Frankfurt.

Dunay, P., 1992, 'Stability in East Central Europe', *Journal of Peace Research*, 29 (1), pp. 1–6.

Fleron, F.J., Jr., Hoffmann, E.P. and Laird, R.F. (eds), 1991, *Contemporary Issues in Soviet Foreign Policy: from Brezhnev to Gorbachev*, Aldine de Gruyter, New York.

Gati, C., 1990,*The Bloc that Failed: Soviet-East European relations in transition*, Indiana University Press, Bloomington and Indianapolis.

Gorbachev, M., 1987, *Perestroika: new thinking for our country and the world*, Fontana Collins, London.

Gorbachev, M., 1988, 'Address at the United Nations' in M. Gorbachev, *Perestroika and Soviet-American relations*, Sphinx Press Inc., Madison, Connecticut, pp. 185–207.

Gromyko. A., 1989, *Memoirs*, Doubleday, New York.

Herring, E., 1992, 'The collapse of the Soviet Union: the implications for world politics' in J. Baylis and N.J. Rengger (eds), *Dilemmas of World Politics*, Clarendon Press, Oxford, pp. 354–83.

Holloway, D. and Sharp, J.M.O. (eds), 1984, *The Warsaw Pact: alliance in transition?*, Macmillan, London.

Jones, C.D., 1981, *Soviet Influence in Eastern Europe: political autonomy and the Warsaw Pact*, Praeger, New York.

Kaznachayev, A., 1991, 'Old relationship is destroyed. What then?, *International Affairs* (Moscow), 9, pp. 20–5.

Khrushchev, N., 1956, 'Report of the Central Committee of the Communist Party of the Soviet Union to the 20th Party Congress' in L.Gruliow (ed.), 1957, *Current Soviet Policies II: the documentary record of the 20th Communist Party Congress and its aftermath*, Atlantic Press,London, pp. 172–88.

Kovalev, A.G., 1988, 'Sdelat' perestroiku glavnym predmetom nashei zhizni', *Vestnik Ministerstva inostrannykh del SSSR*, 3, 10 October, pp. 9–13.

Laird, R.F. and Hoffmann, E.P. (eds), 1986, *Soviet Foreign Policy in a Changing World*, Aldine de Gruyter, New York.

Lenin, V.I., 1915, 'The collapse of the Second International', *Collected Works*, Vol. 21, Foreign Languages Publishing House, Moscow, Lawrence & Wishart, London, pp. 205–59.

Light, M., 1988, *The Soviet Theory of International Relations*, Wheatsheaf, Brighton.

Light, M., 1989, 'Restructuring Soviet foreign policy' in Ronald Hill and Jan Åke Dellenbrant (eds), *Gorbachev and Perestroika*, Edward Elgar, Cheltenham, pp. 171–93.

MccGwire, M., 1991, *Perestroika and Soviet National Security*. Brookings Institution, Washington, DC.

Novopashin, Yu. S. (ed.), 1986, *Mezhdunarodnaya sfera sotsialisticheskikh obshchestvennykh otnoshenii*, IEMSS, Moscow.

Novopashin, Yu. S. (ed.), 1987, *Natsional 'no-gosudarstvennye interesy v sisteme mezhdunarodnykh otnoshenii novogo tipa*, IEMSS, Moscow.

Petrovsky, V., 1986, 'Sovetskaya kontseptsiya vseobshchei bezopasnosti', *Mirovaya ekonomika i mezhdunarodnye otnoshenii*, 6, pp. 3–13.

Petrovsky, V., 1987, 'Doverie i vyzhivanie chelovechestva', *Mirovaya ekonomika i mezhdunarodnye otnoshenii*, 11,: pp. 15–26.

Pravda, A., (ed.), 1992, *The End of the Outer Empire: Soviet-East European relations in transition, 1985–90*, Sage, London.

Rahr, A., 1988, 'Restructuring the Kremlin leadership', *Radio Liberty Research Bulletin*, RL No. 423/88.

Remington, R.A. (ed.), 1969, *Winter in Prague: Documents on Czechoslovak Communism in Crisis*, MIT Press, Cambridge, Mass.

Rosenau, J., 1966, 'Pre-theories and theories of foreign policy' in R.B. Farrell (ed.), *Approaches to Comparative and International Politics*, Northwestern University Press, Evanston, pp. 27–92.

Rubinstein, A.Z., 1991, 'Soviet client-states: from empire to commonwealth', *Orbis*, 35 (1), Winter, pp.69–78.

Sanford, G., 1986, *Military Rule in Poland: the rebuilding of Communist power, 1981–1983*, Croom Helm, London and Sydney.

Shentov, O. (ed.), 1987, *O novom teoreticheskom videnii sotsializma*, Jusautor, Sofia.

Shentov, O. (ed.), 1989, *Modeli sotsializma: istoriya i sovremennost'*, Jusautor, Sofia.

Shevardnadze, E., 1987, Speech to meeting of the Aktiv of the Diplomatic Academy, *Vestnik Ministerstva inostrannykh del SSSR*, 2, 26 August, pp. 30–4.
Shevardnadze, E., 1991, *The Future Belongs to Freedom*, Sinclair-Stevenson, London.
Teague, E., 1988, *Solidarity and the Soviet Worker*, Croom Helm, London, New York and Sydney.
Valdez, J.C., forthcoming, *Socialist Internationalism, Contradictions, and Eastern Europe: ideology and Soviet influence, 1968–1989*, Cambridge University Press, Cambridge.
Valkenier, E.K., 1989, 'Filling in blank spots: Soviet-Polish history and Polish Renewal', *Harriman Institute Forum*, 2 (12), December.
Wallander, C.A., 1992, 'International institutions and modern security strategies', *Problems of Communism*, LXI (1–2), January–April, pp. 44–62.
White, S., 1990, *Gorbachev in Power*, Cambridge University Press, Cambridge.
Zagorsky, A. *et al.*, 1992, *Posle raspada SSSR: Rossiya v novom mire*, TsMI MGIMO, Moscow.

7

The international dimension of democratisation in Czechoslovakia and Hungary

Judy Batt

Introduction

There are two major aspects of the transitions to democracy currently under way in East Europe which differ significantly from the transitions of the South European and Latin American countries previously studied. The first aspect concerns the degree of 'penetratedness' of the politics of the respective cases – that is, the degree to which domestic political development is conditioned by the international context; and the second concerns the relationship between economics and politics.

In an essay on the international aspects of democratisation, Laurence Whitehead notes that in the cases of South Europe and Latin America,

> Local political forces operated with an untypically high degree of autonomy. The international setting provided a mildly supportive (or destructive) background which was often taken for granted and which seldom intruded too conspicuously on an essentially domestic drama. (Whitehead, 1986, p. 5)

When we consider the East European cases, we are forced to conclude that the opposite was true, especially in the pre-transition phase of Communist rule, when politics could be said to have been characterised by a uniquely *low* degree of autonomy. The 'penetratedness' of East European politics was of a qualitatively different order than that identified by scholars pursuing the theme of 'linkage' of domestic and international politics elsewhere. It was not just a matter of 'fusion of national and international systems in certain kinds of issue areas' (Rosenau, quoted by Pridham, 1991, p. 13) but the more or less exact replication of the Soviet model in the East European political systems, and their subordination to the political priorities of the Soviet leadership. The cases of Hungary and Czechoslovakia provide particularly striking examples, both the Kádár and Husák regimes having originated in the Soviet military intervention, replacing reformist regimes which had overstepped the limits set by

Moscow. These limits were subsequently codified in the so-called 'Brezhnev Doctrine' which attempted to define a set of compulsory ideological principles to be observed by all Communist regimes (see Dawisha, 1981).

Soviet domination did not rest at the level of ideology alone but was intitutionalised in the 'leading role of the Communist party', whose leaders were appointed by Moscow and subject to close supervision. A back-up chain of control was also maintained through the security forces which were run directly by the Soviet KGB, and which, in times of crisis, clearly demonstrated that they were answerable primarily to Moscow, not to the local East European Communist leaderships. Furthermore, the military structures were fused in the Warsaw Treaty Organisation, and were unable to operate independently. And the East European economies, about which I will say more later, were tied in to the Soviet-dominated trading bloc under the Council for Mutual Economic Assistance. While Soviet aspirations to institute a unified, supranational system of planning covering all the economies of the regions were thwarted in the 1960s, nevertheless, a high degree of dependence of East European economies on the Soviet Union was achieved which greatly limited room for manoeuvre in economic policy.

In this context, it is hard to separate out the domestic from the international in East European politics. The domestic and international dimensions of East European politics had become fused as a result of the imposition throughout the bloc of a 'model' of economic management, derived from Soviet experience but held to embody universally valid principles of 'socialist construction'. Domestic political developments thus had immediate international implications, and this fusion of the two dimensions was a constant source of tension and crisis. When East European regimes sought to stabilise themselves by reforms which promised concessions to domestic popular aspirations, they immediately ran into conflict with their Soviet masters, on whom their power ultimately depended. Political change was thus only possible to the extent that the Soviet Union was prepared to tolerate it. The transition to democracy was only possible once the entire international structure of the Soviet system collapsed.

The collapse of the Communist regimes was caused by a general systemic failure occurring simultaneously at both the political and the economic levels. Economics and politics are of course linked in all societies, but the linkage in Communist systems was qualitatively different. The Soviet model of socialism entailed the fusion not only of the domestic and the international but also of politics and economics. Private ownership of industrial assets and land was virtually completely eliminated, and the management of the economy was effected through central planning which ensured the domination of political priorities at the expense of autonomous, market-based economic criteria. Enterprises were reduced to the lowest link in a bureaucratic machine, their managers dependent on political connections both with the Communist Party and the ministerial apparatus for their careers. Enterprise performance was measured not by the independent economic judgement of the market, but by fulfilment and overfulfilment of central plan targets prescribed by bureaucratic superiors in the ministries.

But this system proved unable to deliver the economic abundance promised according to the regime's own Marxist ideology, and unable to compete with the economic performance of the rival capitalist West, and thus it could neither satisfy popular expectations nor sustain the military effort on which the international position of the socialist bloc depended. The decision of the Soviet leadership under Gorbachev to introduce radical reforms in the Soviet Union with the aim of making the system work better in fact led to the unravelling of the whole structure of the bloc: the Soviet leaders' admission that the model had failed even in the Soviet Union itself had inescapable implications for Eastern Europe, where this failure had been recognised for years, and where attempts to deal with the problem had been the source of recurrent domestic crises and conflicts with Moscow. Karen Dawisha encapsulates the dilemma: 'Gorbachev realised that the Europeanisation of the Soviet Union could not proceed without the de-Sovietisation of Eastern Europe' (Dawisha, 1990, p. 198).

What are the implications of these East European peculiarities for its transition to democracy? Firstly, in contrast to the South European or Latin American cases, the transition is taking place in a completely changed, extremely fluid and uncertain international context with the breakdown of the Cold War system of competing blocs in Europe. East Europe has gained its freedom and national autonomy, but now suffers from an acute (but not clearly focused) sense of international insecurity. The small countries of East Europe have a deep historical sense of vulnerability derived from the brute fact of their geopolitical position, sandwiched between the much larger, and in the past usually threatening powers, Germany and Russia. The Soviet system has collapsed, but this geopolitical predicament remains, because the chaos to the East creates uncertainty and fear of unpredictable spill-over effects, such as uncontrolled waves of emigration, possible civil wars within or between the former Soviet republics and so on. The insecurity of their present position feeds into the general climate of domestic politics, as former Czechoslovak President Václav Havel put it:

> For a long time now I have been pondering this fundamental question: why at a time when no foreign power threatens us, when no-one interferes in our affairs, and when for the first time in centuries we both as a state and as citizens truly hold our future in our own hands, why do we have so few reasons for joyful contentment? What exactly causes our nervousness, our confusion, our impatience and often even our hopelessness? (Havel, 1992)

A major source of the anxieties expressed by Havel has been the rise of nationalism in the politics of the region, which, as we shall see, has much to do with the uncertainty of the international context and has become one of the main challenges to the transition to democracy in both Czechoslovakia and Hungary.

The second point about the transition to democracy in East Europe is that it is accompanied by the transition to a market economy. There are indeed some similarities in the economic sphere between the East European and Latin American cases, in particular, the problems of debt, inflation and structural adjustment associated with domestic and external liberalisation (see the useful collection of essays in Kövés and Marer (1991). But in many respects, the problems are qualitatively different. The East European economies were not merely over-regulated with an over-blown state sector, but fully state-dominated economies, lacking a developed private sector and even the most basic institutions of a market economy. Moreover, they were geared overwhelmingly to an international trading bloc – the CMEA – which operated separately from the world economy (see Kövés, 1985), and which has now collapsed. The scale of the task of economic transformation and structural reorientation is unprecedented, and likely to take much longer than initially expected. The social costs will be high, and popular confidence in the goal of a market economy cannot be taken for granted. Western aid is a vital condition of the success of the economic transition, but it has so far been much less generous than expected or needed. Thus economic uncertainties compound with the uncertainties of the international context to heighten the difficulties of the democratic transition.

This introduction has set out some of the main general features of the East European transition to democracy. Now it is time to focus more closely on the two specific cases of Czechoslovakia and Hungary, and to highlight some of the differences between them.

The breakdown of Communist rule

Despite the broad common features outlined above, the patterns of breakdown of Communist rule in Hungary and Czechoslovakia display significant differences. In Hungary, the transition was an extended process. The starting-point of the irrevocable decline of the regime can be traced back to the early 1980s (if not earlier), and deliberate moves to inaugurate systemic transition were already being made under Communist rule. Major change began in late 1987, when the leading reformist figure in the Hungarian Socialist Workers' Party (HSWP), Imre Pozsgay, lent his support to the formation of an independent political group, the Hungarian Democratic Forum, and thus signalled his conversion to the idea of resurrecting a multi-party system. The Hungarian transition from 1987 to 1989 was effected by a self-conscious process of negotiation between competing elite groups – the substantial faction of reformers within the HSWP and opposition intellectuals – who shared a common concern to avoid open crisis and complete breakdown of order, as had happened, to the detriment of the interests of both the people and the Communist Party itself, in 1956 (see Batt, 1991, Chapters 2 and 3).

In Czechoslovakia, by contrast, the Communist regime clung on to power right up until November 1989, then collapsed extraordinarily rapidly as a result of mass popular demonstrations on the streets of Prague, Bratislava and other major towns. By the end of December, Czechoslovakia had even overtaken Hungary, with a new 'Government of National Understanding' dominated by non-Communists and a new president, the veteran opposition activist Václav Havel. The compression of events allowed little time for negotiation, and the major impetus came not from elite initiatives but directly from mass pressure from below (see Batt, 1991, Chapters 2 and 3).

The difference between the two countries can be explained by differences in their respective Communist Parties' strategies of rule, which in turn rested on different balances between domestic and international (i.e. Soviet) support. Thus we can see differences in the role and relative weight of domestic and international factors when it came to the breakdown of Communist rule in the respective cases. While both regimes were, as noted above, installed in power as a result of armed intervention by the Soviet Union, the process of 'normalisation' – re-establishing the Communist Party's monopoly of power to the satisfaction of Moscow – took a different course in each case. The Hungarian strategy was defined while Khrushchev was still in power in Moscow. In the early 1960s, the 'thaw' in Soviet politics with Khrushchev's open critique of the legacy of the Stalin era afforded the Kádár regime scope to develop a less ideologically dogmatic, more flexible political style in Hungary, and to introduce reforms of the economic system which, it was hoped, would more effectively satisfy consumer aspirations and thus divert popular energies away from public political activity into the pursuit of private material comforts.

This path of 'normalisation' was not available to Czechoslovakia. The crisis of 1968 had developed out of the failure of the Czechoslovak Communist Party (CSCP) to control political and economic reforms which were in many ways similar in conception to those introduced by Kádár (see Batt, 1988), and which were also being tried out, much more cautiously, in the Soviet Union under Prime Minister Kosygin. The Soviet decision to intervene in Czechoslovakia spelt the defeat of reformist forces not only within the CSCP, but it also affected the political balance within the Soviet Communist Party leadership itself, weakening the position of reformers such as Kosygin. Thereafter, Brezhnev was in a position of unchallenged power in Moscow, and as a result the CSCP also became, and remained to the bitter end, one of the most staunchly and loyally 'Brezhnevite' of all Communist parties, making a virtue out of its heavy dependence on Moscow and its isolation, both political and economic, from the world outside the Soviet bloc.

The nature of the Hungarian regime requires a little more explanation, as the strategy of rule was more subtle and complex from both the domestic and international veiwpoints. Kádár won and retained power after 1956 by assuming a pivotal role as mediator between the demands of Moscow and the aspirations of the Hungarian people; and between internal HSWP factions, comprising hard-line Communists loyal to Moscow and the traditional Soviet model of socialism, and reformists who gave higher priority to adapting that model to meet local needs. Kádár proved able to convince the Soviet leadership, even after 1968, that economic reforms had to be tolerated as the essential means of pacifying Hungarian society and avoiding a repeat of 1956. He thus argued that economic reforms need not lead to political crisis, as in Czechoslovakia, but could in fact serve to win popular support. On the other hand, when addressing his domestic audience, Kádár could point to the regime's political flexibility and its willingness to introduce economic reforms as evidence of its independence from Moscow. At the same time, he could refer to the sad, but unavoidable fact of Hungary's 'geopolitical position' to remind people that the price of being 'unrealistic', or going 'too far' with reform would be a repeat of the national disaster of 1956. The 1968 Czechoslovak crisis and the successive Polish crises were interpreted in this light in Hungary.

An interesting accompaniment to Kádár's strategy of economic reform was a greater degree of openness to the West, made possible by East-West detente in the 1970s, which created a favourable climate for expanding economic links. In addition, the recession in the West spurred on exporters to take advantage of the new markets in the East, while the international financial system, awash with 'petrodollars' as a result of the surge in oil prices after 1973, was only too eager to extend credits to back such exports. It was also assumed in Western financial circles that the Soviet Union would ultimately step in to sort matters out if an East European borrower proved unable to repay credits. Hungary (like Poland) saw this as an opportunity to bring about rapid modernisation of its industrial base, while at the same time improving the lot of Hungarian consumers by means of sharp increases in imports of a wide range of Western products, financed by borrowing.

The viability of this strategy depended on domestic economic reforms proving sufficiently far-reaching to bring about a radical improvement in the productivity, quality and hence international competitiveness of the economy. But this was not the case. In fact, in the mid-1970s, substantial modifications in the Hungarian economic reforms took place which greatly reduced their effectiveness (see Batt, 1988). The net result of this, to put it as briefly as possible, was that by the start of the 1980s, Hungary had accumulated a hard currency debt of similar proportions to that of Poland (see Marer, 1986). And in Poland, this problem led directly to the massive crisis of 1980–81, as the Kádár regime observed in mounting panic. When, as a result of the Polish débâcle, East-West detente broke down, and Western creditors started looking much more closely at their policy of lending to East Europe, Kádár's entire strategy of rule began to unravel. A new, more radical round of economic reform was proposed, but this time, no improvement in the population's standard of living would be possible – quite the reverse, a harsh austerity programme was called for. Reform now threatened the social peace bought in the boom years of the 1970s, but without credible reform, Hungary would find itself cut off from Western financial support and social upheaval would be all the more likely.

But Hungary was also under pressure from Moscow to abandon reform altogether. In the early 1980s, the Soviet Union tried to reassert much tighter control over East European states, blaming the Polish crisis on Western subversion which, it held, had resulted from the Communist Party's abandonment of central control over the economy. Hungary now found itself caught between East and West, tied to Moscow, but increasingly dependent economically on the West as well (see Bauer, 1988). Hungary was forced to choose, and its application for membership in the International Monetary Fund, accepted in 1982, was the first sign of a radical shift in political strategy away from the previous unswerving loyalty to the Soviet line in international affairs.

Kádár appeared to believe he could use a more overt Western orientation, and the resulting conflicts which would inevitably arise between his regime and Moscow, to shore up his popular credibility at home as defender of the 'national interest', and take people's minds off the dire economic situation. In the early and mid-1980s, Hungary successfully cultivated an extraordinarily favourable reputation in the West for its foreign policy independence, economic reformism and human rights record (see Tókés, 1984). The Soviet leadership, amid the throes of gerontocratic political succession at the end of Brezhnev's life and for the following few years, seemed unable to prevent this, but it is symptomatic of the Czechoslovak regime that it steadfastly refused to follow a similar course to take up the opportunity offered for greater independence, but instead launched a vitriolic anti-reform and anti-Western propaganda campaign on behalf of the most conservative, hard-line forces in Moscow directed against Hungary, the GDR, and any other wayward allies (see Gati, 1986).

The contrast between the Hungarian and Czechoslovak regimes was most stark at the point at which Gorbachev came to power. It might have been expected that the impact of Gorbachev's *perestroika* on the two regimes would be very different, but, as it turned out, in the end both were undermined. The challenge posed by Gorbachev for Czechoslovakia was obvious almost from the start – Husak's regime was the very embodiment of Brezhnevism. When Gorbachev's speeches and writings criticising the Brezhnevite 'era of stagnation', and advocating political reform, were published translated into Czech in *Rudé právo*, the CSCP's daily paper, his words resounded with echoes of the 1968 'Prague Spring'. Yet Gorbachev's most fervent supporters in Prague were to be found not in the Party but among the ex-Communist losers of 1968, now forming the ranks of Prague's window cleaners, lavatory attendants and boiler-stokers. The surprise was not that the Husak regime collapsed, but that it lasted right up until the end of 1989 – evidence that Moscow really had decided to abstain from further direct meddling in the affairs of the East European regimes. The final straw for the regime came from the breach of the Berlin Wall on 9 November 1989. After that, the sceptical and notoriously unheroic people of Czechoslovakia had no further excuse not to take action to bring down the regime. A student demonstration on 17 November was met with an extraordinary show of force by the Prague police. Rumours circulated that a student had been killed. In outrage, almost the entire population of Prague surged onto the streets, sustaining their protest for several days while the CPCS Central Committee met in emergency session to try to work out where it was going and how it could preserve its power. Apparently, the question of putting down the popular revolt by force was raised, but the representatives of the army pointed out that without Soviet backing, they were simply not capable of carrying through such a large-scale operation on their own. On the other hand, the CPCS completely lacked a credible alternative leadership of reform Communists who could retrieve the situation peacefully. After that was acknowledged, Communist power rapidly melted away. The small group of intellectual dissidents, led by Václav Havel, found themselves hastily cobbling together an alternative leadership and organising the popular masses on the streets into a ramshackle impromptu movement, Civic Forum, to bring some order into the situation and to take over government.

In Hungary, the advent of Gorbachev was enthusiastically greeted by the burgeoning ranks of committed reformers within the HSWP: since they shared both his domestic and his international objectives, it now appeared that the way was open for them to tackle the mounting domestic crisis by pursuing radical economic reform and further developing their good relations with the West. But in fact, Gorbachev precipitated not reform but the total collapse of the regime by undermining Kádár's pivotal position. Under Gorbachev, the limits of the possible in the field of reform were no longer clear, but wherever they were, they were certainly much wider than Kádár himself could tolerate. As a result, Kádár was increasingly exposed as a major obstacle to reform, and so he lost his role in the Party as a 'centralist' mediator between extremes, and lost his credibility with the people as the 'best leader possible in the circumstances'. The period from 1985 to early 1989 was one of intense internal conflict within the HSWP, which the party reformists won. They set about consolidating their position in power by re-opening the deeply emotive and politically explosive issue of 1956. In so doing, they discredited the older generation within the party, and Kádár personally, and at the same time, raised popular expectations of radical change. Other dramatic gestures were the tearing down of the 'Iron Curtain' on the border with Austria in spring 1989, allowing East German refugees to transit via Hungary to the West, and setting up the Round Table to negotiate the transition to multi-party democracy with representatives of opposition groups. Many of the party reformists were for some time under the illusion that their courageous actions would guarantee them the leading role in Hungary's political life even after the transition to multi-party democracy. As the 1990 elections were to show, the relatively calm way in which the people watched and responded to these momentous changes did not mean apathy and readiness to continue to be ruled by Communists for the sake of 'stability'.

In conclusion to this section, we can perhaps say that in the case of Czechoslovakia, the international factor – change in Moscow – was decisive in bringing down Communist rule. The nature of the Husak regime was such that it had all but smothered an autonomous domestic sphere of politics, with the result that internally-generated pressures for change were very weak within the party and diffuse and disorganised in society. A really forceful challenge only emerged in response to the collapse of Communism in all the neighbouring countries. In Hungary in the 1980s, the economic and political crisis of the 1980s generated intense domestic pressures for change, not least within the HSWP itself; a dramatic and possibly bloody social revolt was feared by all sides. But the international factor here too was decisive in ensuring the peaceful nature of the final denouement of Communist rule.

The 'return to Europe'

In 1989, East Europeans summed up their aspirations for change in the phrase 'return to Europe', which captures nicely the complex of domestic/international and political/economic interconnections involved in the transition to democracy in this region. The 'return to Europe' was to mean, in domestic terms, the establishment of 'normal', understood as West European-style , institutions: a pluralist liberal-democratic political system and a market economy which could offer both consumer affluence and a developed welfare state. As a result, people expected that a 'normal', West European way of life – in particular, standard of living – would relatively rapidly follow. The legitimation of the new democratic political order would thus depend to a significant extent on economic performance, rather as before. The new governments were well aware that, in the short to medium term, their populations would have to undergo a painful shock generated by the economic and social dislocations involved in the transition from a state socialist to a market economy. So they sought to divert popular aspirations into other channels, emphasising the non-material and international aspects of the 'return to Europe'. In order to legitimate their rule, the new governments proclaimed adherence to a set of values, held to be distinctly 'European' (respect for human rights, individual liberty, tolerance of diversity as well as democratic principles of political organisation), and sought to distinguish themselves from the old Communist regimes. Western recognition of the new governments as equal partners, and the promise of rapid integration into Western international institutions, played a very important role in their legitimation by providing some kind of seal of approval or guarantee of their credibility *vis-à-vis* their own societies.

At the same time, the 'return to Europe' had an outwardly-oriented purpose. The new governments also sought to use their demonstrated commitment to 'European' values in the domestic arena as an argument for Western support in various fields – first of all for economic and financial aid for the transition to the market, but, no less importantly, for some kind of security guarantees in the post-Cold War world. Without such support, they argued, the success of the democratic transition would be thrown into doubt, the West's commitment to the values it professed would be revealed as a cynical sham and a great opportunity would have been lost to the detriment of the West's own long-term economic and security interests.

In this section, we will draw out some of the differences between Czechoslovakia and Hungary in their respective 'returns to Europe'. Firstly, we will look at the way in which the foreign policy and security dimension and external economic dimension interacted with domestic political developments. Although there is much in common between the two states in this respect, nevertheless some differences can be observed, which to a large degree are the inheritance of the respective states' recent past, as identified in the previous section. Secondly, we will look at the role of nationalism in the democratic transition in the two countries, which draws on both the international and domestic dimensions.

The foreign policy security dimension

The general conditions of foreign policy-making in the two countries were in some respects different, which at times produced divergent emphases and approaches.

In Hungary, there was a much greater continuity in foreign policy from the last years of Communist rule. This was because of the way in which the foreign policy reorientation towards the West had been used in the 1980s as a means of sustaining the regime's domestic credibility (see Reisch, 1990). The culmination of this trend had come in 1989 with the decision of the last Communist Prime Minister and Foreign Minister, Miklós Németh and Gyula Horn, to open the border between Hungary and Austria, which precipitated the attempted flight to the West via Hungary of vast numbers of East German citizens. The Hungarian decision in September 1989 to allow them to leave directly undermined the Honecker regime and led to the dismantling of the Berlin Wall, and thus of the postwar order in Europe. There is no doubt that this historic gesture was aimed simultaneously at the domestic audience as well as the foreign, and indeed it had a great impact on Hungarian opinion – polls showed that Németh and Horn were personally hugely popular. But this did not translate into the hoped-for level of electoral support for the Socialist Party (as the reform wing of the HSWP renamed itself in September 1989) in the spring 1990 elections (11 per cent of votes cast – see Batt, 1991, p. 123). However, Horn retains a prominent role in political life as a respected parliamentary deputy and leader of the HSP fraction. (Németh found his reward abroad with a key position in the new European Bank for Reconstruction and Development in London).

The new government under József Antall also wished to use foreign policy for the purposes of domestic legitimation, but it found it politically inconvenient to admit to continuity in the foreign policy area, yet somewhat difficult to demonstrate a radical break with the past. Many of the grand symbolic gestures and realignments, such as dismantling the Iron Curtain, establishing diplomatic relations with Israel, hosting the CSCE Cultural Forum, joining the IMF, establishing a special relationship with the European Community and being a founder member of the Pentagonale etc., had already taken place under their Communist predecessors. It was in many respects a hard act to follow, but nevertheless there were certain lines which could be pursued to great effect, the chief among them being seen to be at the forefront of the moves to disband the WTO and securing the earliest possible departure of Soviet troops from Hungary. Thus full sovereignty was finally won back: for the first time since 1944 there were no foreign troops on Hungarian soil, and the key popular demand of 1956, 'Russians go home!' had been achieved (see Reisch, 1991).

In its relations with the West, Hungary enjoyed the advantage of an established good reputation, and was first of the post-Communist states to be admitted to full membership of the Council of Europe. In fact, being 'first' or at the forefront in developing new links with Western and European institutions appears to be an important psychological undercurrent in current Hungarian foreign policy. In the Kádár era, the regime gained much credibility at home from its recognition in the West as the leading reforming country. The new government appears to fear that this competitive edge over its neighbours might be lost as they too embark on radical reforms, and it appears to think that this would be a bad thing for its domestic political credibility. This undercurrent feeds into relations within the Central European region, for example, injecting a competitive rather than collaborative spirit into such regional initiatives as the Višegrad group, set up to coordinate the approaches of Hungary, Poland and Czechoslovakia towards, among other things, the European Community. Hungarians feel that their economic reforms are further advanced than those of their neighbours, and that they are likely to be held back by dealing with the EC in tandem with them. In the view of Rudolf Tókés, a senior adviser to the Hungarian Foreign Ministry, 'The advantages that may be gained through unilateral actions with the West vastly outnumber the advantages that may be gained through triangular cooperation' (see Tókés, 1991, p. 110).

It was much easier for the new Czechoslovak government than for the Antall government to present its foreign policy as diametrically opposed to what had gone before. The new regime launched into a vigorous effort to restore its international position after more than twenty years of isolation, including an exhausting schedule of foreign visits, approaches to join key international organisations such as the Council of Europe, the Pentagonale, the IMF (see Obrman, 1990). Czechs and Slovaks discovered that Havel, their new head of state (a man of whom remarkably few had heard until 1989), enjoyed great international prestige which was clearly an asset to the country, helping to bring in vast numbers of tourists and promoting an intense proliferation of cultural and educational exchanges and a variety of other links. Czechoslovakia, in particular Prague, suddenly found itself a very fashionable place, in stark contrast to its dismal reputation of the previous twenty-odd years.

A distinctive feature of Czechoslovakia's foreign policy in the early months after the collapse of Communist rule was the role of a certain moralistic idealism which reflected in part President Havel's own position, and in part the legacy of dissent in the 1980s, when the Charter 77 activists had established links with Western peace movements in opposing the siting of a new generation of missiles – both Soviet and American – in Europe. A strand of neutralism was observable in 1990 on questions of East-West relations in the Cold War era. Czechoslovakia shared with Hungary the traumatic national memory of Soviet invasion, and the breakup of the Warsaw Pact and the withdrawal of Soviet troops from its territory correspondingly occupied a central place in its new foreign and security policy. But it differed from Hungary in calling for the dissolution of *both* blocs, NATO as well as the WTO, and the withdrawal of US as well as Soviet troops from Europe. This stand was gradually abandoned in the course of 1990, but a distinctively idealistic strand could still be detected in Czechoslovakia's high hopes of the evolution of the CSCE into an effective pan-European security framework.

In contrast to Hungary, one consequence of the rapidity and radicalism of the political change in Czechoslovakia in 1989 was that the new government lacked a ready team of reliable and sympathetic professional diplomats and foreign policy advisers. This accounts for a certain naïvety which caused some of the new government's early policy initiatives to backfire, such as Havel's offer to mediate in the conflict between Israel and the PLO, which was not greeted with international enthusiasm; Havel's admission that injustices had been perpetrated by the Czech side in the expulsion of the Sudeten Germans after 1945, which enraged the older generation of his fellow countrymen who retained bitter memories of the war; and the Federal Assembly's decision to ban all arms sales, immediately threatening the employment of large numbers, especially in Slovakia, in an industry dominated by former nomenclature managers hostile to the new regime.

The external economic dimension

The economic transition involves at once domestic and external dimensions: the restoration of a market economy is intimately linked with opening up to the world market. The main points of contrast here between the two countries derive from the differing economic legacies of their Communist pasts; but it is also worth noting that despite these differences, they also share important basic problems.

Hungary's two decades of economic reform have given it a head start on the rest of Eastern Europe in several respects which are crucial to the reintegration of its economy into the world economy. The greater degree of openness to the world economy over the past two decades means that, in some important respects, Hungary has less far to travel than Czechoslovakia, whose Communist regime chose after 1968 to turn the economy back to the traditional Soviet, highly centralised, model, which also implied economic introversion and heavy dependence on the CMEA market (see Table 7.1).

In terms of legislation, Hungarian company law, commercial and foreign investment law was already radically overhauled in 1987 and 1988 to bring it into line with West European norms (see Sárközy, 1988). The taxation system was reformed, with the introduction of a system of personal income taxes and VAT. This has created an environment which Western investors see as more stable and predictable, and the result has been a much higher inflow of foreign direct investment into Hungary than into any other country in the region. Western multinational companies,

Table 7.1 Distribution of foreign trade with Europe

(% total)	*Hungary*		*Czechoslovakia*	
	1986	*1990*	*1986*	*1990*
EXPORTS to:				
CMEA	55.1	29.0	56.4	43.4
USSR	33.9	18.0	33.4	25.2
EC	17.3	35.0	16.0	26.5
Germany, West	8.5	20.0	7.7	12.8
East	6.4		6.8	4.2
Austria	5.3	6.5	3.9	5.9
IMPORTS from:				
CMEA	51.2	32.0	59.3	44.4
USSR	30.9	20.0	35.5	21.6
EC	22.5	39.0	16.4	23.8
Germany, West	12.4	18.0	8.3	13.3
East	6.7		7.5	8.2
Austria	6.2	9.2	4.7	9.7

Source: Economist Intelligence Unit

when establishing themselves in the region, tend to begin by 'testing the water' in Budapest, and then establish their regional headquarters there. All of this began to have a visible effect on the city as early as the first half of the 1980s, and contributed to the awareness of Hungarian people that their country was in some sense in the lead in 'returning to Europe' well before the events of 1989. In addition, the two decades of reform had an important impact on Hungarian managers and economic officials, who absorbed to a great degree an understanding of market-oriented economics and business practices as a result of growing direct contacts with Western firms and financial institutions.

Despite the differences in their respective economic starting positions, the adjustment of the industrial structure to the demands of external liberalisation has been painful for both countries, and the impact of the collapse of trade with the Soviet Union has been severe. Industrial output has fallen: in Hungary by 8.5 per cent in 1990, 19 per cent in 1991, and 15 per cent (estimated) in 1992; in Czechoslovakia, where reforms only began to be introduced in 1991, industrial output fell by 23 per cent in 1991, and a further 9 per cent in 1992 (see *Economic Trends in Eastern Europe*, 1992; EIU, *Country Reports*, on Czechoslovakia and Hungary for the relevant years). The industrial recession has been accompanied by unemployment, which rose to over 11 per cent in Hungary and 6 per cent in Czechoslovakia by the end of 1992. As we shall see below, the unequal distribution of this between the Czech Republic, with less than 3 per cent unemployment, and Slovakia, with 11 per cent, had major political implications.

Hungary inherited from the economic failures of the past a very high level of external debt ($20.6 bn gross in 1989, almost $2,000 per capita), which is a major obstacle to rapid improvement in its domestic economic performance (see Young, 1989). Czechoslovakia, on account of the caution of the Communist regime in dealings with the West, had a relatively low level of debt, at $7.9 bn gross in 1989 (just over $500 per capita). However, here, too, the contrast between the two countries is not as stark as it first appears. Czechoslovakia's advantage was bought by the previous regime at the cost of future generations – by neglecting investment in the modernisation of its economy, and by continuing with outdated energy-intensive and highly polluting production processes, it had effectively borrowed against its own future (see the comparative economic study of Hungary and Czechoslovakia by Dyba, 1985). A sharp rise in borrowing thus seems an inescapable concomitant of the transition in Czechoslovakia, implying that here too, the adjustment cannot be made without a relatively long period of restricted domestic consumption.

The implications of these economic issues for the transition to democracy in each country are, in a general sense, rather obvious. Both governments are faced with an acute political challenge: their legitimacy is very much bound up with the promise of the 'return to Europe', and foremost in the minds of their electorates is the aspiration to the West European standard of living. But the means to that end – the transition to a market economy and the ensuing economic openness – seem to require a further extended period of economic retrenchment, which is hard for people to accept because it is more severe and more extended than expected. This threatens to undermine the credibility and authority of the new governments. The temptation for weak governments is to make concessions in economic policy in order to soften its social impact; but the result of such concessions is likely to be a slowdown in the economic transition with knock-on effects for the 'return to Europe' in the sense of achieving international economic reintegration on the basis of liberalisation and competitiveness.

Nationalism and the democratic transition

The rise of nationalism in Eastern Europe since 1989 can be seen as an inevitable response to the peculiarities of its multi-dimensional transition discussed above. It is, firstly, a reaction against the former high level of 'penetration' of the political system, which involved the forced imposition of an alien model designed to obliterate national identity and to subordinate national interests to those of a foreign power. A major precondition of establishing democratic politics in these circumstances is the redefinition of the community to which the state must become answerable. The definitions of the political community and of citizenship in modern democratic politics in Europe is intimately bound up with the notion of the nation. Eastern Europe's 'return to Europe' sometimes appears to have been conceived as the replacement of Communist internationalism with another set of universal, abstract principles, those of liberal individualism, but in practice these principles have always assumed the prior existence of a national political community as the basis for legitimation of states:

> Democracy in Western Europe turns upon the existence of strongly cohesive collective identities which are centred on nationalism . . . Liberal democracy has almost everywhere been parasitic on nationalism. Democracy possesses no theory or force of its own capable of either generating or explaining the very ties of attachment upon which its workings in practice depend. Without a 'body' whose politics can be democratically ordered, party-politics contains no substantive coherence or principle of continuity. (Keens-Soper, 1989, p. 694).

The perennial problem for Eastern Europe has, however, been a non-contiguity of national identities with the territorial boundaries of states, with the result that awareness of national identity is heavily skewed towards ethnic and racial characteristics, to the detriment of the civic component of national identity – that is, the idea of a community based on equal political rights. The predominantly ethnic understanding of nationhood is very hard to reconcile with liberal-democratic politics, because implicitly it recognises full citizenship rights only for the majority ethnic group. Ethnic minorities tend to be treated as anomalous and problematic, even when they have inhabited the territory for centuries.

The redefinition of an authentic national identity is taking place through the rediscovery of history, which leads on to the rediscovery of the arbitrariness and injustice with which most existing state borders were established. This ties in to the second feature of Eastern Europe's transition, *the breakdown of the existing states-system in Europe*, which has created a peculiarly insecure and fluid international environment, raising questions about the immutability of state borders. The intimate connection between the transition to democracy and redrawing state borders was clear at the very outset, with the opening of the Berlin Wall and the subsequent reunification of Germany. The process has continued to work its way through the collapse of Communist rule in the Soviet Union and Yugoslavia which immediately led on to the collapse of those states themselves as multinational entities.

The third element of the situation is the *political impact of the economic transition*. New democratic governments find themselves in the difficult position of imposing economic policies in the name of the long-term 'national interest' which in the short and medium term have a very severe impact on the material welfare of large groups of their electorates. Nationalism can be used effectively by governments as a means of justifying the sacrifices their economic policies demand; but it can also be used by opponents of the new governments, who point to the role of outsiders – experts from the IMF, Western bankers and multinational companies – who appear to be determining policies to suit their own interests at the expense of the people.

The place of nationalism in Eastern Europe's transition to democracy is thus highly ambiguous. On the one hand, it is a natural part of the process of redefining the basis of state legitimacy, and can serve to shore up fragile new democratic institutions as societies pass through the stresses of the economic transition. On the other hand, it can be used to divert societies away from 'Europe', undermining the authority of democratically elected governments and blocking the economic transition. Let us turn to discuss these issues in the cases of Hungary and Czechoslovakia.

The importance of nationalism to the legitimation of the new regime in Hungary was clearly demonstrated by József Antall, leader of the Hungarian Democratic Forum which won the election in spring 1990. Presenting the programme of his government to the Hungarian parliament, Antall declared that he spoke as representative of the interests of '15 million Hungarians'. The population of Hungary is 10.5 million – the rest live mainly in Transylvania (2 million), which is part of Romania; in the Vojvodina (400,000), which is part of Serbia; in Slovakia (600,000); and in the Ukraine (200,000). The situation of these minorities has always been a matter of deep concern to most Hungarians resident in Hungary, but this concern has inevitably been heightened by the current situation, with civil war in Yugoslavia, the breakup of the Czechoslovak state and the emergence in Romania of extremist nationalist parties and a government prepared at times to play on Romanian nationalist sentiment. An estimated 50,000 refugees are now being cared for in Hungary, most of them Hungarians fleeing from Vojvodina and Transylvania.

Hungarian nationalism in the interwar period was military chauvinist and revisionist (see Barany, 1969), but a deep sense of the injustice of the Treaty of Trianon which established the existing frontiers in 1920 was held by nearly all shades of political opinion apart from the Communists, and continues to be held today. The question here is not whether nationalism will play a central role in Hungarian politics, but whether it will be nationalism of a more moderate variety which can coexist with and support the transition to democracy. Antall's claim was interpreted by the Romanian and Slovak governments in particular as a revival of traditional Hungarian revisionist nationalism, but, in my view, it should rather be read in the context of the task Antall sees himself facing, that of establishing his government's domestic authority. He appears to be responding to genuine popular feeling which is not necessarily revisionist. Mainstream Hungarian nationalism today is the product of substantial evolution over the recent period.

This started with the experience of the Second World War, which was perceived as a national disaster brought about by fanatical nationalists, and the events of 1956 demonstrated a convergence between nationalism and democratic values: '. . . conspicuously absent from the Revolution of 1956 was the taint of revisionist irredentism, the hard core of World War II Magyar nationalism' (Barany, 1969, p. 303). After 1956, the Kádár regime was extremely wary of using nationalism as a means of increasing its legitimacy, but instead, it did develop a new sense of Hungarian national self-identity centred on economic reform and, especially in the 1980s, on acting as a 'bridge' between East and West. This went some way towards incorporating (albeit not explicitly) some of the notions of the interwar populist-nationalist intellectual current, by playing on the idea of Hungary's 'special' nature, which had to be defended by achieving a degree of independence (even neutrality) from superpower politics, and by finding a 'Third Way', neither capitalist nor Communist, appropriate for its unique character. As the economic situation deteriorated in the mid-1980s, there were some signs that the regime was prepared to use national feeling, particularly against Romania, as a form of diverting domestic attention. (It has to be said as well that the behaviour of the Ceauşescu regime at this time made some form of response from the Hungarian government unavoidable.) But in the course of the 1980s, and even more so since 1989, Hungarian foreign policy, as argued above, has become overtly pro-Western. The strategy for dealing with the problems of the Hungarian minorities is centred on working through existing multilateral structures, in particular, through the CSCE process, within which Hungary acquired much useful experience in the past decade.

But if these structures prove inadequate in future for protecting national minorities, there is obvious scope for the re-emergence of a more militant form of nationalism which could in turn tilt the domestic political balance back towards the interwar patterns of authoritarianism. Revisionist currents certainly exist: for example, a leading member of the HDF, István Csurka, published an openly anti-Semitic and implicitly revisionist pamphlet in September 1992; supporters of Csurka in the HDF managed to secure the election of four of their faction to the party's Executive in January 1993 (see Pataki *et al.*, 1992). Although it seems unlikely that extreme nationalism will take over a dominant position in Hungarian politics, even the more moderate variant of it propounded by Antall tends to have a deleterious effect on political development in the region. The Hungarians appear to be chronically insensitive to the way in which their pronouncements are interpreted in Romania and Slovakia, both of whom have bitter memories of mistreatment at the hands of Hungary within living memory. Their over-reactions then set in train a vicious circle of mutual recriminations and misunderstandings which strengthen the hand of nationalist demagogues on all sides and could easily lead to regional conflict.

In multinational Czechoslovakia, the resurgence of Slovak nationalism brought about the division of the state. As in the Soviet Union and Yugoslavia, the advent of open politics appears to have undermined the legitimacy of the existing federal structures, even though in the Czechoslovak case, in clear contrast to the Soviet Union and Yugoslavia, there is no history of imperialist domination or mutual ethnic blood-letting in the relations between the two nations. The concept of a 'Czechoslovak' national identity has not proved sufficiently robust to withstand the self-questioning which has accompanied the opening up of free debate (see Batt, 1993, Chapter 1). Thus what had been domestic politics has now been shifted to the plane of international relations with the final separation into two states on 1 January 1993. The international context played a vital role in this development: Slovak nationalists clearly took the international recognition of Slovenia, Croatia and the Baltic states in the course of 1991 as a signal that their own aspirations for independent statehood could at last be realised.

But the economic factor was the main motor of the rise of nationalism in Czechoslovakia. While in Slovenia, Croatia and the Baltics, the case for economic self-government was made in terms of ending the draining off of national resources to subsidise weaker economies in federations dominated by Communist centralists who were blocking the transition to a market economy, in the case of Slovakia, the case for economic self-government has been made in terms of pursuing a different pattern of economic transition from the radical neo-liberal one devised by Prague politicians and imposed on Slovakia regardless of its disproportionately high social costs for that republic. Slovakia's economic plight has much to do with its economy's structural disproportions, inherited from the programme of industrial development and modernisation implemented by the Communist regime, particularly (ironically) by the post-1968 'normalisation' regime dominated by Slovaks, who were committed to overcoming Slovak economic backwardness. This programme was financed by the transfer of resources from the stronger Czech economy: one study claims that transfers from the Czech lands accounted annually on average for 14.4 per cent of national income distributed in Slovakia between 1950–70, and for 8.6 per cent on average between 1971–88 (Hanzlová, 1992). While extraordinary progress was made in terms of equalisation of the standard of living and the quantitative indices of development, in qualitative terms, which only come to the fore with the reintroduction of the market and reintegration into the world economy, Slovak industrialisation was a disaster. Slovak industries were very heavily geared to defence production for the Warsaw Pact, which no longer exists, and to meeting the demands of the Soviet market, which has collapsed.

In these circumstances, it is by no means clear that the government of an independent Slovakia will be able to deliver on its promises to bring about a less painful economic transition than that offered within the framework of a common Czechoslovak state. Predictably, the common front which Slovak politicians were able to forge in opposition to Prague has fallen apart now that the goal of separate statehood has been achieved. The economic issue has now moved to centre stage in Slovak politics, and intense conflict can be expected not only between, but within, parties, particularly within the governing party, the Movement for a Democratic Slovakia. On the one hand, Slovak economic survival and future prosperity requires heavy dependence on international economic and financial support. This will be subject to political conditionality, which may be hard for nationalists to swallow, especially as the policy prescriptions handed out by the international financial institutions are likely to differ very little from those formerly imposed by Prague. But divisions among the nationalists on economic policy are apparent: the Slovak Nationalist Party is evolving towards a right-wing position on economic issues; Prime Minister Měciar, leader of the MFDS, is committed to a statist, avowedly 'left-of-centre' approach, and occasionally seems to believe that Slovak prosperity can be best assured by resurrecting its trade links with the former Soviet republics; others within his party may be more prepared to adapt to the demands of economic integration with the West.

There remains the possibility that a Slovak nationalist government facing this difficult economic situation will be tempted to divert attention from material issues into the emotionally charged area of national identity, by fomenting conflict with the large Hungarian minority. The international repercussions of this could be far-reaching. Slovakia would not only damage itself by forfeiting Western financial support and investment; it could generate a threat to its own security. A substantial proportion of the Hungarian minority lives in compact territories directly adjoining Hungary. In the period 1939–45, when a separate Slovak state was last in existence as a result of Nazi Germany's dismemberment of the Czechoslovak First Republic, those territories were returned to Hungary. The Hungarian minority has been relatively contented with its lot in postwar Czechoslovakia, but is apprehensive about its prospects in the new Slovak state. Crass extremism on the part of Slovak nationalist politicians could provoke the very crisis they claim most to fear – the demand for secession by Hungary-majority areas in south Slovakia.

Conclusion

Hungary and Czechoslovakia, two neighbouring states in the heart of Europe, have shared many of the historical vicissitudes which flow from their common geopolitical predicament. Both have been extraordinarily open to the international environment. And yet there have been striking contrasts between them in the ways in which their domestic politics have adapted and responded to international pressures. Their mutual relations, moreover, have been much more often characterised by conflict than cooperation, mutual sympathy and support. This is particularly disturbing today, when Hungary and the new Slovak state embark on essentially the same task of political and economic transition, but find themselves diverted by nationalist conflicts to the detriment of that transition in both countries.

References

Barany, G., 1969, 'Hungary: from aristocratic to proletarian nationalism' in P. Sugar and I. Lederer (eds), *Nationalism in Eastern Europe*, University of Washington Press, Seattle.

Batt, J.R., 1988, *Economic Reform and Political Change in Eastern Europe*, Macmillan Press, Basingstoke and London.

Batt, J.R., 1991, *East-Central Europe from Reform to Transformation*, Francis Pinter for the Royal Institute of International Affairs, London.

Batt, J.R., 1993, *Czecho-Slovakia from Federation to Separation*, Chatham House Discussion Paper No. 46.

Bauer, T., 1988, 'Deceleration, dependency and "depaternalisation": some considerations concerning the changes of the Soviet Union and Eastern Europe in the coming decades', *Acta Oeconomica*, Vol. 39 (1–2), pp. 155–69.

Bruszt, L., 1990, 'The negotiated revolution in Hungary', *Social Research*, 57 (2), pp. 365–88.

Dawisha, K., 1981, 'The 1968 invasion of Czechoslovakia: causes, consequences and lessons for the future' in K. Dawisha and P. Hanson (eds), *Soviet-East European Dilemmas: coercion, competition and consent*, Heinemann for the RIIA, London.

Dawisha, K., 1990, *Eastern Europe, Gorbachev and Reform* (2nd edn.), Cambridge University Press, Cambridge.

Dyba, K., 1985, 'Adjustment to international disturbances: Czechoslovakia and Hungary', *Acta Oeconomica*, 34 (3–4), pp. 317–37.

Ecomomic Trends in Eastern Europe, 1992, Kopint-Datorg, Budapest, 1 (1).

EIU (Economist Intelligence Unit), various years, *Country Reports*, on Hungary and Czechoslovakia, London.

Gati, C., 1986, *Hungary and the Soviet Bloc*, Duke University Press, Durham NC.

Hanzlová, D., 1992, 'Ekonomická realita Česko-slovenských vztahů', *Ekonom*, 36 (2), pp. 22–3.

Havel, V., 1992, 'President diagnoses ills and reviews successes in New Year speech', *BBC Summary of World Broadcasts*, EE/1268, pp. B/1–5, 3 January.

Keens-Soper, M. 1989, 'The liberal state and nationalism in postwar Europe', *History of European ideas*, 10 (6), pp. 689–703.

Kövés, A., 1985,*The CMEA Countries in the World Economy: turning inwards or turning outwards*, Akademiai Kiado, Budapest.

Kövés, A., and Marer, P. (eds), 1991, *Foreign Economic Liberalisation: transformations in socialist and market economies*, Westview Press, Boulder,San Franciso and Oxford.

Marer, P., 1986, 'Hungary's balance of payments crisis and response 1978–84' in US Congress Joint Economic Committee (ed.), *East European Economies: slow growth in the 1980s*, US Government Printing Office, Washington DC.

Obrman, J., 1990, 1990 'Czechoslovakia: putting the country back on the map', *Radio Free Europe Report on Eastern Europe*, 1 (52), pp. 10–14.

Pataki, J. *et al*, 1992, 'Political storm in Hungary', *Radio Free Europe/Radio Liberty Research Report*, 1 (40), 9 October, pp. 15–29.

Pridham, G., 1991, 'Democratic transition and the international environment: a research agenda', CMS-Occasional Paper No. 1, Centre for Mediterranean Studies, University of Bristol.

Reisch, A., 1990, 'Primary foreign policy objective to rejoin Europe', *Radio Free Europe Report on Eastern Europe*, 1 (52), pp. 15–20.

Reisch, A., 1991, 'Free of Soviet military forces after forty-six years', *Radio Free Europe Report on Eastern Europe*, 2 (30), pp. 21–32.

Sárközy, T. (ed.), 1988, *Foreign Investments in Hungary: law and practice*, Lang Ltd., Budapest.

Tókés, R.L. 1984, 'Hungarian reform imperatives', *Problems of Communism*, 33 (5), pp. 1–23.

Tókés, R., 1991, 'From Višegrad to Kraków: cooperation, competition and coexistence in central Europe', *Problems of Communism*, 40 (6), pp. 100–14.

Whitehead, L., 1986, 'International aspects of democratisation' in G. O'Donnell, P.C. Schmitter and L. Whitehead, *Transitions from Authoritarian Rule*, Part III, Johns Hopkins University Press, Baltimore and London.

Young, D., 1989, October 1989, Hungary – debt versus reform' *The World Today*, 45 (10), pp. 171–5.

8

Communism's weakest link – democratic capitalism's greatest challenge: Poland

George Sanford

Introduction

Since the collapse of Communism in Eastern Europe in 1989, and even more so after its demise and the breakup of the USSR in 1991, a number of scenarios have been presented for the developing shape of the New Europe. Buzan *et al.* (1990) and Hyde-Price (1990) identify the following range of, by no means exclusive, outcomes; the conservative EC/NATO consolidation and extension scenario; that of EC-based political, economic and security integration; variants of German-dominated Europe; a Russian nationalist-authoritarian backlash with expansionary consequences; the collapse into multipolar rivalries and nationalist conflicts in both Eastern and Western Europe; and the development of general pan-European frameworks to provide a favourable environment for a wide range of nation states. The ending of the bipolar division of Europe has also presupposed the integration of what used to be Communist Eastern Europe in different ways and at varying levels with European frameworks.

Eastern Europe, in its widest sense, had previously been regarded as a monolithic whole (Soviet bloc or External Empire) in Eastern Europe and the Inner Empire of the ring of non-Russian Republics within the USSR. This space has now become highly differentiated. The dominant criteria adopted for distinguishing between individual national experiences have been the degree and prospects of domestic democratisation/marketisation and the consequent likelihood of integration with the EC. Poland, thus, finds itself within the most favoured Central European constellation with Hungary and the Czech Republic, all of which gained EC Association in December 1991. Unlike the more questionable case of Slovakia, their nation-building problems also include, at worst, a residual degree of national consolidation. In 1993 it seemed that Bulgaria and Romania, who gained EC Association in December 1992 and March 1993 respectively, were, possibly with independent Slovakia, well ahead of the Baltic states and in a different category to a residual grouping of ex-Soviet European republics such as Belorussia, the Ukraine and Moldava. The turmoil in Yugoslavia made prognostication difficult. Slovenia seemed more favourable than Croatia which, again, had a totally different level of domestic consolidation and external stability than Albania or Macedonia (Skopje), let alone Bosnia.

The above pecking order is completely *ad hoc*. The EC itself has never been quite so clear in its responses to Eastern European developments; but it can be taken as a rough rule of thumb for indicating Poland's quite favoured position in the wider regional context. One may also add that the above groupings correspond roughly to rankings by level of alleged cultural civilisation which are more popular on the European continent than in Anglo-Saxon countries. The latter express them more in terms of potential for capitalist democracy but specialists reiterate traditional distinctions. On the one hand, there is Catholic Central Europe with its 'Western' values and the similar but Scandinavian-Germanic mode of the Baltic states and on the other, the collectivist-authoritarian traditions of the Orthodox in both the Ottoman-influenced Balkans and the ex-Soviet controlled Slav Republics. Such perceptions may be regarded as over-schematic, but they highlight the importance of traditional political cultures in moulding the general processes of democratisation and marketisation unleashed in the region since 1989. One can, therefore, argue that the region's systemic transformation towards capitalist democracy and Western-style pluralist societies is a long-run inevitability; significant aspects of the transitional process and, even, the outcome will, however, be more than marked by the differentiated local factors. The latter aspects, which include broad historical traditions, the national experience under Communism, the socio-economic and cultural level at the entry point into the transformation process, the composition of post-Communist elites, the degree of national consolidation which subsumes the questions of ethnic minorities and disputed frontiers as well as the country's strategic position, are well illustrated by Poland's current experience.

The discussion of Poland's path away from Communism towards democratic capitalism and of the complex interplay between the domestic-cultural and external support factors is also significant for the following more specific reasons:

1. Developments within both its Communist state and national society and the relations between them in the three decades before 1989 produced a process which accelerated the bloc-wide collapse of Communism. It also revealed the structural constraints and new challenges to post-Communist democratisation and marketisation at their starkest. Poland's penetration by Western political, economic and cultural pressures accelerated from 1956 onwards. There is, therefore, one of the strongest and clearest connections between external influences and domestic transformation in Poland's case.
2. The Poles, with large justification, consider themselves part of

European civilisation. This favourable starting off point assisted the 'Organic Rejection' of Communism and the initial transition to a democratic framework; but it does not necessarily facilitate the resolution of current economic and social problems. The absence of significant national minorities and seriously threatened frontiers also means that the central democratisation and marketisation processes are not complicated, as in much of the Balkans and the ex-USSR, by the primary problem of nation-state building. The Communist experience of postwar modernisation had also produced an open and plurally differentiated society by the 1970s. But the Communist system, while producing many original responses to its continuous crisis after 1976, proved unable to accommodate the subsequent pressures for a civil society. Fully articulated state-society links, including the essential elements of popular sovereignty and political representation based on free elections and a competitive party system, became possible after 1989. But much of the necessary groundwork including the bases for a constitutional *Rechtsstaat* had emerged during the 1980s. That is why the 'rupture', when it came, could be negotiated so relatively painlessly in 1989.

3. Poland, as a medium-sized European state, with the equivalent population and potential of Spain, merits consideration of its specific features just as much as for its wider impact and significance as for the general processes mentioned above.

Poland's road: nationalist-authoritarianism and socio-economic modernisation

Poland was the weakest link in the Soviet bloc in Eastern Europe. It provided one of the most difficult national environments in which to establish Soviet control, let alone in which to build Communism (Kolankiewicz and Lewis, 1988). In fact, its comparatively limited political terror and incomplete Stalinisation provoked a massive social reaction which transformed the system in important respects in 1956. Gomułka, an authoritarian Communist with a nationalist-domesticist streak, accepted the consequences of the Polish 'October'. He abandoned the half-hearted collectivisation of agriculture, the Soviet Stalinist strategy of restructuring society and the attempts to control the Roman Catholic Church and the intelligentsia. The rank and file membership of the ruling Polish United Workers' Party (PZPR) were never socialised properly into Soviet socialist values and proved an unreliable support for Communist leaderships in the great confrontations with Polish society of 1970, 1976 and 1980–1. Although Communist leaders used force as in Poznań in June 1956, on the Baltic seacoast in December 1970 and in martial law repression, Gomułka, Gierek and Jaruzelski all wanted to maintain their autonomy from the Kremlin. But in order to implement their particular realistic conceptions of Polish patriotism they had to develop a wide range of innovative forms of crisis management. This normally involved compromises with society and the gradual abandonment of mainstream Soviet-Leninist values and practices.

Poland, thus, never became anything like a totalitarian state on the Soviet model and a full-blooded satellite of the Kremlin power-holders (Sadowski, 1991). After 1956 it increasingly became a pluralist-authoritarian system; the leadership camouflaged its nationalist-domesticism by manoeuvring between the Kremlin and Polish society to preserve its power. Ideological belief and commitment dwindled away. The Communist elite became openly materialist and corrupt under Gierek, but in a cynical and good-natured, not tyrannical, way. It lost its cohesion and social prestige especially amongst the workers. It had few reserves of ideological or general legitimacy to fall back on once Gierek's consumerist strategies failed. In terms of development theory, Poland had, by 1980, become a demographically youthful, dynamic, well-educated and stratified society with traditional Polish cultural and social values predominating over Soviet Communist ones, except in ritual mouthings at the very top. The great achievements of the Gierek decade were thus the maturation of Polish society and its opening up to the world in economic, cultural and travel terms (Lepak, 1988); but the stoking up of socio-economic stresses and the insufficient response by the exclusionary political system provoked the massive outburst of 1980.

The split between the monopolistic Communist state and the anything but monolithic, modernising society, which was managed elsewhere in the Soviet bloc fairly successfully in various ways until the late 1980s, was, however, aggravated by Poland's highly specific historical experience. Its tradition of excessive individualist democracy harked back to the 'Golden Freedom' or 'Anarchy' which is often considered to be the prime reason for Poland's partition and loss of independent statehood in the eighteenth century (Gomułka and Polonsky, 1990, Chapters 1–3). On the other hand, Russia tyranny after the failure of the 1830 and 1863 uprisings, the horror of Nazi occupation and the pressure of early Soviet Communist rule all produced and reinforced what in various forms can be described as the Polish national and Catholic counter-community opposed to a German or Russian/Soviet-dominated state. This ensured Poland's survival against its occupiers; but such aspects of the political culture were unhelpful once the Poles regained independent statehood. Interwar Poland is now much praised, but it failed to solve the country's modernisation dilemmas or to assure her military security and independent statehood. It veered between the extremes of a politically fragmented and unstable parliamentary democracy and, after Piłsudski's *coup d'état* in May 1926, an exclusionary political authoritarianism. The latter had little real control over Polish society which was divided into hostile political, socio-economic and, even, given that a third of the country's population was made up of national minorities, ethnic camps. The task of national and social integration was, therefore, not completed before the Second World War and Soviet Communist rule dictated a return to the previous opposition pattern. By the mid-1970s this assumed the form of the self-organisation of society. The tactic, as applied by the Workers Defence Committee (KOR), provided a model for Solidarity's development as a social movement and a political force as well as a free trade union in 1980–1. What proved a superbly effective force in confronting, and eventually wearing down and defeating, Communist power, again, proved a destabilising force in the post-1989 early democratisation stage.

One important aspect of the foregoing, partly cause and partly consequence, was that Communist Poland became remarkably open to the outside world. After 1956 tourism, guest-worker movements and links with Polish communities abroad (*Polonia*) expanded, particularly in the 1970s. So did trade with non-Communist countries and the attempt to import Western technology and to create dynamic export-led economic growth. Gierek's mismanagement led to a $20 billion trade deficit by the outburst of the 1980 crisis and partial dependence upon the capitalist world economy. Polish intellectual and cultural life flourished despite this. Extensive links were maintained with the non-Communist world as evidenced by the number of widely available Western plays, films and publications. Censorship was relatively light and mainly directed at a clearly understood number of taboos concerning the Soviet Union. The growth of domestic dissidence was tolerated. Unfavourable, and often unrealistic, comparisons between the quality, freedoms and living standards in Poland and the West, therefore, developed. Poland in this respect, as in so many others, thus entered the most dangerous pre-revolutionary stage of a decaying authoritarianism in General Crisis when reforms merely stoked up further demands. But Poland, as one of the most liberal Communist systems, along with Hungary, also acted as an important conduit for the introduction of non-mainstream Leninist-Stalinist ideas and practices into the Soviet bloc. Poland was, therefore, 'penetrated' in two very different and conflicting respects, by both Soviet control-mechanisms on the elites (see the chapters in this volume by J. Batt and M. Light) and by countervailing Western influences on society. From 1980 onwards Poland became the weakest and most disruptive element within the Soviet-dominated Warsaw Pact and Comecon section of the Communist world (Bromke, 1989).

The decomposition of Communist power: from Solidarity to the Round Table

One of the most confusing aspects of the post-1980 political scene is that the two quite separate strands of attempted intra-system reformism and anti-systemic overthrow and transformation ran very closely in parallel. The workers' upsurge which produced Solidarity in summer 1980 initially claimed to be primarily concerned with correcting the 'deformations' of socialism. But free trade unions and social and political pluralism were unacceptable to the stagnant Brezhnev leadership. It nipped any serious possibility of the PZPR leadership becoming dominated by socially supported and genuinely reformist figures, like Tadeusz Fiszbach, in the bud through the threatened military invasion of early December 1981. Subsequent Soviet political, economic, military and psychological pressure ensured that the process of Leninist-Democratisation was controlled by the leadership of PZPR First Secretary Stanisław Kania and Prime Minister Wojciech Jaruzelski. Competitive elections for delegates and officials at the July 1981 Ninth Congress and the promulgation of a most far-reaching programme for intra-system Communist reformism were kept in check (Sanford, 1983). Solidarity, worn down by a series of local and other confrontations, backed down in the national crisis which followed the beating up of three of its activists in Bydgoszcz in March 1981. With Polish society being tired out by the almost complete economic collapse both the PZPR and Solidarity leaderships were unable to find common ground even for continuing negotiations in early August 1981. The latter, as demonstrated by David Ost, could never quite bring itself to accept political incorporation in exchange for major reforms; there were, however, moments in the mid to late 1980s when it looked as though a deal on a corporatist basis might be achieved (Ost, 1990).

Jaruzelski concentrated party, state and military power in his hands in the final preparations for martial law, after replacing Kania in October 1981. The Solidarity Congress of September-October 1981 debated its organisation and policies, elected a new National Committee (KK) with Wałęsa as its chairman and passed a wide-ranging, but under the conditions of the time, rather Utopian, Programme for a Self-Managing Republic (Sanford, 1990). It was, however, hopelessly divided over immediate short-term tactics. Its leadership responded to the hardening PZPR line with demands for referenda on self-management and a new electoral law; but these were curtailed by the declaration of the State of War on 13 December 1981.

It has been argued that Soviet opposition was the prime reason for the failure of Solidarity and the PZPR to achieve a historic compromise in 1980–1. Further, it has also been argued that even had such a deal been struck, the Soviet Union would have invaded Poland as it had Hungary in 1956 and Czechoslovakia in 1968. The geopolitical argument of overwhelming Soviet regional control on fundamental systemic-ideological issues was also the apologia of the Kania-Jaruzelski camp, both then and now (Rachwald, 1990: Rensenbrink, 1988). Solidarity used similar arguments to clear itself of any responsibility for the 1981 débâcle and to justify its emphasis on ensuring the long-term survival of its moral-symbolic values during the 1980s. The contrary argument, quite apart from the Communist reform and corporatist theses, is that Poland with its 38 million population, traditions of resistance and crucial strategic position was a much more daunting proposition than Hungary or Czechoslovakia; much had also changed by 1981 in East-West relations and within the USSR itself. We shall never know for certain, but the USSR and its Polish allies certainly backed down in Summer 1980, played for time and continued to do so right up till Wałęsa and his Catholic advisers lost their nerve over Bydgoszcz. Genuine workers' leaders of an anti-Soviet, Western socialist sort, like Gwiazda, Rulewicz, Jurczyk and Modzelewski not only opposed Wałęsa's messy and undemocratic internal running of the union. They also doubted his confused belief that 'self-limitation' would allow free trade unions and pluralist social organisations to survive (Barker, 1986). A firm Solidarity line strengthening the PZPR's pragmatic-reformist wing and achieving a compromise, as all social confrontations had done since 1956, might have forced the ageing Brezhnev leadership to accept a Eurocommunist solution in 1981. Would this have precipitated the onset of Gorbachev's intra-system reformism? History, however, ruled otherwise and the balance moved decisively towards the transformation and the replacement, not the reform, of the Communist system by the end of the 1980s.

I argue that there was an important conflict within the Soviet bloc, of which the Polish case before Gorbachev was the most intense, over the possibility, extent and type of intra-system Communist reformism. Poland produced the most developed theoretical model of Leninist-Democratisation within the Communist Party itself (Hahn, 1987). But the attempt to destroy Solidarity's rival model of social self-organisation through martial law repression and to cow society did more than merely shift power from the party to the political-military elites (Sanford, 1986). It has been argued that Jaruzelski's regime should be considered as a type of authoritarian, initially semi-military, system with technocratic inclinations which can be seen as having many similarities with Latin American or Far Eastern dictatorial-modernising systems.[1] It monopolised power but was quite open to the specialist and educational elites running a pluralist and divided society, howbeit one with weakly organised independent social groups. Consequently the promised 'reform from above' got stuck and the ideal of self-managing and self-financing enterprises was not achieved. Martial law failed to exterminate the Solidarity leadership cores or to bury the memories of the 1980–1 social experience. Economic reform also created austerity and additional social discontent through huge price increases from early 1982 onwards.

The Jaruzelski regime, therefore, failed to break the stalemate, although there were moments when it seemed close to doing so. It gained, at best, limited and pragmatic social acceptance for its consultative-authoritarian reforms. After martial law it adopted incorporationist policies and a National Unity rhetoric and even came to accept the Solidarity slogan that economic reform would not work without social support. The regime-opposition struggle, therefore, assumed new forms during the middle to late 1980s. Jaruzelski's social-consultative bodies gained some intelligentsia support; intellectuals played important mediating roles in the state-society conflict. The ex-Solidarity opposition was increasingly tolerated and allowed to reorganise in 1985–6 although it never regained the mass support of 1980. Once the Jaruzelski regime had committed its economic marketisation policy, from the November 1987 referendum onwards, to a National Agreement strategy, its ultimate fate became less dependent upon its own efforts. Soviet bloc developments, especially the fate of Gorbachev's *perestroika*, and the repercussions of the changing East-West relationship became crucial factors (Gerrits, 1990; Carnovale and Potter, 1989).

This dimension also entails discussion of the relationship between the

East-West conflict in the 1980s and the process of Communist system transformation and replacement. Western elites, especially Reagan's and Thatcher's, had no interest in helping Communism to survive through reform, however major. Conservative ideological and political interests utilised the thesis of Communism's varied shortcomings in terms of economic failure and political autocracy as well as of its irreformability in their domestic conflicts with Social Democratic rivals. But in order to achieve these goals they had to balance sticks against Communist elites, like economic sanctions against Jaruzelski's martial law regime, with the carrot of various inducements purporting to show the higher attractions of the Western world for their societies.

The abdication of Communist power in Poland in 1989, therefore, needs to be set against the wider backdrop of a number of processes on the international scene which continued in one form or other for almost two decades. The first was West German Ostpolitik, which led to the legal-diplomatic confirmation of Poland's western frontier and the normalisation and improvement of Polish-West German relations. An important side effect was that the diminution of the so-called German revanchist threat weakened one of the strongest and genuinely felt arguments in Poland favouring the Polish-Soviet alliance. The second was the detente process in East-West relations which included SALT as well as a whole succession of other disarmament negotiations. The third was the Conference on Security and Cooperation in Europe (CSCE). The Polish role in the latter two was more important and was much more genuinely supported by Polish public opinion than is often appreciated in the West. There is insufficient space to document this thesis here but this has been amply done in numerous publications by the Polish Institute of International Affairs (PISM) in Warsaw.[2] What is better known is the way in which the Third Basket of the 1975 CSCE Helsinki Conference launched the issue of civil and human rights as an almost autonomous factor in the East-West conflict. It encouraged East European opposition movements to Communism, notably KOR and Solidarity in Poland, mobilised large sections of Western public opinion in their support and enabled Western governments to raise the issue in their political and economic negotiations with the Communist states. Conversely it fuelled the neo-liberal political propaganda offensive of the early 1980s within Western political systems themselves; it strengthened the rebirth of Hayek-Von Mises-Popper types of arguments that non-market systems were not only economically disastrous failures but also inevitably political tyrannies which sacrificed individual rights and liberties in the chimerical search for social Utopias. Western Social Democrats, being no friends of Soviet Stalinism, went along with this offensive but, apart from ruling Socialist Parties, notably those in France and Spain, generally failed to differentiate their own line and values sufficiently clearly. They were, consequently, hard hit by the backlash against Communist systemic failure which the political right everywhere hastened to equate with the death of democratic, as well as Leninist, socialism.

Although the radical transformation of both Polish Communism and its relations with society long predated Gorbachev, his appearance had important consequences for the final stage of Communism in Poland (Żukrowska, 1990). Once he had established himself, and certainly from 1987 onwards, the conservative wing of East European Communism found itself ideologically and politically on the defensive (Pravda, 1992). Worse than that, from their point of view, the abandonment of the Brezhnev Doctrine meant that both psychologically and *de facto* Communist elites and their supporting police, military and other *apparats* knew that they now really were on their own in facing their societies. Dramatically improved East-West relations, disarmament agreements and major reform within the USSR itself transformed the Cold War atmosphere which had petrified the possibility of change and divided Europe into two hostile camps for so long. In the short run this caused the post-Husak, Jakeš, bunker in Czechoslovakia to dig in and something similar occurred in Honecker's East Germany, although there was greater confusion in Bulgaria; but in Poland, and Hungary, the reform wings were now given a free run.

Mechanisms of power-transfer

The process of 'Negotiated Revolution' which led to the abdication of power of the Communist elites in Poland was accelerated by the strikes of spring-summer 1988. This decided the PZPR plenum in late August to break the 1980s' political stalemate. Interior Minister Czesław Kiszczak was delegated to negotiate an anti-crisis pact; this would incorporate the 'constructive' sections of the opposition in parliament, and even in government, within a revised national front in order to undercut social opposition to the costs of the much needed economic reform (Sanford, 1992). Secret discussions stalled during the autumn over the extent and time-scale of the proposed democratisation and marketisation and the way in which the opposition (i.e. Solidarity) would be legalised, despite the appointment of a reformist government led by Mieczysław F. Rakowski. The post-Solidarity opposition had always maintained its unity by holding out for an ultimately complete systemic transformation while negotiating on specific aspects. The PZPR, on the other hand, argued that everything was negotiable except its ultimate hold on power; but even this could be bargained down to a fifty per cent plus arrangement as in 1944–7. The issue remained ambiguous till the last but the Round Table took place because of two important developments within each camp. Wałęsa formed his Civic Committee on 18 December 1988 provoking an irrevocable split with his 'Fundamentalist' rivals who eventually formed 'Solidarity 80'. The PZPR replaced many of its major 1980s' notables with outright reformers in the first part of its Tenth plenum a few days later: the plenum's second session in mid-January took the historic decision to accept political and trade union pluralism (a coded phrase for the re-legalisation of Solidarity on its own terms), to democratise the PZPR and to embark on the Round Table without prior guarantees on its limits.

The course of the Round Table negotiations of 6 February to 5 April

1989, including the now published secret deals struck at the Magdalenka Villa between the leading figures, has been discussed elsewhere (Sanford, 1992, pp. 14–19, 50–68). What concerns us here is the long and extremely detailed agreement, set out by different sections, which was finally hammered out. The painfully argued political deal was that the Sejm (Lower House of Parliament) would be dissolved. The opposition would be allowed to contest 35 per cent of its seats in the contractual election which would follow. As the PZPR would contest less than half, the balance of power in the new Sejm was to be held by its minor party allies, the ZSL (United Peasant Party) and the SD (Democratic Party). On the other hand free elections would take place for the newly re-established Senate (Upper House). Although the issue was disputed later, the top leaders on both sides accepted that Jaruzelski would become the first incumbent of a more executive type of Presidency of the Republic to be elected by both parliamentary chambers. The independence of the mass media and of the judiciary were also agreed on after much controversy; but it was symptomatic that the OPZZ (originally government-sponsored trade unions) and Solidarity clashed with each other, rather than with the Communist leadership, over the compensation levels of wage-indexation while leaving vague the details of marketisation.

The Round Table Agreement represented an unprecedented historic compromise. It was envisaged as initiating a four-year transition period towards full democracy, pluralism and marketisation under conditions of general, if loose, Communist domination during which the PZPR would learn how to maintain its rule through competitive political methods. Where political power would ultimately reside and who would control the new mixed post-Soviet Communist system at the end of that time was left open and ambiguous on purpose in order to make immediate agreement possible. The answer to the question came much sooner and in a totally unexpected and devastating form as a consequence of the June 1989 elections and, even more so, in the collapse of the East European Communist systems in late 1989.

The June 1989 election, despite its contractual character for the Sejm, was the last great plebiscite on the Communist system; as such it denuded it of its last vestiges of legitimacy thus undermining the self-confidence of its leadership for good. Civic Committee candidates won 99 of the hundred Senate seats and all 161 Sejm seats available to it.[3] Humiliatingly, only two of the 35 Government-Coalition notables on the National List were elected while regime candidates were mostly returned on the second ballot with very low support (see Jasiewicz and Żukrowski in Sanford, 1992). About 50 of the latter, elected with Civic Committee endorsement, became potential allies. Jaruzelski was, therefore, barely elected as President on 19 July while the Sejm was unable to confirm Kisczak as Prime Minister. Wałęsa's early August proposal that Solidarity should head the new government then became possible when the ZSL and SD changed alliances. Tadeusz Mazowiecki, a social-Catholic and *Znak* Sejm-Deputy during the 1960s and Wałęsa's close adviser became Poland's first non-Communist Prime Minister since 1947. He headed a Grand Coalition, however, as Communists retained control of the Interior and Defence ministries and also held two other posts. Only the collapse of Communism elsewhere allowed his government to move on from power-sharing within the framework of the Round Table contract to dismantling the Communist system itself in late 1989 and early 1990.

Dismantling Communism

One should note the almost total absence of actual, as against the underlying threat, of violence, apart from some strikes and demonstrations, in Poland's 'Negotiated Revolution'. The transfer of power was carried out in a wholly legal and parliamentary manner. It was confirmed in the constitutional amendment of December 1989 (Sokolewicz in Sanford, 1992). This abolished the PZPR's leading role, expunged the commitment to socialist values and transformed the Polish People's Republic into the Polish Republic. The PZPR wound itself up in January 1990. Its two successors SdRP and PUS, elected young and uncompromised leaders. They declared their return to European social-democrat traditions and condemned the Soviet-Leninist experience.

The establishment of the Rule of Law entailed the depoliticisation of such bodies as the army and the police though the new rulers maintained some old bad habits in their running of state-controlled radio and TV. Officials from the Communist period such as judges, procurators, policemen, both secret and ordinary, and administrators, both national and local, were verified and, where necessary, dismissed, retired or sidetracked. Communist politicians were gradually replaced by Solidarity and other opposition, or uncompromised specialist, figures but the no-victimisation spirit of the Round Table generally prevailed. Despite Wałęsa's calls for an 'acceleration' of the dismantling of the Communist state and the replacement of its personnel, the resignation of the Communist Ministers, Kiszczak from the Interior and Siwicki from Defence in July 1990, and of Jaruzelski from the Presidency, marked only the end of this particular stage (cf. White, 1991, pp. 155 ff.). The de-Communisation issue was revived by the National-Christian Union (ZCh-N) Minister of the Interior, Antoni Macierewicz, who tried to reveal secret files in spring 1992 on political figures who had allegedly collaborated with the security services. Democratisation naturally permitted the organisation of an incredibly wide range of new political and social organisations. Many of the bodies, publications and institutions associated with the Communist party faded away.

The demise of Communism in Poland, like its establishment, was made possible by external factors. The decline and withdrawal of the Soviet imperial guarantee under Gorbachev was decisive in her case as elsewhere in Eastern Europe. The Polish and Soviet Communist elites had tried to counterbalance this by basing their relations on rational security and economic collaboration arguments and by rewriting the 'blank spots' in their histories (Sanford in Pravda, 1992). Other factors like the decline of the German threat, the improved East-West atmosphere and the greater feeling of security following Gorbachev's disarmament and domestic Soviet reform drives were also important. But the Polish Communist elites had already embarked on negotiating a mixed system which easily developed into a unique form of political transition. By controlling the manner and speed of their abdication from power and by ruling out political reprisals through the Round Table they secured a favourable exit from the political scene.

The Round Table Agreement between the incorporationist wing of the Solidarity elite and the Communist reformers also structured the first post-Communist phase until well past the first fully free election of October 1991. It allowed Poland to democratise in its own way while resisting many of the new external pressures from a Western and world capitalist system direction. After all, one of the reasons for the peaceful outcome had been that almost all sides agreed that democratisation was necessary in order to break the political stalemate of the 1980s by giving government a real legitimacy and, therefore, social approval for its decisions. The building of a market economy was accepted but the speed and the manner in which it would be done and, even, its final shape was still an open question. One of the key issues of the initial post-Communist stage was the extent to which Balcerowicz' neo-liberal section of the new elite would be able to dismantle what the Polish sociologist Włodzimierz Pańków calls the 'social-democratic infrastructure' inherited from Communism.[4] But contrary to many Western assumptions, and in many quarters expectations, the new Polish democracy proved capable of defending its national interests by making its own policies against at least some of the new external pressures; this reaction against economic dependency and the absence of the compensation of a Marshall-type aid programme became clear, certainly by the time of the Olszewski government in early 1992 and was clearly reflected in the results of the September 1993 election.

Building democracy and the market system

Some economic restructuring had preceded political democratisation but the really qualitative changes followed it. Finance Minister Leszek Balcerowicz brought the growing hyperinflation under control through 'shock therapy' in late 1989 and achieved IMF-backed currency stabilisation (Blazyca and Rapacki, 1991). This opened up the way for a privatisation programme which was rapid and successful as far as the small business sector was concerned; but the eventual fate of larger enterprises, and especially the heavy industry sector, raised greater difficulties. The first three post-Communist governments, under Mazowiecki, Bielecki and Olszewski, were undecided in their industrial policies and uncertain whether to aim for social market or extreme neo-liberal solutions as advocated by the IMF and the Harvard professor, Jeffrey Sachs. The immediate economic consequence of marketisation under deflationary conditions was an initial shrinkage in GNP of the order of 30 per cent and huge unemployment which rose to 2.6 million (about 14 per cent) by late 1992 as the result of the closure or slimming down of businesses. Its effects were particularly harsh in single-industry dominated areas like coalmining basins or the textile city of Łódź. Marketisation caused continual price rises, growing austerity and cuts in living standards. Low purchasing power and the difficulty of raising credit blocked the expansion of the private sector but the most important consequences were political. Disappointment with the lack of economic benefits, apart from for the favoured, but somewhat narrow, new entrepreneurial class, first manifested itself in social apathy and political disengagement. Electoral turnouts fell from 60 and 53 per cent in the two ballots of the 1990 Presidential election to 43 per cent (plus 5.6 per cent spoilt votes) in the first fully free parliamentary elections of October 1991. Growing socio-economic discontent and alienation, manifested in the growth of Poujadist type forces such as Stanisław Tymiński's success in the 1990 Presidential election, raised fears that full-blooded neo-liberal economic policies threatened democracy. Many concluded that Poland needed to work out its own distinctive economic development strategy, even a degree of protectionism, and not one that was dictated largely by external, notably IMF, pressures.

The defeat and dismantling of Communist power is conceptually quite different from the subsequent stage of building and, eventually, entrenching, democracy. Here one should note the following points about the latter. Firstly, Poland has a highly specific tradition of democracy which has often been challenged by an equally individual form of authoritarianism. This meant that institutions such as the Sejm, the courts and even the minor political parties survived the Communist period and immediately assumed a new life and reality under democratic conditions. Parliament had been the central focus of the 1919–26 system; even under Communism the theory of its constitutional sovereignty coexisted with the reality of PZPR hegemony implemented through control of the electoral process. Likewise Roman Law codes maintained a tradition of regular procedure in both the administration and the courts. The institutional framework for the new democratic system was, therefore, already in place and was deeply entrenched in Polish values. Communism in its final phase of attempting to build a *Rechtsstaat* had also produced such bodies as the State and Constitutional Tribunals and the Spokesman for Citizens' Rights (Ombudsman) which now assumed a deeper reality. This aspect, coupled with high educational levels and an ingrained, even excessive, tradition of personal rights and liberties, provided a much more favourable environment and initial starting-off point for democratisation than in the ex-USSR/Balkans.

Secondly, the above did not foreclose the issue of where power was to lie in the new system. The dispute, using French examples, over whether it was to be an assembly-dominant system as in the Third Republic, an executive-dominated Presidential one as in the Fifth Republic or whether a compromise could be struck between the two rumbled on throughout the first post-Communist stage (Sanford in White, 1991). It was bedevilled by the controversy over Wałęsa's quarrelsome personality, limited abilities, huge ambitions and role as President, which has been more destructive and destabilising than is normally assumed in the West. The result, reflecting this basic lack of agreement, was that the promulgation of a new constitution just kept on being postponed. The original 1952 Communist draft was revised in successive amendments before the Sejm adopted the 'Little Constitution' in August 1992.[5] All this strengthened the wholly evolutionary character of Polish political change.

Thirdly, there were similar disagreements over the most desirable electoral law and type of party systems. The 'War at the Top' for the Presidency between Wałęsa and Mazowiecki in 1990 eventually produced the Centre Party (PC) and Democratic Union (UD); contrary to initial predictions these parties failed to aggregate the Christian-Democratic and Social-Democratic wings of the Solidarity conglomerate successfully. Other formations such as the Liberal-Democratic Congress (KLD) of the second democratic Prime Minister, Jan Krzysztof Bielecki, the Confederation for an Independent Poland (KPN) and the Christian-National Union (ZCh-N) all emerged as major forces (Sanford in Szajkowski, 1991). The PZPR-successor SdRP also established itself as did two peasant alliances, one developing out of the ZSL and the other out of Rural Solidarity and splits in the former. This political fragmentation determined that an electoral law based on proportional representation without any threshold should be adopted for the October 1991 election. The noted Polish psephologist, Stanisław Gebethner, however, rightly points out that the electoral law only slightly exacerbated the fragmentation of the party system.[6] The subsequent elections results, with the leading party receiving just over 12 per cent of the vote and nine parties holding between 27 and 62 seats, merely confirmed that Poland was, politically, a highly divided nation.[7] The statement that 29 parties were represented in the Sejm is, however, misleading although the picture is bad enough without exaggeration; nine individually elected Deputies only represented themselves or were associated with other parties while another nine parties only had between one and seven seats apiece (totalling 34), so the strongest ten parties held 417 out of the 460 seats. Polish traditional values prefer that such divisions should be expressed openly; but this extremely accurate form of democratic representation had predictably negative consequences as in 1919–26.

Jan Olszewski (ZCh-N) had great difficulty in negotiating and then, maintaining, his government coalition. His last two months as Premier were spent in failed talks with the UD, KLD and KPN about broadening his support. When he fell in summer 1992 these earlier discussions facilitated the emergence, after the Pawlak interlude, of Hanna Suchocka (UD), an ex-SD Deputy of the Communist period, as Poland's first woman Prime Minister. Pressure from the Presidential Palace (*Belweder*) for greater decree powers and control over the armed forces had precipitated the crisis which led to the dismissal of Defence Minister, Jan Parys, for claiming that a military coup was being prepared, and to Olszewski's downfall. A fairly high electoral threshold which aimed to streamline the party system somewhat in the next election had emerged by the time Wałęsa dissolved the Sejm in May 1993.

Lastly, many Polish academics feared that there were strands in Polish culture which favoured nationalism, strong-man leadership, populist-authoritarianism, the 'Strong State' and national unity in reaction to the anarchic *Sejmocracy* discussed above (Connor and Płoszajski, 1992). Potential saviours of the nation abounded, such as the KPN chieftain Leszek Moczulski, the Party 'X' leader Stanisław Tymiński, not to mention a number of National Democratic extremists. Wałęsa's credibility, however, had been eroded substantially because of his inconsistency and vacillation. He could not decide whether he wanted to be a 'Father of the Nation' above politics and safeguarding the new democracy, a de Gaulle or, *in extremis*, a Peronist type of figure. If he desired the democratic dictatorship role he bungled very badly in his disputes with the Sejm and the UD in 1991 which prevented him from building a majority and thus defining a strong presidential office in the new constitution. He also, initially, lacked the nerve and the skill to call on the electorate to give his presidency parliamentary support by backing his own party as in Gaullist France. On the other hand, despite the support of capable advisers in his Presidential Office, he refused to accept the lesser, but still very useful, role of a constitutionally arbitrating Head of State. He thus got the worst of both worlds for himself, and more importantly for his country. The 'Great Electrician' made the mistake of believing that prestige and charisma could substitute for an institutional base but Poland was nothing like a post-independence African state. However, the Western elites who had built up his global image through the award of the 1983 Nobel Peace Prize and continual mass media adulation saw him (probably mistakenly) as an essential guarantor of the democratic capitalist course.

The Return to Europe and the hard road to the EC

Brzezinski's 'Organic Rejection' theory argued that incorporation in the Soviet bloc and the attempt to build Communism was at odds with Poland's traditions and natural inclinations.[8] The idealised picture of Western democracy, freedom and economic prosperity was also a crucial part of the Polish opposition's propaganda and mindset in the 1980s. It allowed it to contrast the reality of the failed socialist Utopia with a glowing image of the West. It popularised the simple-minded Solidarity myths of the 1980s that merely getting rid of Soviet economic exploitation and political tyranny would release the huge energies of the Polish people; this would resolve all problems in a trice and allow Poland to take its rightful place in the European community of nations. This drive, as illustrated by Rupnik and Garton Ash, was abetted by major intelligentsia spokesman.[9] The bulk of the educated classes were, however, aware that their interests and special social position were, arguably, better served by socialist allocation than by the market; they, therefore, like their Civic or New Forum counterparts in Czechoslovakia or East Germany, often preferred a 'Third Way'. Communism's collapse, however, removed a whole range of Soviet barriers and restraints which led to an important psychological feeling of normalisation. The state-society split was replaced by an initial atmosphere of national unity favouring systemic political and economic transformation. The distinguished Polish sociologist, Andrzej Rychard, has demonstrated how the Second (mid-1980s onwards) Solidarity was legitimised, after 1989, by the values of the First Solidarity of 1980–1; both workers and peasants, in particular were, however, aware that the latter's marketisation policies would hit their interests very hard (Sanford, 1992). But this was quickly replaced by the beginnings of normally organised social and political conflicts and divisions over domestic politics. Disillusionment with what many Poles came to regard as the 1989 'dud prospectus' also became prevalent. The Eurobarometer poll, held in ten post-Communist East European states in autumn 1991, showed that only 27 per cent of Poles were satisfied with the growth of their democracy as against 50 per cent who were not, the second lowest figures. The Poles were also the most pessimistic about their political and economic prospects. Only 20 per cent thought that change was going in the right direction as against 58 per cent who recorded negative responses. Poland also registered the least support for the market apart from Russia and Romania (*Polityka*, 15 February 1992).

The Poles, however, were certainly more at ease with their new international environment. Personal financial restraints meant that very little actually changed in terms of travel, tourism or labour-emigration. For example, it became more difficult to receive British visas in the first two years after 1989 than before, although visas were belatedly abolished on both sides in early 1992; as in most things this was somewhat later than in the Hungarian and Czecho-Slovak cases. The slogan of an 'Open Europe without Frontiers' also assumed a different ring when the threat of massive refugee and labour movements loomed on Poland's eastern and southern frontiers. There is, however, no doubt that the Poles welcomed the dismantling of the postwar division of Europe and the collapse of Communism in the Soviet sphere overwhelmingly. The potential dangers of German reunification aroused powerful public tremors but these produced only a muffled articulation by parties mainly outside the Solidarity consensus. Public opinion was reflected in the late 1980s' debates attacking the very concept of 'Eastern Europe', later scepticism for regional collaboration with Czecho-Slovakia and Hungary, fear of Euro-region proposals such as for the Carpathians and the determination to express Poland's role in a pan-European sense if EC entry were blocked.[10]

Continuity in post-Communist foreign policy was assured by Krzysztof Skubiszewski, an independent law professor, who remained at the Foreign Ministry from September 1989 onwards through the life of the first four governments of the democratic era. He gained great respect for his balance and caution, especially during 1989–91 before the Warsaw Pact, Comecon and the USSR broke up. In particular, he worked to transform the Warsaw Pact into a purely political and defensive alliance counterbalancing the new uniting Germany. He was criticised for being much slower than the Hungarians and the Czecho-Slovaks in demanding the withdrawal of the Soviet garrison; but this and the related dispute over compensation, was a marginal and largely symbolic issue. That full withdrawal was only set for 1994, although almost completed by late 1992, was less important than the maintenance of good relations with the USSR's successors. His 'two-track' policy towards the non-Russian nationalities, although attacked by the independence and nationalist parties, especially the KPN, also safeguarded Poland's options while the inevitable dissolution took place without irritating sensitivities in the newly independent Republics. Apart from Lithuania, Poland's relations with all its newly independent neighbours from Estonia to the Ukraine, therefore, got off to an unexpectedly positive start given the deeply ingrained suspicion of Poland because of her erstwhile historical and socially dominant role in what had been for centuries her eastern borderlands (*kresy*).

The EC established official relations with Comecon and promised collaboration with its members in its Luxemburg Declaration of 25 June 1988. Poland's rapid moves towards reform were rewarded with preliminary negotiations, during the autumn, for the bilateral trade and cooperation agreement, promised there. The EC Rhodes Summit of December 1988 confirmed the political will for a more active economic policy to encourage reform in Eastern Europe and the Commission drew up detailed proposals. Poland lagged behind Hungary, whose agreement was signed in September 1988, while hers only came a full year later on 19 September 1989.[11] But in practice the Community dismantled its quantitative restrictions on trade with these countries during 1990, much sooner than the envisaged date of 1995. Integration into the EC system of generalised tariff preferences also gave some Polish sectors, such as environmental protection, energy, financial services and occupational training, the sort of tariff reductions which were normally only given to developing countries. Such initiatives were supported by OECD; the G-24 meeting in Brussels in December 1989 granted Poland a one billion dollar stabilisation fund and promised similar aid for other East European countries moving towards capitalist democracy. Despite much talk and a whole plethora of measures such as debt rescheduling, and even a major degree of debt-forgiveness for Poland by the Club of Paris, the promised comprehensive Marshall type of plan for rapid reconstruction never materialised. This had the political and psychological effect already mentioned, although the one-off assistance measures did eventually add up to quite an impressive total. On the other hand, the previously mentioned Eurobarometer poll revealed an undiscerning popular enthusiasm for Europe which was confused with the EC. About half the Poles wanted to join it immediately and most of the remainder within five years (*Polityka*, 15 February 1992).

The EC was preoccupied at this time with the issues of its deepening through the Single European Act leading up to 1992 and Commission President Delors' initiatives for European Monetary Union. It also realised that even the Czech Lands and Hungary, who had more favourable prospects for achieving the conditions for full EC membership than Poland, were unlikely to do so much before the early years of the new century. Prior applications were also likely from ex-neutral, but fully democratic and economically advanced, states with the ending of the division of Europe, the collapse of the USSR and the EC's swallowing up of EFTA; Turkey and Cyprus were also on the long agenda of EC widening (see J. Pinder's chapter in this volume). The issue was, naturally, bedevilled in the early 1990s by the clash over whether deepening through the Maastricht Agreement should precede widening or whether Europe should remain a loose confederation with dominant national governments benefiting from the Subsidiarity principle; the latter concept would more easily permit its quicker extension to include the most favoured democracies of Poland, Czecho-Slovakia and Hungary and even the Baltic states and Slovenia (M. Ostrowski in *Polityka*, 23 November, 1991).

The result, hardly surprisingly, was a compromise. The European Council in Strasbourg in December 1989 took decisions which allowed the EC Commission in February 1990 to offer the three East European states, which were irrevocably building democratic capitalism, a form of associate membership designed to achieve the closest political and economic relations outside full membership. These aims were again confirmed by the Dublin Summit of April 1990. As far as Poland was concerned, the EC declared the political will to develop its bilateral trade agreement towards association if Warsaw continued to liberalise and marketise her economy and to strengthen the constitutional rule of law and its multi-party system. In practice, the issue was complicated by the fears of France and the Mediterranean members of the consequences of such an eastward shift on the southern and agricultural balance of the EC.[12] The negotiation of Poland's EC Associate status took place in seven rounds of talks beginning on 22 December 1990 and ending with the initialling of the agreement on 22 November 1991. (*Rzeczpospolitia*, 16 December 1991). Despite last-minute Spanish reservations on East European steel imports, the Agreement was signed by Deputy-Premier Balcerowicz on 16 December 1991, at the same time as the Czecho-Slovak and Hungarian agreements (*Rzeczpospolita*, 17 December 1991).

The document, comprising 119 articles in 9 sections, stated in its preamble that 'Poland's ultimate goal is to become a full member of the Community'.[13] The Community as a whole, though, did not then pledge itself to Poland's eventual full membership thus lessening the Agreement's political significance.[14] All the Agreement did was to commit the parties to a political dialogue designed to integrate Poland gradually into the EC framework. Two equal stages over a ten-year preparatory period were envisaged for the earliest attainment of full membership under the most favourable conditions. Free trade, apart from in agricultural products, would also be achieved in this time. The speed and terms of tariff reduction for various industrial goods were regulated 'asymmetrically' in Poland's favour as the EC reductions were more immediate and extensive than hers; a number of contentious issues – investment and capital flows, competition policy, labour mobility, the rights of Polish workers within the EC and the transfer of pension and social security benefits – were also settled.

Balcerowicz praised the concessions which he had gained in the agreement (*Rzeczpospolita*, 19 December 1991): the formal asymmetry of the EC concessions offered a range of short-term benefits such as technical, financial and training assistance, immediate access to the EC market and aid from the European Investment Bank and the PHARE (Poland-Hungary Economic Restructuring) programme established in 1989 and widened subsequently; Poland generally had longer than the three-year period of grace before reducing its own tariffs, but the EC would reduce its charges on 55 per cent of Poland's industrial exports to it to zero as of 1993 and on the remainder including chemicals, cars, porcelain, glass and textiles on a descending scale arriving at zero by 1998 and in some cases sooner. On the other hand, it was admitted that the Common Agricultural Policy raised insuperable difficulties for resolving Poland's agricultural exports within the Association framework. Press discussion centred on typically EC bones of contention such as quotas for Polish veal and mushroom exports; but the philosophical keynote underlying the document was that both sides would have to demolish their mutual Cold War barriers. The size of Poland's task in adapting her laws to meet EC integration norms was reflected in estimates that over 7,000 Polish legal regulations would have to be revised. A wide range of diplomas, statistics and practices needed to be standardised. The country had to build up a wholly new stock exchange and banking, financial, telecommunications and service infrastructure almost from scratch.[15] Poland with its declining GNP, high inflation rate and huge budget deficit and Public Debt could also only blanch at the longer-term vision of Maastricht-type requirements. All this naturally aroused domestic Polish fears and opposition. Some political spokesmen were willing to prolong the time-horizon for full integration in order to retain greater control over the social consequences of closing down antiquated sections of the state industrial sector as well as palliating the consequences of agricultural transformation. The agreement was ratified decisively by the Sejm in July 1992 by 238 votes to 78 and 20 abstentions (and overwhelmingly by the Senate by 75 votes to one with six abstentions); but the negative voices reflected the growth of a sizeable backlash against the costs of EC entry favouring Poland's pan-European and regional activities.

Official Polish sources did their best to emphasise the benefits of association with the EC which participated in 37 per cent of world trade. But they could not obscure the magnitude of the economic transformation required in their country. This is illustrated by comparisons between Poland and the EC's national members, which despite necessary qualifications, is most starkly pointed up by the fivefold GNP per capita differential with Spain (see Table 8.1).

The official Polish line was that the long-term goal of full membership offered Poland its only real chance of becoming a fully developed partner of the European family with high living standards and economic growth levels. Access to superior technology, the inflow of foreign capital investment and competitive market disciplines were essential to get rid of Communist monopolies. But official prognoses, drawn up by Jacek Saryusz-Wolski, the Plenipotentiary for European Integration, of the effect of mutual customs liberalisation on Poland's EC trade in manufactures were discouraging (*Rzeczpospolita*, 19 December 1991). Poland, as

Table 8.1 Comparison of GNP and GNP per capita

Country	*Population (millions)*	*GNP (billion $)*	*GNP per capita (thousand $)*
Poland	38.2	89.4	2.3
Spain	40.0	487.1	12.5
Denmark	5.1	125.5	24.4
France	56.4	1,190.2	24.1
Germany	79.5	1,648.8	20.1
Greece	10.0	67.3	6.7
Italy	57.7	1,077.5	18.6
Portugal	10.5	59.5	5.6
UK	57.2	979.9	17.1
Czechoslovakia	15.7	42.0	2.7
Hungary	10.6	31.6	2.9

Source: Rynki Zagraniczne, 7 December 1991

a weaker partner, would benefit much less from trade liberalisation than the more advanced EC economies. The negative trade balance would be worsened by inward capital flows and the introduction of superior technology as well as by the agricultural restrictions. The official view was that there was no alternative if foreign confidence was to be maintained and domestic authoritarian-populist challenges to be fended off. Only thus could Poland build the normally functioning and competitive market economy essential to safeguard democracy, a pluralist open society and gain full EC membership. Wolski forecast much 'stop-and-go' in Poland's relations with the EC but felt that short-term difficulties would be more than balanced by the rapid development of Poland's natural resources and high-quality, but cheap, labour force. A more efficient Poland would thus be able to re-expand her trade with erstwhile 'captive' Comecon markets, which had totalled well over 60 per cent but had shrunk with the introduction of hard currency exchanges in 1990.

General official optimism could not wish away the specific problems. Poland's traditionally strong export sectors in steel, coal, textiles and leather goods raised particularly sensitive issues for the EC as her export profile was so similar to the EC's already established southern members (J. Mojkowski in *Polityka*, 14 December 1991). Much of Polish industry, with low Soviet efficiency levels, was unlikely to survive EC industrial policy and competition from EC exports following tariff reduction.[16] Even with favourable external investment and restructuring at higher productivity levels the Foreign Trade Ministry (MWGZ) estimated that EC demand for Polish industrial goods might only increase by about 15–20 per cent (*Rynki Zagraniczne*, 7 December 1991). This would be scant compensation for the loss of economic sovereignty as such matters as exchange rates and industrial policy now had to be discussed with EC partners.[17] The picture was also very mixed on the privatisation front once the easy job of clearing out the small firms was well on the way. PHARE in 1992 helped

Fiat to acquire a 90 per cent stake in FMS and to pledge $2 billion for rebuilding the car plant; another Italian firm, Lucchini, took a majority stake in Huta Warszawa, Poland's largest steelworks. Suchocka's privatisation programme, despite some signs of economic upturn and her successful visit to London in spring 1993, was much opposed, and even rejected initially, by the Sejm. Poland's 'ontological opening' towards the building of 'political capitalism', therefore, faced grave, although not insuperable, political, economic, cultural and external obstacles (Staniszkis, 1991).

The eternal enemies? Germany and Russia and the European solution

Poland's independence in modern times has been assured by simultaneous German and Russian weakness as in the 1920s and endangered by their resurgence and understanding as in the 1930s. We now need to discuss whether the eternal verities of Poland's geopolitical situation have been transformed by German reunification and the breakup of the USSR in the early 1990s (B. Rychlowski in *International Affairs Studies*, 1991, No. 2). The perception of an external threat or of an insecure international environment hinders democratic consolidation and encourages authoritarian responses; the development of a benign European framework, on the other hand, can be posited as being an important supportive factor in the building of a democratic system in Poland.

The 79-million strong united Germany which emerged legally on 3 October 1990 was the world's third strongest economy after the USA and Japan; it also dominated the EC, producing about 30 per cent of its GNP. It had given Poland all the legal-political guarantees concerning the inviolability of Poland's western frontier on the Oder-Neisse and promises of future good-neighbourliness that were diplomatically possible.[18] But disputes between Bonn and Warsaw over Poland's participation in the negotiations leading to the agreement of 12 September 1990, which necessitated a 'Two plus Four' formula, and over Kohl's pandering to domestic right-wing nationalist and expellee forces kept Polish fears alive.

The newly dominant Solidarity elites were, however, committed to the idea of Polish reconciliation with a united Germany within the framework of a uniting Europe (Tomala, 1991). They saw German unification emotionally in terms of the ending of Communist rule in Eastern Europe and as finally healing the consequences of the Second World War, primarily the continent's division. They considered that West Germany would digest East Germany and quickly become a force for European stability and development. The new Germany would think in larger European terms rather than be swayed by parochial grievances against Poland. This was held to invalidate Polish fears of domination by the German colossus; such occasions as Wałęsa's official visit to Germany in March–April 1992 were used to highlight the theme that Poland's road to Europe as well as her security depended upon German support within the EC and NATO and their mutual inclusion within such reinforced and extended structures

(*Gazeta Wyborcza*, 31 March 1992). Wałęsa, true to form, provided domestic critics with further ammunition for their case that he was demeaning his high office by getting irritated during a press conference and talking about chamber-pots! One may also note that the Polish-German Treaty of 17 June 1991 had done more than reconfirm the big questions on borders and security. Its framework for friendly bilateral collaboration bore fruit in such areas as youth exchanges and the sensitive issue of the German minority in Poland.

Both traditional left-wing and right-wing opinion remained sceptical. They pointed out how huge funds had flowed from Germany to ensure the success of German minority parties in the 1991 election; they also regarded calls for joint sovereignty Euro-regions in such sensitive border areas as Gdańsk, Pomerania and Silesia as dangerous (*Polityka*, 18 January 1992, p. 12). Whether Poland will be able to live with the inevitable spread of German economic, political and cultural influence and whether the Germans will exercise sufficient self-restraint remains to be seen. It is true that Poland's future survival depends on the continuation of a democratic, non-revisionist Germany just as much as what happens in the ex-USSR. Historians will remember, however, that Polish-German reconciliation was regarded in exactly the same way at Locarno in 1925 but that this is now viewed as the first step towards appeasement of German nationalism. Have the parameters really changed and will the current European endeavour prove genuine and prevent history from repeating itself?

Interwar Poland was destroyed once its balancing act between her two equally dangerous eastern and western neighbours had been undermined by their mutual agreement through the Ribbentrop-Molotov Pact. It is still too early to be definite on the shape of the post-USSR states-system; but it is likely that only the weakest of the newly independent states will continue to participate in common (Russian-dominated) political, economic and security arrangements. Poland's priority in any case will be to establish friendly and collaborative relationships with her closest neighbours in the East. These include the three Baltic states (Estonia, Latvia and especially Lithuania), Belorussia and the Ukraine; she no longer has a common border with Russia apart from the residual oddity of Kaliningrad. Belorussia started off as a somewhat artificial creation and its initial elites accepted Russian 'protection'. But it faced few threats, unlike the strife over Moldava, and could still evolve domestically and change its external orientation.[19] The post-USSR Republics also had a mass of frontier and national minority disputes and arguments over the division of ex-Soviet assets (Z. Brzezinski in *International Herald Tribune*, 16 September 1991). Poland was, however, favoured by the fact that her eastern border was largely unquestioned both within Poland and by her neighbours. Her only major difficulty, which Skubiszewski handled with great restraint, was with Lithuania over the ill-treatment of the Polish minority.

One of the major threats to democratisation in Eastern Europe will undoubtedly be the problem of national minorities. The international community and European public opinion expect standards in this respect which cause great difficulties for sensitive, newly sovereign, national majorities. Apart from small German and Ukrainian minorities, Poland is spared the problem of having to combine nation-building with democratisation with all the political overload and human suffering which the former may entail. The following comments on the Baltic states are designed to illustrate the point. They all have substantial Russian and other minorities with the dominant nationality only being 65 per cent in Estonia, 53 per cent in Latvia and 80 per cent in Lithuania (1980). In a perfect world these countries would guarantee minorities full political rights to endeavour to build a consociational and, where necessary, a multi-ethnic Swiss type of democracy. Clumsy Western pressure to this end can, however, endanger the democratisation process within the dominant national majorities. In the extreme Latvian case there can obviously be no national Latvian state unless the Latvians are allowed to establish the dominance of Latvian language, culture and political values in the initial phase, at least. The dilemma is that the Latvians would probably prefer to sacrifice democracy to their own form of nation-building, even Integral Nationalism as in the interwar period, if the choice arose. As we have seen in the Polish case, similar threats to democracy can also be envisaged as arising from a reaction to the social costs of marketisation. Combine the two and one gets such phenomena as the backlash against Sajudis, favouring successor-Communist Social Democracy, in the 1992 Lithuanian election.

Polish attention since 1989 has centred on its *Westpolitik* and to a lesser extent on regional and Hexagonal initiatives with its neighbours to the south. Only the KPN were initially primarily interested in developing a viable policy in areas of traditional Polish regional interest to its east.[20] This is a legitimate, and even sensible, concern but, as in the interwar period, it has been traduced by domestic opponents and ill-informed Western opinion. In its moderate form it has much to offer Poland in terms of political and economic influence in the Baltic, Belorussia, the Ukraine and even Russia. The Poles have the linguistic and temperamental capacities and traditional know-how and links to penetrate the region. Much of the historical animus against them has also faded in just the same way that their own anti-German phobias have declined. But more ambitious schemes for a Polish-led *intermarium* (Baltic-Black Sea) federation are likely to remain as chimerical as in Piłsudski's time and for the same reason; the local nationalisms see no reason to prefer Polish hegemony, however loose, civilised and even mutually beneficial it might be, to that of Russia. They would only be forced into it by a basic threat to their existence which one cannot at the moment envisage. Like the Poles themselves, the new post-Soviet nations would prefer to go for Europe rather than some halfway regional staging post; but their democratisation and marketisation processes are bound to take longer and to be even more complicated than those of the Central European four if only because Republics, such as Belorussia and the Ukraine, have to combine them with basic nation-state building as well. This may well impel them towards transitional regional initiatives for organising the space between Germany and Russia. The Ukraine thus made favourable noises about joining the Višegrad arrangement, a Carpathian Euro-region (grouping parts of south-east Poland, Romania, Hungary, Slovakia and the Ukraine) and even Baltic-Black Sea proposals in early 1993. But their initial situation was aggravated by the fact that 70 per cent of Belorussia's and 39 per cent of the Ukraine's economic cooperation links were with the rest of what had been the USSR (M. Wolf, *The Financial Times*, 29 September 1991). This economic dependence, the fear of stimulating Russian minority unrest and the absence of Western security guarantees made them very cautious about even appearing to act as a *cordon sanitaire* against Russia. Despite all this, however, they can only benefit from Poland's experience and direct assistance. Her diplomatic support will also counterbalance inevitably stronger German and Russian pressures.

The great conundrum is the new Russian Federative Republic. The same processes as elsewhere in Eastern Europe seem to have triumphed with the failure of the August 1991 coup. So did Russia's abandonment of her imperialist tradition of the last three centuries in favour of the reconstruction of a more limited modernised and democratic state. Enormous economic and security challenges were posed by the collapse of the command economy, paralleling Poland's situation in the early 1980s; but this was aggravated by the emergence of the independent Republics and the breakup of intra-USSR links and patterns of cooperation. Skubiszewski, in his report to the Sejm's Foreign Affairs Committee in March 1992, typically saw Poland's priority as being to anchor herself within NATO and American-Western conservative frameworks of European security as quickly as possible.[21] He was rightly criticised at this session by KPN chairman, Leszek Moczulski, for not having an Eastern policy. All that Skubiszewski had to offer was that Poland was most concerned with the liquidation of the Soviet nuclear arsenal, to establish good relations with all her newly independent neighbours, to involve them in ongoing pan-European disarmament and security negotiations and to protect Polish minorities in the ex-Soviet Republics. He warned that political and national minority conflicts and vast refugee movements might mean that 'Poland will become the last stable state, free of conflicts with its neighbours, on the eastern side of the continent and having to its east a situation of growing chaos'. The treaty of collaboration and good-neighbourliness with Russia which he promised, regulating the final withdrawal of Soviet troops from Poland, was signed by Wałęsa during his official visit to Moscow in May 1992 (*Polityka*, 30 May 1992).

It is clear that Poland wanted to disentangle itself from what had been the Eastern Communist camp as quickly as possible (Pravda, 1992, Chapter 9). The transitional stage, readjusting her primary relations towards Western structures, however, proved more long-drawn out than expected (A. Krzemiński and W. Władyka in *Polityka*, 13 July 1991). The Russians, although they had abandoned their hegemonic ambitions in Eastern Europe, still had legitimate security concerns about Poland's moves towards NATO (*Wprost*, 16 June 1991). Walentyn Falin's memorandum on Russia's relations with East-Central Europe also made it clear that Moscow could still exert powerful economic pressure in the supply of raw materials and fuels (*Polityka*, 8 June 1991). Comecon's disintegration and the shift to hard currency trading, however, caused Poland's trade with the USSR to decline from 41 per cent in 1988 to 25 per cent in mid-1991 and to decline even further, thereafter. Politically, the Poles had a confused and generally passive wait-and-see attitude to the breakup of the USSR.[22] Solidarity politicians claimed that only now that Poland had regained full national sovereignty would she be able to rebuild an Eastern Policy (*Rzeczpospolita*, 1 October 1991). Skubiszewski wanted to realise this sovereignty in 1989–91 by freeing Poland's links with the USSR and the Warsaw Pact of ideological and hegemonic aspects while retaining their defensive features. The collapse of both, however, strengthened his Western orientation; he wanted to do no more than negotiate treaties establishing Poland's relations with Russia and the USSR successor Republics on the basis of full equality and good-neighbourliness and to avoid Poland being dragged into the post-Soviet morass (*Życie Warszawy*, 24 July 1991).

In terms of southern policy Poland established good and quite developed trilateral regional links with Hungary and Czecho-Slovakia. These were confirmed in the Višegrad and Kraków summits of their leaders in February and October 1991.[23] The Western powers tended to treat them as a bloc, as states most likely to build democratic capitalism successfully; but their interests, while providing a basis for the successful regulation of small, but useful, issues such as transport and tourist links or the establishment of a Central European University, were too disparate, and even competitive, for thoughts of regional federations to be considered seriously.[24] One can also add that the emergence of two independent Czech and Slovak states in January 1993 raised no problems for Poland. Historically, it has always had greater sympathy for the latter. The Višegrad Triangle, along with the Hexagon (Italy, Austria, Hungary, Yugoslavia, Czechoslovakia and Poland), plans for collaboration with the Baltic states and the rebirth of a Hanseatic-sounding League of Baltic Towns, were positive and useful, but, nevertheless, still secondary and subsidiary supports to the main Westward thrust of Polish policy in the post-Communist world.[25]

What security and which democracy for the new Poland?

Post-Communist Poland would seem to have an unprecendentedly favourable security position and international environment as it does not have any obvious enemy or threat (Kuźniar, 1992). It could easily, however, get caught up in the backwash of the nationalist and regional conflicts of post-Communist Eastern Europe, especially refugee movements; above all it faces the prospect of growing German political and economic domination (Wnuk-Lipiński, 1991, pp. 37–44). Its ruling elites considered that the country's interests would be best served by linking post-Communist Poland to the unipolar system of limited American dominance, in the short run, while working for the multipolar European conception in the longer run (Stefanowicz in Wnuk-Lipiński, 1991). There were, therefore, two main thrusts in post-Communist Poland's security policy after the dissolution of the Warsaw Pact. The first was to work to develop the CSCE framework (Rotfeld, 1990). The second, most strongly articulated by Premier Olszewski, was to enter an enlarged 'NATO-bis' which might also include the Ukraine and Belorussia.[26] These developments, which deserve separate studies in themselves (see E. Herring's chapter in this volume), were abetted by Poland's initially unreserved drive for full integration in the world capitalist economy by meeting IMF and GATT requirements in full. Poland also, belatedly, joined the Council of Europe in November 1991.

With the fall of Communism came a great debate about the nature of democracy. An *essentialist* debate paralleled earlier discussions of totalitarianism and pluralism in comparative Communist studies. Could democracy assume a wide variety of forms going beyond the diversity of mere institutions and mechanisms? In particular, the Fukuyama thesis raised the issue whether liberal democracy was its most superior single form; or was it just a response to the highly specific evolution of some favoured countries who had produced the right sort of political culture to support it? European and Third World, unlike British, North American or Commonwealth, specialists tended to take a more relativist view which incorporated a wider understanding of populist forms of democracy.[27] The main thrust of the former tendency was, however, the debate about the relationship between democracy and the market. The latter was usually closely identified with capitalism and with attacks on the practicability of market-socialism. The dominant Western elites and their supporters among the initial post-Communist neo-liberal Polish elites were only interested in achieving the collapse of Communism if it permitted the building of the capitalist form of democracy. Whether on grounds of interest or value they felt that there could only be one form of democracy and that, within certain limits, it had to be capitalist. The East-West systemic struggle of the 1980s, therefore, had a left-right domestic dimension as far as West European politics was concerned. Hence communist democratic reform efforts were ridiculed by Western politicians and the popular press. They could not digest such phenomena as the Polish Communist elite thinking that it could participate in free elections successfully and the Romanian and Bulgarian successor-Communists actually winning them in 1990. Much of the political struggle, both domestic and international, during the 1980s was designed to squeeze out theoretical alternatives like the Polish working-class programmes for strong free trade unions, genuine cooperatives and workers' self-management. In the event, what was remarkable was the speed with which domestic East European electorates moved on from the systemic choices of 1989–91 to resolving intra-system socio-economic orientations by democratic means. The Christian-Nationalist camp in Poland also hastened to get its favoured measures such as the criminalisation of abortion passed as there were already signs that Catholic influence was waning. Claus Offe has argued that the current democratic transitions in Eastern Europe are fundamentally different from the post-Second World War cases in Germany, Italy and Japan or mid-1970s Spain, Portugal and Greece. His case why the former should be regarded as wholly original phenomena is based on the simultaneity and profundity of the three different nation-building, democratisation and economic dimensions of transformation.[28] His conclusion parallels the central thesis in this chapter that the democratic and market-capitalist aspects are not inextricably linked and that a 'democratic blockage' is emerging to the form of economic transition desired by external neo-liberal elites and their initially dominant domestic allies. The Polish case, however, suggests that some sort of social-democratic compromise, however, unavowed and even in a Christian-Democrat, or corporatist form, may be the outcome in East-Central Europe in order to assuage popular discontent over the time-scale and delayed benefits of the transformation. Suchocka's Democratic Union based government claimed that it wanted a social market economy with a social security 'safety-net' balancing its privatisation and industrial restructuring measures. But the social consensus required to steer Poland through its first post-Communist decade while preserving democracy emerged in the novel form of a democratic veto on 'wild marketisation' in the September 1993 election. The Poles voted in a Peasant Party and successor-communist majority and a social democratic government committed to a more socially-defined and gradual form of marketisation with a, consequently, longer drawn-out and more native-based transition.

The external environment in the form of the East-West systemic conflict and the decay and abandonment of Soviet hegemony was the essential enabling factor in bringing about the political abdication of Communist power in Poland. While not depreciating its significance this study has, nevertheless, emphasised the contribution of Poland's domestic evolution since 1956 to the outcome. Poland's 'Negotiated Revolution' also remains an important factor conditioning the national path taken by the democratisation and marketisation processes since 1989. There continues to be a highly complex and fairly balanced interplay between external and domestic factors in Poland's post-Communist development just as there was in the latter period of Communist rule.

Notes

1. This was implication of the 'Realist' case for the Jaruzelski regime's reform potential. Cf. A. Walicki, 1985, 'The Paradoxes of Jaruzelski's Poland', *Archives Européens de Sociologie*, Vol. 16, No. 2, pp. 167–92.
2. In particular the works by Adam D. Rotfeld: *Od Helsinek do Madrytu. Dokumenty KBWE*, 1983, PWN, Warsaw. *From Confidence to Disarmament*, 1986, PWN, Warsaw. *Międzynarodowe czynniki bezpieczeństwa Polski*, 1986, PWN, Warsaw.
3. Z. Pelczynski and S. Kowalski, 1990, 'Poland', *Electoral Studies*, Vol. 9. No. 4, pp. 346–54. P. Lewis, 1990, 'Non-competitive elections and regime-change', *Parliamentary Affairs*, Vol. 43, No. 1, pp. 90–107.
4. W.Pańków, 1990, 'Transformations in the Polish social environment in the 1980s', *Journal of Communist Studies*, Vol. 6, No. 4, December, pp. 174–8.
5. W. Sokolewicz, 1992, 'The Polish constitution in a time of change', *International Journal of the Sociology of Law*, Vol. 20. This was not the end of

the story as there was another round of Sejm-Senate disagreement before the final text was promulgated in late 1992.

6. S. Gebethner, 'Gdyby była inna ordynacja'. I am much indebted to the author for letting me have a mimeograph preview copy of this authoritatively detailed analysis.
7. G. Sanford, 1993, 'Delay and disappointment: the fully free Polish election of 27 October 1991', *Journal of Communist Studies*, Vol. 9, Nol. 2, June, pp. 107–18.
8. Z. Brzezinski, 1990, *The Grand Failure*, Macdonald, London.
9. T. Garton Ash, 1991, *The Uses of Adversity*, Granta Books, Cambridge; J. Rupnik, 1989, *The Other Europe*, Weidenfeld & Nicholson, London.
10. Cf. K. Krzystofek, 1990, *Uniwersalistyczne i pluralistyczne wizje pokojowego świata*, PISM, Warsaw; Kukliński, 1991; Kostecki, 1991.
11. The full text is reproduced in *Materiały i dokumenty BSE*, No. 5, February 1992, Sejm Chancellery, Warsaw; for commentaries on its detail see *Życie Gospodarcze*, 1 October 1989 and the interview with Dr Andrzej Olechowski, the main Polish foreign trade minstry (Ministry for Economic Collaboration with Abroad, henceforth MWGZ), negotiator in *Polityka*, 21 October 1989.
12. *Biuletyn Ekonomiczny*, 30 September 1991; G. Bernatowicz, 1991, *Eastern Europe and the European Mediterranean countries*, PISM Occasional Papers No. 25, Warsaw.
13. The document's provisions are discussed in English in *Poland Today*, No. 3, 1991–2, pp. 26–8 on the basis of the fuller summary of the text in *Rzeczpospolita*, 19 December 1991.
14. See the comments by MGWZ State Secretary, Olechowski, who negotiated its commercial sections, *Polityka*, 12 December 1991.
15. Jolanta Adamiec, 1992, 'Droga krajów postkomunistycznych do EWG', *Materiały i dokumenty BSE*, No. 4, 12 January 1992, Sejm Chancellery, Warsaw.
16. A. Karpiński, 1986, *Restrukturyz acja gospodarki w Polsce i na świecie*, PWE, Warsaw, pp. 250–4.
17. J. Głòwacki, 1972, 'Procesy integracyjne w Europie Zachodniej a polska polityka przemysłowa', *Raport BSE*, No. 17, March, Sejm Chancellery.
18. For the documents on the various stages of this process including the Polish dimension see *Zjednoczenie Niemiec*, November 1990, PAP, Warsaw.
19 For domestic criticisms of the Minsk government's pro-Russian and pro-German inclinations and the democratic opposition's case for a Polish-Scandinavian orientation see *Gazeta Wyborcza*, 8 April 1992; for documents and commentary on the emergence of independent Belorussia, see *Białorus Czas odrodzenia*, Błyskawica-PAP, September 1990, Warsaw.
20. See the KPN's Fourth Congress material held in March 1992; *TezyProgrammowe KPN* and *Apel IV Kongresu KPN do społeczeństw i sił politycznych krajów Międzymorza*.
21. *Biuletyn Komisji Spraw Zagranicznych*, No. 243/1 kadencja, 17 March 1992, Sejm Chancellery.
22. On the wider challenge of defining the aims and strategy of Polish foreign policy see R.Kuźniar in *Sprawy Międzynarodowe*, Vol. xlv, No. 1–2 (1992).
23. R.L. Tókés, 1991, 'From Višegrad to Kraków', *Problems of Communism*, November – December.
24. Cf. R. Zięba, 1992, 'Nowy Regionalizm w Europia a Polska', *Sprawy Międzynarodowe*, Vol. xlv, No. 1–2.
25. I am grateful to Dr Tomasz Knothe for letting me have a mimeograph copy of

his paper on 'Poland and the Baltic Sea region'. Here he distinguishes between the European, the *Intermarium* and the 'positive equilibrium' between Germany and Russia schools of thought in Poland.

26. See the interviews with Jerzy Milewski, the Presidential State-Secretary for National Security in *Glob 24*, 3–5 April 1992, and with German Defence Minister, Gerhard Stoltenberg, in *Prawo i Życie*, 4 April 1992.
27. Cf. the symposium on 'Prospects for Democracy' in *Political Studies*, XL, Special Issue (1992). For the latter critique see Laurence Whitehead, 'The alternatives to "Liberal Democracy": a Latin American Perspective', pp. 146–59. Cf. Adam Przeworski, 1991 *Democracy and the Market. Reforms in Eastern Europe and Latin American*, Cambridge University Press, New York.
28. Claus Offe, 1992, 'Vers le capitalisme par construction démocratique'. La théorie de la démocratie et la triple transition en Europe de l'Est'. *Revue Française de Science Politique*, XLII, No. 6 (December), pp. 923–42.

References

Barker, C., 1986, *Festival of the Oppressed. Solidarity, reform and revolution in Poland*, Bookmarks, London.

Blazyca, G. and Rapacki, R. (eds), 1991, *Poland Into the 1990s. Economy and society in transition*, F. Pinter, London.

Bromke, A., 1989 *Stosunki Wschod-Zachód w latach osiemdziesiątych*, PISM, Warsaw.

Buzan, B. *et al.*, 1990, *The European Security Order Recast. Scenarios for the post-Cold War era*, Pinter, London.

Carnovale, M. and Potter, W., 1989, *Continuity and Change in Soviet-East European Realtions. Implications for the West*, Westview Press, Boulder.

Connor, W. and Płoszajski, P. (eds), 1992, *Escape from Socialism. The Polish route*, IFIS Publishers, Warsaw.

Gerrits, A., 1990, *The Failure of Authoritarian Change: reform, opposition and geopolitics in Poland in the 1980s*, Dartmouth, Aldershot.

Gomułka, S. and Polonsky, A. (eds), 1990, *Polish Paradoxes*, Routledge, London.

Gołembski, F., 1991, *Czynnik społeczny w kształtowaniu współczesnych stosunków międzynarowych*, PISM, Warsaw.

Hahn, W.G., 1987, *Democracy in a Communist Party. Poland's experience since 1980*, Columbia UP, New York.

Hyde-Price, A., 1990, *European Security after the Cold War*, Macmillan, London.

Kolankiewicz, G. and Lewis, P., 1988, *Poland, Politics, Economics and Society*, F. Pinter, London.

Kostecki, R. (ed.), 1991, *Eastern Europe in Transition: a chance or a threat to peace*, IPRA Research Team on Changes in Eastern Europe-PISM, Warsaw.

Kukliński, A., 1991, *Poland in the Perspective of Global Change. Globality versus locality 1*, Polish Association for the Club of Rome, Warsaw.

Kukułka, J. and Zięba, R., 1992, *Polityka zagraniczna państwa*, Wydawnictwo Uniwersytetu, Warszawskiego, Warsaw.

Kuzniar, R. (ed.), 1992, *Krajobraz po transformacji. Środowisko międzynarodowe Polski lat dziewięċdzięsiatych.* Instytut Słosunków Międzynarodowych, Uniwersytet Warszawski, Warsaw.

Lepak, K., 1988, *Prelude to Solidarity. Poland and the politics of the Gierek regime*, Columbia UP, New York.

Multan, L., 1991, *Evolution of the military order in Europe*, PISM Occasional Papers No. 29, Warsaw.

Ost, D., 1990, *Solidarity and the Politics of Anti-Politics*, Temple UP, Philadelphia.

Pastusiak, L., 1991, *Polska a Zachód*, PISM, Warsaw.

Pravda, A. (ed.), 1992, *The End of the Outer Empire. Soviet-East European relations under Gorbachev, 1985–90*, Sage-RIIA, London.

Pridham, G. (ed.), 1991, *Encouraging Democracy. The international context of regime transition in Southern Europe*, Leicester University Press, Leicester.

Rachwald, A., 1990, *In Search of Poland. The superpowers' response to Solidarity, 1980–89*, Hoover Institution Press, Stanford.

Rensenbrink, John, 1988, *Poland Challenges a Divided World*, Louisiana State University Press, Baton Rouge.

Rotfeld, A., 1990, *Europejski system bezpieczeństwa in statu nascendi*, PISM, Warsaw.

Sadowski, Z. (ed). 1991, *Społeczeństwo po-totalitarne. Kierunki przemian*, Polskie Towarzystwo Współpracy z Klubem Rzymskim, Warsaw.

Sanford, G., 1983, *Polish Communism in Crisis*, Croom Helm, London.

Sanford, G., 1986, *Military Rule in Poland, 1981–83*, Croom Helm, London.

Sanford, G., (ed.), 1990, *The Solidarity Congress, 1981. The great debate*, Macmillan, Basingstoke.

Sanford, G., 1992, *Democratisation in Poland 1988–90. Polish voices*, Macmillan, Basingstoke.

Staniszkis, J., 1991, *The Dynamics of the Breakthrough . The Polish experience*, University of California Press, Berkeley.

Szajkowski, B., (ed.), 1991, *New Political Parties of Eastern Europe and the Soviet Union*, Longman, London.

Tomala, M., (ed.), 1991, *Zjednoczenie Niemiec. Aspekty międzynarodowe i polskie*, PISM, Warsaw.

White, S. (ed.), 1991, *Handbook of Reconstruction in Eastern Europe*, Longman, London.

Wnuk-Lipiński, E., (ed.), 1991, *Świat postkomunistyczny: diagnoza in prognozy*, ISP-PAN, Warsaw.

Żukrowska, K., 1990, *Determinanty przemian systemowych w Polsce*, PISM, Warsaw.

Index